THE
ARCHITECT'S
GUIDE
TO
COMPUTER-AIDED
DESIGN

THE ARCHITECT'S GUIDE TO COMPUTER-AIDED DESIGN

MARK LAUDEN CROSLEY, AIA

WITHDRAWN

JOHN WILEY & SONS

NEW YORK
CHICHESTER
BRISBANE
TORONTO
SINGAPORE

Text and Cover Design by Karin Gerdes Kincheloe

Cover illustration by Lloyd Martin

Library of Congress Cataloging in Publication Data:

Crosley, Mark Lauden.
The architect's guide to computer-aided design.

Bibliography: p.
1. Architectural design—Data processing.
2. Computer-aided design.   I. Title.
NA2728.C75   1988   720′.28′40285   87-13308
ISBN 0-471-62433-0
ISBN 0-471-85336-4 (pbk.)

Printed in the United States of America

10 9 8 7 6 5 4 3 2

FOR CLAUDIA

PREFACE

Virtually everyone involved in architectural design is being affected by the arrival of computers into the profession. Very soon most of us will be using computers daily, so it is vital that the concepts and techniques of computer-aided architecture are widely understood. The design professions are being transformed, and it is crucial that the talents of all involved, from students to principals, be applied to the task. We are entering new territory; this book is a guide to the exploration of that territory.

The Architect's Guide to Computer-Aided Design is intended for architectural designers, managers, drafters, and students, as well as people working in landscape and urban design, architecturally related engineering, and construction. The book covers a broad range of drawing, design, and management issues, because we assume that these are important to everyone involved in the practice of architecture.

A guide should help you foresee some of the shortcuts and dead ends you could encounter, so I have tried to include both helpful tips and some pragmatic thoughts about some of the problems that computers are bringing to architecture. I also indulge in some speculation as to where architectural practice and architectural computer programs are headed in the near future.

ARCHITECTURE ON SMALL COMPUTERS

Why small computers? Although size is less indicative of a computer's capabilities than it once was, it is microcomputers or *personal computers* that have planted computer-aided design firmly in the architecture world. Larger, more expensive computers are not feasible for small and medium-sized architectural firms, and they have proved too big a burden even for some large firms. High-cost computer systems tend to create the "ticking meter" syndrome: a firm must limit the computer to its most productive uses, such as drafting, and minimize creative work, which has less tangible results. In many cases, expensive systems are turned over to computer drafting specialists, and the equipment is often operated two or three shifts a day.

The Architect's Guide is based on the premise that computers should be available to virtually all the participants in architectural practice. They can be used at most stages of the design process, and graphics can be meshed with many nongraphic functions. If everyone in a firm is to have open access to computers, then low-cost equipment is clearly required. Fortunately, small computers are simultaneously becoming more affordable and more powerful and thus more practical for use in architecture.

BEGINNERS AND EXPERTS

The Architect's Guide is not a computer user's manual or a tutorial for learning computer-aided drawing. Instead, it is a guide to fundamental and advanced tactics that you can use to get the best possible results in applying computers to architecture. Whether you are a beginner or have extensive computer experience, it is intended to help you to take full advantage of the computer's assistance in visualizing and organizing your work.

For the architect who is unfamiliar with computer terminology and routines, the book will serve as a primer on what is available, how to use it in an architectural workplace, and what to expect as computer technology and the profession itself evolve. Part One and Part Three require no hands-on experience; the remainder will help you as you learn to design and draft with the computer's aid.

For more experienced computer users, *The Architect's Guide* can help provide an overview of computer use in architecture that goes beyond the use of any one system. It should help in pushing your use of computers beyond basic drafting into design and fields like building material specification, cost estimating, and project management. While the book focuses on graphics, there are discussions of a number of other aspects of architectural practice.

A BROAD-BASED APPROACH

There is a remarkable range of computers and programs that are useful to architects. There are enough similarities in graphics programs, in particular, that we can conduct a generalized discussion that is applicable to many different systems. There are, of course, differences in capabilities and especially in terminology, but our discussion of *design strategies* is applicable to most architecturally-oriented computer-aided design and drafting programs. If you are using a system that does not include some of the capabilities mentioned, remember that graphics programs are evolving rapidly, and you will probably be using more sophisticated programs in the near future.

In our discussion of two-dimensional drawing, I have used, primarily, terminology associated with AutoCAD, one of the more capable and popular programs. Many other programs use the same or similar terms, and the glossary should prove helpful in applying the text to a large number of different systems.

WHERE TO START

The Architect's Guide to Computer-Aided Design is organized into three sections.

Chapters 1 through 3 contain an orientation to computer-aided architecture, including an introduction to computers and an examination of the various features of programs for drafting and design. This section will be most helpful if you are starting out, and

it may contain some interesting information even if you have some previous experience. Chapters 2 and 3 should be particularly useful in you are choosing or upgrading a computer-aided design system, or if you expect to in the future.

Chapters 4, 5 and 6 are an exploration of how to use computer-aided drafting and design *effectively* in the practice of architecture. We assume here that you have learned (or are learning) the rudimentary skills of computer-aided drawing, with the help of user's manuals, tutorials, and hands-on use. In these chapters we cover the strategies that enable you to reach beyond the capabilities of manual drawing and design.

Chapters 7 and 8 examine the impact computers are having on the architectural profession in general, and on the architectural workplace in particular. These chapters may be of special interest to professionals who are planning the direction of a firm, but should be informative as well to the designer or student who is interested in the future of architectural practice.

DESIGNING THE FUTURE

Computer-aided architecture is already extraordinarily useful, but it has room to grow enormously in the future. Designing computer programs is an ongoing process: the program you use today will probably be revised and improved many times in the next few years. Graphics programs, in particular, are evolving rapidly, becoming more capable, better suited to architecture, and integrated more effectively with nongraphic operations.

Architects are not entirely at the mercy of software designers. There is tremendous competition in the computer-applications marketplace, and some of this competition is directed toward trying to provide new, enticing architectural tools. Most computer programmers are not architects and sometimes fail to see ideas that are obvious to architects. They often rely on suggestions to produce computer tools that are well suited to architecture. Thus, the more you know about the potential of computer-aided architecture, the better equipped you are to ask for new and better tools. Most software developers encourage and respond to suggestions.

The Architect's Guide is intended to help you start thinking about what you can do with computer assistance. As you read it, try to use it as a springboard for your own ideas. As you explore new territory, you may open new paths for others to follow.

A PERSONAL VIEW

As an architect who enjoys drawing, I was once skeptical of computer-aided design: I feared it was a *replacement* for drawing. Only after I began to use CAD did I realize that computers can *supplement* familiar skills in remarkable ways. Computer-aided architecture is not without problems, but, if used well, it is a tool that can add to the creative spark that is so important to architecture.

Like many other architects, I became interested in CAD as a labor-saving device. Once I began using a CAD system, I began to discover tricks for *designing*—tricks that enabled me to do things that were impossible by hand. Rather than replacing architects, as many of us initially feared computers might do, it became clear that CAD was providing new capabilities and freeing us to spend more time on design. The realization that computers were significantly extending architects' powers lead to this book.

And, incidentally, I still enjoy drawing by hand.

Mark Lauden Crosley

ACKNOWLEDGMENTS

Many people have contributed ideas, drawings, and tools to this book.

Adel Foz had the foresight to look to microcomputer-based CAD when it was in its infancy; David Wallace, Peter Floyd, and Thomas Green at Wallace, Floyd Associates were daring enough to try it; and the firm has contributed drawings to the book. Other contributing architects include Richard Buday of Buday Wells, Architects; Blake Mason of Arch-1; Phil Bernstein of Kaplin, McLaughlin, Diaz; Dennis Neeley and Terry Lofrano of Neeley/Lofrano, Inc., and David Baker Associates. Thanks also to Brian Cacchiotti and Lisa Gee, and to Sharon Gallagher for much advice.

David and Eric Robinson were kind enough to allow the use of the drawings of their house, which I designed using AutoCAD and MegaCADD software.

Assistance was provided by many software developers, listed in Appendix B. A number of individuals in the CAD industry were instrumental in the book's development. Joe Oakey, Joe Woodman, and Karen Kershaw were especially helpful. Valuable contributions were made by Otto Buckholz, Dianne Dempster, Lloyd Martin, Martin McCloskey, and Hiroshi Takaki. Thanks to Marty McConnell of Houston Instrument for arranging the use of an HI plotter, with which most of the illustrations were plotted.

Valuable contributions were made by a number of readers, including Edward Allen, William Glennie, Tony Gualtieri, Jack A. Kremers, Barbara-Jo Novitski, Rick Roman, and Claudia Stern. Some added ideas, some added clarity, and most added encouragement.

A capable team at John Wiley and Sons is responsible for the transformation from manuscript to the product at hand, a process that is almost as complex as the design of a building. Thanks to Judith R. Joseph for initiating and guiding the project; to Elizabeth Doble for ably coordinating the editorial and production processes and patiently responding to an author's whims; to Cindy Funkhouser for managing production with care and good humor; to Karin Kincheloe, who crafted stacks of text and drawings, page by page, into a polished book design; and to the many others at Wiley who contributed.

If there is anything that links these people together, it is a concern for quality. I have found these architects, CAD developers, readers, and publishing people to share a sense of craft which I have seen applied to different areas of expertise. They have shown in many ways that an overriding concern for quality is the ultimate guide.

M.L.C.

CONTENTS

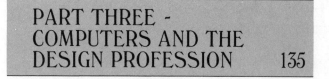

THE
ARCHITECT'S
GUIDE
TO
COMPUTER-AIDED
DESIGN

COMPUTER-AIDED DESIGN BASICS

PART 1

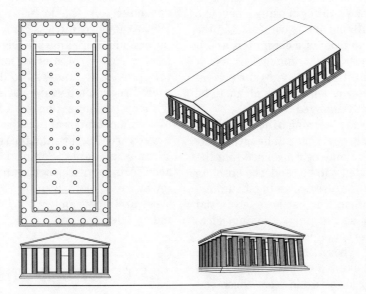

GETTING
ORIENTED

CHAPTER 1

A wave of new tools is descending on the architectural profession. Computers are changing the ways we draw and the ways we use information. These tools have the potential to make the labor of architecture more productive, but, more importantly, they promise to transform the way we design.

Computer-aided drawing and information management systems are now within reach of virtually every designer and drafter. Sophisticated computers (*hardware*) and programs (*software*) can now be purchased by even the smallest design firms, giving them capabilities for design and production that only the largest offices could afford just a few years ago. An understanding of computer-aided design will soon be essential to the practice of architecture.

CHANGES: PERSONAL AND PROFESSIONAL

The design professions have never been quick to change, and it is a major step to begin using a new tool like a computer. Virtually no one is comfortable the first time they sit down in front of a computer, and it takes time to just get used to it, much less use it productively. Even more difficult, though, is overcoming the fear that your way of working is about to be drastically and irrevocably changed.

When you've spent years learning to do something one way, learning a totally new way can be intimidating, even frightening. You may be concerned that the skills you have accumulated will be rendered obsolete or that you will never learn to use a drawing technique that seems completely alien. Furthermore, an initial encounter with a whirring, beeping, flashing, electronic beast can be unnerving. Drawing with such a tool, using a typewriter keyboard, or perhaps a plastic "mouse," is obviously not like drawing with a pencil. In fact, it requires a different attitude from those you have acquired through pencil drawing. This is not as bad as it sounds.

Once you overcome the possible trauma and inevitable fumbling, you may come to a sudden realization that the new drawing process is familiar, after all. You may find that, at times, computer-aided drawing is closer to the way you *think* about design and drafting than hand drawing is; not always, but sometimes. The more you can use your thinking method to supplement your drawing method, the more you will benefit from (and enjoy) drawing with the assistance of the electronic beast.

✓ In fact, if applied to the right situation, computer-aided drawing can help you produce work that is not only quicker, but better. It can save much repetitious pencil pushing, to be sure, but it can also help increase accuracy and eliminate errors in drafting. It can help you produce more design studies in a day than you could otherwise produce in a week. It can even be used interactively with good old fashioned hand drawing. Like any other tool, it can be used well or badly.

COMPUTER-AIDED ARCHITECTURE

Not long ago, only specially trained "CAD operators" could use computers for design and drafting. It was so difficult to learn to use a firm's computer-aided draw-

ing tools that most architects never considered it: cadres of computer drafters reigned over the equipment.

This is no longer true. As drawing programs were developed for the low-cost microcomputers of the 1980s, they became less complex than their minicomputer and mainframe predecessors. (They also became less expensive.) Memorization became less important; intuitive, easily understood drawing techniques took over. Programs became easier to use "off the shelf," without customization or additional programming. Most important of all, programs oriented specifically toward architecture and the related design professions became available. Some of these were written by architects-turned-programmers, with a helpful bias toward architectural design techniques. Now, any and every architect can learn to use computer-aided drafting and design.

THE PROOF IS IN THE DRAWING

It's easy to sit down and draw lines, curves, and circles; you barely need to read the user's manual to do these simple tasks. It's even easy to draw three-dimensional shapes, then turn them into orthogonal drawings. With practice, you can do most operations faster than by hand, and more accurately. It's a bit like learning to play a musical instrument: it takes some fumbling before you become comfortable enough to produce something easily and well. When you master it, it feels natural.

Yet this is only the beginning. Computer-aided design offers tools that go far beyond anything you can do by hand. In order to use these tools effectively, you must learn to organize drawing layers, create and use drawing libraries, and plan sequences of drawings. If these concepts are unfamiliar, don't worry. These are the **design strategies** that let you take architectural design and drafting into new territory.

WHAT IS CADD? CAD? CAD/CAM?

The acronyms applied to the use of computers in architecture are somewhat ambiguous. The two "D"s in CADD stand for "design and drafting," and they can, of course, be very different things. Drafting is often a means to design, as any architect who has developed details during working-drawing production knows. But in general, *drafting* is a highly standardized process, with a high level of accuracy required, while *design* refers to the entire process of conceptualizing and documenting a project, including all stages of drawing. Design, of course, includes many non-graphic aspects, and many of these can take advantage of computer assistance, as well (Figure 1-1).

The term *CAD* (one "D") is used to refer to computer-aided ("CA") *drawing* or *design*. In this guide, we are interested in many aspects of design, though we will focus on graphics. Thus, we use *CAD* to refer to **computer-aided design**, with the understanding that this includes drawing, drafting and modeling, as well as the management of information. Drawing, in all its forms, is the architect's primary tool. Most of our discussion here will center on drawing, but we will frequently mention the various non-graphic aspects of design. One of CAD's most significant advantages is its ability to directly link drawings to the information that is represented by graphic images, such as lists of building materials, construction specifications, and cost data.

The term CAD/CAM adds **computer-aided manufacturing**, a concept that at first seems generally irrelevant to the architect. Nevertheless, when designers use computers to specify partition systems, window units, and pre-engineered building elements, the distinction may seem less clear. When design and engineering drawings go straight to a fabricator's computer to be translated into shop drawings, the distinction begins to disappear completely.

DATABASES AND DRAWING PROCESSORS

How does a computer actually assist in making drawings? In computer terminology, a collection of organized information is called a *database*. Any drawing is, of course, highly organized information, which can be stored electronically as numbers representing points, lines, angles and such in the machine's memory. The software allows each piece of information to be recalled or modified by the user to create an electronic drawing that can be printed on paper using a plotter.

A good drawing program insulates the user from having to think too much about the organization of the database, and translates instructions into easy-to-understand terms that relate to drawing, rather than to database management. CAD programs are sometimes compared to word processors, which let you write without concern for the appearance of your document, then turn your writing into a polished manuscript without retyping. The analogy is a good one, since word processors free the user from the mundane tasks required in handling text, and a "drawing processor" helps you draw your work once, then adapt it to your presentation needs.

The evolution of text-handling computer programs, such as sophisticated text formatters, spelling checkers, and typographic layout programs illustrate how CAD programs are developing. These tools can prepare text for publishing and check spelling, spacing, and page design. In a similar way, sophisticated CAD programs can help develop and check designs using predefined "rules" (such as dimensions or structural requirements) and stock drawing parts that may be selected as needed. Ideally, such a system should be able to link and automatically cross-check individual drawings to ensure complete consistency: this is the potential of a powerful *three-dimensional* database manager. When an entire object is stored as a single file of information, individual drawings can be extracted like snapshots of views of the object. The end result of such a process is an essentially unlimited number of drawings of an electronic "model," each drawing completely consistent with the others.

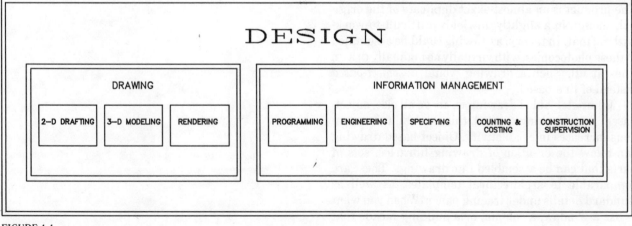

FIGURE 1-1

HOW IS CAD DIFFERENT FROM TRADITIONAL METHODS?

It's possible to use computer-aided drawing without really taking advantage of its capabilities. Even some experienced CAD users have simply transferred all their manual-drawing habits over to the computer. It's like buying an airplane and driving it down the highway, rather than learning to fly. It requires an effort to learn to fly, but if you don't bother you might as well stick with your car.

Computer-aided design programs offer a wide variety of features, in many different combinations. Some of these are common to most sophisticated, architecturally oriented programs. It is particularly important that you learn to take full advantage of the particular features of your software. We will examine, here, some of the general concepts that are most important to using CAD effectively.

Objects

Sketching and drafting manually are "line-based" drawing techniques; they involve placing lines, one at a time, on paper, until a whole image is created. The order of line drawing may be based on any number of factors, such as direction, line weight, or ink-drying time, but it is still one line at a time. Sometimes this is the best way to draw, as when sketching, in which every line may carry a special meaning, or when you are deciding on dimensions, one line at a time.

Often it is more useful to think in terms of objects or patterns. For example, you might use an already drawn image as a reference beneath tracing paper, instead of drawing it from scratch. When tracing, there is no need to completely rethink the object, only to draw it (line by line). Going a step beyond tracing, an object or detail can be photocopied and stuck onto a drawing, actually eliminating the effort of redrawing. The product is an almost-exact duplicate of the original, though in a slightly unwieldy, difficult-to-work-with format. In theory, a drawing could be assembled of these photocopies, with virtually no manually drawn lines at all. Such a drawing would be *object-based* instead of line-based.

Computer-aided drawing is, above all else, object-based. As a working method, this can lead to tremendous increases in productivity. Object-based drawing can allow the creation of drawing libraries, sets of parts that can be assembled into drawings. These are comparable to architectural templates, as well as standard details under tracing paper. When you want to use a window, a column, or a building facade that

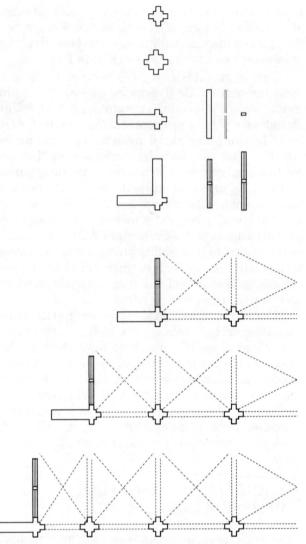

FIGURE 1-2   These simple forms and several others were used to assemble the cathedral in Figure 1-3.

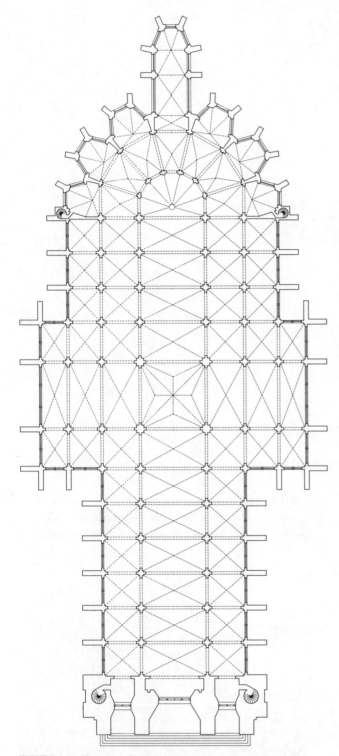

FIGURE 1-3 The plan of the cathedral at Amiens was assembled from a small number of repetitive forms.

you have drawn previously, you can simply add it to a drawing rather than redrawing it. If you need to change or adapt a previous version, this is often easier than starting from scratch. Forms and details can also be drawn "on the fly," then repeated a number of times within a drawing, or even transferred to another drawing.

Instead of taking time to redraw objects that have already been designed, you can insert them in seconds, without breaking your train of thought. By assembling complex drawings from libraries of predrawn objects, you can conduct elaborate design studies very rapidly. The church in Figure 1-3 was assembled very rapidly from the forms illustrated in Figure 1-2. These forms, which represent actual physical forms, could be stretched or compressed to reflect different material sizes or column spacings. Thus, when you want to use a form that you have drawn previously, you can use it almost instantly, making the thought-to-paper process more direct. Object-drawing can allow mindless repetition and lazy use of standard details, but it also offers a means to evaluate your ideas almost as quickly as you conceive them.

Mass Reproduction

Line-drawing is also, by definition, an additive process. Drawings are constructed by adding single elements, again and again. Even photocopy repetition is additive, sticking down image after image. Drawing with computer assistance is, on the other hand, more like multiplication, because a single line, image, or an entire drawing can be reproduced any number of times, with little more effort than adding a second copy. This has several implications that go far beyond timesaving.

Mass reproduction of drawing elements makes possible exact reproductions, in great quantities, *located* very accurately. For tasks like drafting centerlines, multiple columns, lighting layouts and window walls, the benefits of this are obvious (Figure 1-4). Mass reproduction of finely drawn details and patterns can enable you to produce drawings that might not have been practical, or even possible, by hand.

There are also design implications inherent in the use of mass reproduction. While it can encourage the efficient use of repeated elements, it can encourage a repetitive sameness, since it is often easier to rubber-stamp large numbers of identical elements onto, say, a facade, than it is to articulate individual, varied elements. This is one of many examples we shall see of a tool that can be used creatively, as it might have been

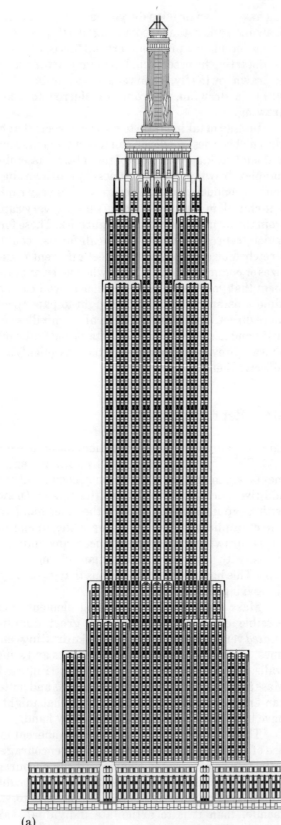

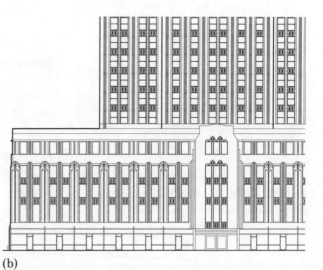

FIGURE 1-4 The elevation of the Empire State Building (a and b, detail) was assembled from a few simple elements, such as windows and vertical elements, repeated over and over. Creative Technologies, Inc.

(a)

(b)

in the design of the cathedral and Empire State Building, or abused by a careless designer.

Layers and Other Collections

When you wish to erase or move part of a manual drawing, such as a room full of furniture, you must erase each piece, one at a time. If you want to be able to look at a plan with and without furniture, you must make copies of your drawing or use multiple overlays of tracing paper. CAD, on the other hand, lets you collect groups of elements that you can control through a single action. You can copy a roomful of furniture into another room, or you can plot a plan without its furniture.

By collecting parts of your drawing into groups, it can be drawn as if on many sheets of paper, cut into pieces, and assembled in new forms. Most CAD programs include a facility for separating parts of your drawing into tens or hundreds of **layers**, as if they were transparent overlays. As a design tool, you may use layers to view only the portions of your work in which you are currently concerned; using layers as a production tool, you may display and plot the same drawing many different ways, for different purposes.

Cycles

Just as a designer often goes back and forth between large and small scales, drawings produced with computer assistance can be constructed in a way that might be described as cyclical. The first, simple parts of a drawing can be assembled, then you can return and develop the details. As a drawing is assembled from these elements, little or no line-drawing need be done.

When a drawing has been constructed of repeated elements, it is easy to make repeated changes. For example, if round columns are to be replaced by square columns throughout an entire building, this single decision would require massive amounts of redrawing for a large building. In Figure 1-5*a* and *b*, the round column symbols are transformed into rectilinear columns: all the columns in the drawing are then automatically transformed. When the floor details are added to the "bay" elements (Figure 1-6), the entire church is instantly paved (Figure 1-7). With computer assistance, the change must be made only once for each type of object; period. Again, this is more than a drafting aid; this is much closer to the way a designer *thinks*.

The advantage of this cyclical process is in the creation of a drawing made up of parts over which the drawer has a tremendous amount of control. It also

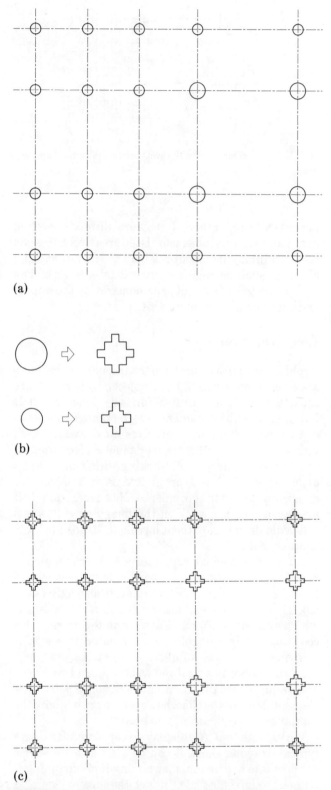

(a)

(b)

(c)

FIGURE 1-5   This detail of the church plan illustrates how the columns might have been transformed from circular to cruciform shapes. After the building is laid out, as in *(a)*, the round column symbol is replaced *(b)* with the new symbol, resulting in the automatic substitution of all the columns *(c)*.

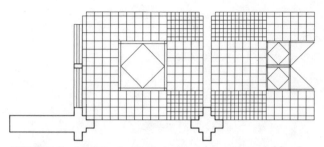

FIGURE 1-6   A column bay with paving patterns substituted for the dashed overhead-lines.

permits a designer to work at several different levels of detail almost simultaneously. Used creatively, this can result in immediate feedback between different types of work, such as relating entry details to an urban design analysis of a street or demonstrating the impact of dimensional changes on a site plan.

Real-World Scale

Architectural drawings have traditionally been small scale representations of large objects. Only rarely are construction details drawn full size, since a whole building must be documented by a manageable set of drawings. A computer perceives *all* drawings as if they were drawn full-scale, using inches, feet, meters, or whatever units you are working with. Only when a drawing is displayed or plotted is it reduced, or expanded, for your convenience. However, when it is displayed you can work on the image *as if* it was a full-scale drawing, without having to "translate" it to another scale.

Two-dimensional computer-aided drawings are based on an x- and y-axis coordinate system. Every point has an x and y value that relate to an origin point, 0,0. Three-dimensional drawings add a third, z-axis, which extends "up" and "down" from the origin. This coordinate world enables the computer to see your drawing as if it was a full-sized object. As you work, you can display an axis if you wish (Figure 1-8), or you may inquire as to the coordinate location of a drawing element. Most of the time, however, you can ignore the computer's coordinate system entirely.

Although the CAD display screen is smaller than a typical drawing sheet, it can be used as a telescopic window into a drawing, magnifying it or shrinking it without regard for scale. In fact, the idea of "scale" is almost meaningless when you work on an electronic drawing, since you can move from a view of a whole building to a larger-than-life sized view of a detail in second. You can work at *real-world* scale: it's your viewpoint that changes.

When designers work on paper at a specific scale,

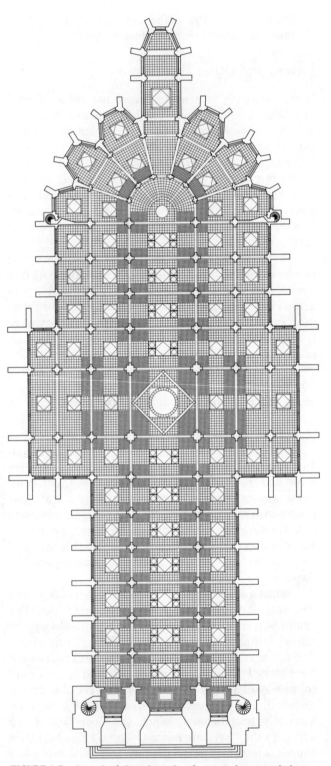

FIGURE 1-7   As each of the column bay forms in the original plan (Figure 1-3) is replaced with a bay with a paving pattern, all the bays are automatically transformed, and the entire building is paved.

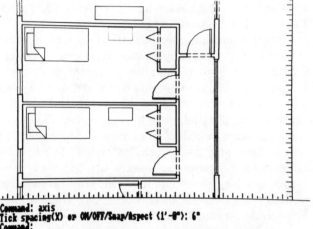

Command: axis
Tick spacing(X) or ON/OFF/Snap/Aspect (1'-0"): 6"
Command:

FIGURE 1-8   This photo shows an axis of *x* and *y* coordinates displayed on the AutoCAD screen. As with most programs, the screen display of the axis and grid is optional, but all drawings are nevertheless located on a similar coordinate system, even if it is invisible to the user.

they often become adept at estimating distances at that scale with great precision. This is an important design skill, since it enables a designer to accurately estimate sizes without stopping to measure. An infinitely variable CAD display interferes with this skill, but less than you might expect. Whenever your drawing contains objects of a known dimension, such as walls or plumbing fixtures, they will serve as references with which you will quickly learn to estimate distances. Even when no such references are visible, a continuous on-screen display of coordinates, in whatever units you specify, enables you to easily measure distances with great accuracy. You can also inquire as to the distance between two points or the length of an object.

Speed and Feedback

Increased efficiency is often cited as a reason to bring computers into the design process. An experienced CAD user can generally produce a drawing, from scratch, somewhat faster than a manual drafter, but the difference may not be dramatic. The real time savings comes from using drawing libraries and from *revising* drawings, drastically reducing redrawing time.

As we have noted, the elimination of repetitive steps through the use of symbols and drawing libraries supports a designer's way of thinking better than traditional methods do. Thus, *design*, as well as production, is more efficient. In addition, object-based drawing (and the ability to quickly substitute alterna-

tives) provides rapid feedback that gives you new opportunities to experiment and test ideas. The ability to quickly assemble and change drawings encourages design exploration. Seeing the implications of a change in a repeated element can remove some of the guesswork from the design process. If you can look at more alternatives, presumably you are more likely to find better alternatives, earlier in the course of a project.

Planning

Complex drawings that use layers, drawing libraries, and cyclical design techniques require a good deal of planning. A drawing that looks identical to a manual line-drawing may have a tremendously complex internal structure, a structure that is completely invisible. Thus, the advantages of CAD are not free; they come at the expense of having to actually design the drawing.

The amount of planning that must go into a drawing is related to the purpose of the drawing: from the start, you should have a clear set of goals for a drawing. Beyond that, it is important to know what level of detail is important, what size the drawing should be when plotted, and, most importantly, to have a good idea of the relationships between the parts of a drawing. If these things are considered, a simple drawing may remain simple, and a complex drawing may be prevented from becoming unwieldy or muddled.

Manual drawing does not generally require as much preliminary planning, and this is one reason why it will never be entirely replaced by the computer. Sometimes, choosing the right pencil and paper is the only decision you want to make before drawing something.

Intelligent Drawings

Since a drawing is stored in the computer as a database, why should this data be limited to graphics? It needn't be: labels, descriptions, and quantities can be included in a drawing, as well. You can attach this information to each object that you place in a drawing, and you may display the data or hide it, as you prefer. When you want to list the various objects you have used, you may create tables of parts complete with descriptions, quantities, cost estimates, or all of these. You can then sort them according to, say, type, location, or manufacturer.

"Intelligent" drawings are much more than drawings. When you have enough information at hand (including predrawn graphics and manufacturer's data), you can produce drawings, schedules, specifications, and cost estimates almost simultaneously. You can eliminate the extra effort and opportunities for error that are inherent in doing these independently.

Interaction

One of the most enticing promises of computer-aided design is the prospect of being able to sit down with a client and design a project while discussing it. In terms of complete buildings, this may be more of a client's fantasy than an architect's dream, since designers often prefer to work out ideas in private, checking for feasibility before presenting solutions to a client. However, in cases in which an architect has previously worked out major elements, such as specialized building types or repetitive building systems, and assembled appropriate libraries of drawings and symbols, interactive design is not an unreasonable possibility. It is even more feasible for designing parts of projects such as office layouts, landscape plans, or details of residential designs such as kitchens. Once a library of drawings is available, it is a fairly simple matter to drag, say, workstation and partition symbols around a drawing or to substitute cabinet types in a kitchen plan. On an easy-to-use CAD system, this process is so straightforward that clients can take over and try it themselves.

THREE-DIMENSIONAL DRAWINGS AND MODELS

Two-dimensional drawing software is essentially an extension of traditional drawing practice. When a third dimension is added, opportunities arise for working methods that could not have been imagined before the arrival of electronic drawing.

Many microcomputer-based CAD systems provide the ability to project simple two-dimensional drawings into a third dimension, allowing plans to become volumes, elevations to become walls, and so on. Views can be selected in orthographic modes (all parallel lines remain parallel) or true perspective. This technique is often called $2\frac{1}{2}$-dimensional **projection**, in which lines and points are "extruded" to give the appearance of volumes. Images are generally displayed as *wire-frame* shapes, in which lines are used to outline planes and forms (Figure 1-9a). Hidden lines behind the foremost planes can be automatically removed, providing more realistic views (Figure 1-9b). Some programs allow on-screen surface shading, and a few allow shadow studies by providing a user-selected light source.

Until recently, *true* three-dimensional imaging has been the province of mechanical engineers armed with mainframe computers. The appearance of three-dimensional **modeling** for architects promises to have an extraordinary impact on the design professions. Three-dimensional models allow the creation of drawings that are *interrelated* in plan, section, and elevation, such that changes in one are immediately reflected in all the others. The result is an accurate three-dimensional representation of all the information that has been drawn; the model can be viewed from any point, inside or out (Figure 1-10, *a–c*).

Accurate views are only the beginning of the potential of three-dimensional modeling. New two-

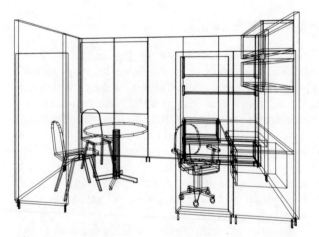

(a)

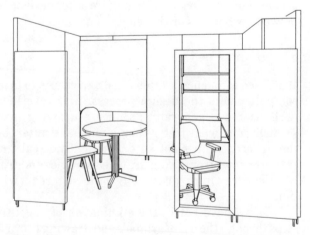

(b)

FIGURE 1-9   *(a)* A three-dimensional wireframe model. *(b)* With hidden lines automatically removed. MegaCADD, Inc.

(a)

(b)

(c)

FIGURE 1-10 This three-dimensional model was used to create
perspective views from numerous angles, and orthogonal views, such as *c*,
were used to produce elevations. David Baker Associates, Architects.

dimensional drawings can be obtained simply by cutting the model at any point, in any direction. "Cutaway" perspectives or axonometrics can likewise be created. Although modeling is a relative newcomer to computer-aided architecture, it holds enormous potential for transforming design and drafting.

THE CHANGING DESIGN PROFESSION

A new medium is never an addition to an old one, nor does it leave the old one in peace.[1]

In writing about the impact of "extensions of man," Marshall McLuhan declared emphatically that new tools change the nature of work. Furthermore, these extensions change the men and women who wield them.

Architectural design and drafting is one of the most traditionally practiced professions; in many ways, it is the same craft that it was a hundred or more years ago. The introduction of computers into architectural practice is bringing changes that are potentially as jarring as the appearance of the printing press was to the bookmaking craft of the Middle Ages.

Printing from movable types was the first mechanization of a complex handicraft, and became the archetype of all subsequent mechanization.[1]

For years, the printing press was applied to the imitation of hand lettering. Designers and drafters tend to do the same thing in applying computer graphics to architecture, using familiar manual strategies for organizing and producing work. Of course, it isn't immediately obvious how to use a new medium most effectively, and it takes time to learn. In a few years, the notion of drafting with a pencil, one line at a time, will seem as quaint as hand lettering a book. Until then, we are in period of transition, during which we must learn to use unfamiliar "extensions," not because they are inevitable or because of future promises, but because they are useful even as we stumble into better and better ways to use them.

Typography was no more an addition to the scribal art than the motorcar was an addition to the horse.[1]

The printing press brought new forms of typefaces, book designs, illustrations, bindings, and, most important of all, the publishing industry itself. The medium evolved as the tools grew less constraining;

simultaneously, as the literate audience grew, the *content* changed, and our current literary forms evolved. Computer-aided architecture is bringing a similar transformation, demanding not only new skills but also new premises and principles. Nevertheless, it will continue to be architects, not computer programmers, who produce architecture. The important question is: can we use computers to produce better architecture?

In amplifying and extending the written word, typography revealed and greatly extended the structure of writing.[1]

Electronic design extensions can similarly be used to amplify and extend drawing, the most fundamental design tool. As we will see, computer graphics can indeed reveal the structure of architecture, in both two and three dimensions. By extending our powers of visualization and our capabilities for exploring and documenting designs, computers may lead us into the architectural equivalents of Gutenberg's *Bible*, *War and Peace*, mass-marketed best-sellers, or comic books, but they will certainly lead us into new territory.

EFFICIENCY AND QUALITY

As computers make architectural practice more productive and versatile, they are changing the very concepts of drawing and design. Many architects worry that familiar techniques will be replaced with mechanistic, insensitive methods, and that design work will be taken over by computer specialists. These are reasonable concerns: tools are supposed to serve their user's goals, not define them.

The craft of drawing is a fundamental part of the practice of design. From sketch to draft, drawing serves as a means of both exploring ideas and communicating them. It is a way to *simultaneously* record, refine and explain what we see or imagine. It is crucial that a new drawing tool supports this process—if it fails, then the design process can be crippled.

Compared to hand drawing, computer-aided drawing is often somewhat mechanistic. It is difficult to produce the nuances that are possible with hand and pencil, or to use a computer to sketch on a napkin in a restaurant. Hand sketching will always be an important part of designing. Nevertheless, there are times when the computer's capabilities can help to explore and communicate more effectively than a pencil or

[1] All quotes given here are from Marshall McLuhan, *Understanding Media: The Extensions of Man*, New American Library, 1964, pp. 155–162.

pen. The key is to know when computer assistance is appropriate, and when a pencil can do a better job. The computer's role is not limited to drafting, nor should hand drawing be limited to sketches on napkins: the two are most effectively used together, throughout the design process.

Tools that increase efficiency can also be used to lower quality. Computer-aided drawing will be no exception. Yet, it is a mistake to believe that high efficiency and low quality are somehow linked. The urge to produce *as much* as possible *as quickly* as possible may lead some to cut corners. Architects face tremendous pressures to produce physically sound, visually attractive, functionally useful buildings, at an often low level of compensation. By increasing efficiency, a similar level of quality may be reached with somewhat less effort; better still, the same level of effort may improve the product. The most compelling reason for using computer-aided design may be to improve the quality of our work.

HOW DIFFICULT IS LEARNING?

Learning computer-aided design skills is like learning to play a musical instrument: if you have the inclination, you may love it; if you don't, you won't. Be patient: the fumbling period that is inherent to learning often scares people away. Practice without time pressure, doing the kind of drawing you enjoy. Start with simple tasks, but be sure you take some time to try some drawing that takes advantage of the capabilities of your software. Even if you are not planning on working regularly with CAD, your learning time is well spent if you will be working with people who will. It is important that everyone on a project have some idea of the capabilities and limits of the tools that are being used.

Learning time varies tremendously with the "friendliness" of the software. "Friendliness," the ease with which a program accommodates a newcomer, may be a cliché, but it is especially important for architectural computer programs: you have a right to expect programs to be relatively easy to learn and use. A particularly difficult program requires a specialist to use it, and too much specialization is inconsistent with the generalized set of skills required by the architectural profession.

The amount of time it takes to learn to use a CAD program also varies, of course, with your own inclination and the amount of time you spend using it. With a reasonably easy to learn program, some degree of comfort usually comes within days; a reasonable degree of competence within weeks; speed follows not long behind. If you are using particularly difficult software, comfort may take a few weeks, competence months. Either way, some experienced guidance, from fellow CAD users or good references, can help tremendously. Keep in mind that learning about CAD should go on indefinitely, since you will always be thinking of (and borrowing) new drawing strategies.

If you are one of those people who just can't stand to be around computers, take heart. Computers may revolutionize the design professions, but as they do, both the software and the hardware will become far less machinelike. In the very near future, drawing with electronic assistance may be nearly indistinguishable from good old fashioned sketching, except that the results of a few sketch sessions may be remarkably like a finished product.

HARD AND SOFT CHOICES

CHAPTER 2

The technology of small computers has developed rapidly, and architecturally oriented computer programs have followed at a dizzying pace. Architects entering the CAD world often feel like bumpkins entering a department store for the first time. Making smart choices seems difficult, at best.

Even after choosing a computer-aided design system, you can expect it to evolve as technologies progress and your needs change. Thus, you may be building a system long after you choose a software package and your first computer. To make wise choices in assembling and maintaining the system, you need to know a few things about each of the individual parts. Even if you are using someone else's CAD system, it's important to be knowledgeable regarding the various parts: you may need to tinker with the hardware, set up the software, or suggest new additions to the system.

AN EVOLVING TECHNOLOGY

It helps to know some recent history. Only recently have computers with graphic capabilities become affordable for most architectural firms. In the 1970s, a few large architectural and engineering firms began using expensive mainframe computers for drafting, often using programs that were written for the automobile and aerospace industries. These programs were not well suited to architecture, so a few design firms such as Skidmore, Owings, and Merrill and Hellmuth, Obata, and Kassabaum wrote their own software. By the mid1970s, **minicomputers,** smaller, somewhat less expensive machines, were available that enabled a firm to link as many as a dozen workstations through a single computer, at a somewhat lower cost.

By the late 1970s, software developers like Intergraph and Computervision began to adapt their minicomputer software, originally developed for use by engineers and industrial designers, for architects. These two-dimensional drafting systems still cost hundreds of thousands of dollars to set up and were difficult to learn to use, but many large design and engineering firms decided that computer-aided drafting was useful enough to justify the expense. Unfortunately, they often had to keep drafters working two or three shifts a day in order to pay back their investments.

MICROCOMPUTERS

With the introduction of low-cost "personal" (single-user) **microcomputers** around 1980, the stage was set for a graphics revolution, and electronic drafting software was quickly developed for the new machines. Personal computers were relatively slow and had stringent memory limitations, so minicomputer software could not be adapted directly. Instead, a whole new generation of drafting software was born.

The first microcomputer CAD systems were, compared to minicomputer and mainframe systems, rudimentary and slow. AutoCAD (developed for IBM-compatible PCs), PCAD (which became CADvance), and CADApple (written for Apple computers, adapted to IBM compatibles as Versacad), were the first programs to gain popularity. Like the early large-system graphics programs, these were intended to be "general use" computer-aided drafting programs, not specifically designed for architects. With hardware prices below $10,000, including plotters, and software under $2,000, adventurous designers were willing to overlook some deficiencies. Meanwhile, the minicomputer drafting systems were proving that CAD did indeed have a

role in the design professions; ironically, much of the interest that they generated was directed to the evolving personal computer-based systems.

Almost by definition, microcomputers are capable of less than larger minicomputers. But while they could not equal the speed and capacity of bigger machines, equipment like the IBM-AT pushed personal computers into the CAD big leagues. And a funny thing happened as the PC CAD systems grew up: the software designers, able to learn from larger systems, were forced to write more efficient, compact programs, and they began to produce software that could seriously compete with much more expensive systems.

The distinctions between minicomputers and microcomputers have broken down as the former become smaller and less costly and the latter become more powerful. Gradually, there has been a trend toward "machine independence," so that programs can be used on different kinds of computers and peripheral equipment. Increasingly, large and small systems can work together, but for firms with limited budgets, microcomputer-based systems are becoming a standard tool for drafting, modeling, and a number of other architectural applications.

COMPARING CAD PROGRAMS

A program is a set of instructions that tells the computer what to do. It translates *your* instructions into words or graphics. A graphics program tells the computer how to interpret **primitive** drawing elements like a line or a circle. It then tells the machine how to actually draw images on a display or a plotter. Finally, a computer-aided drawing program provides an array of "commands" that let you manipulate the elements you create.

DIFFERENT WAYS TO DRAW

Computer-aided drawing programs can be lumped into several categories.

Painting with Pixels

An image is "drawn" on a computer display screen by lighting thousands of dots (**pixels**) on the screen, according to the program's instructions. A program that maps these pixels individually, storing an image as a grid of dots, is based on **bit-mapped** graphics, or

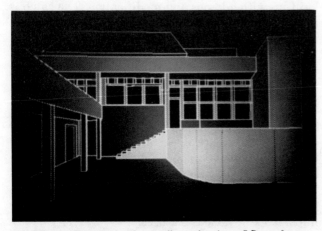

FIGURE 2-1 This image was initially produced as a 3-D wireframe model, then translated into a bit-mapped image and "painted" with MegaCADD's Illustrator software. The program also enables you to create animated "shows" from a series of images.

Imaging systems are programs that can capture and manipulate images from other sources, such as other graphics programs or still images from a video camera or recorder. Pictures of buildings, sites, and people; line-drawings; and shaded renderings can all be combined, stretched and shrunk, cut and pasted together, and displayed or printed. Although these systems are not appropriate for drafting, they can be valuable in preparing presentations and may be used to assemble collages and design studies. Some imaging systems enable you to combine graphics with text, which can be useful in preparing proposals, brochures, and reports.

Vectors

Most programs for architectural design and drafting are based on **vector graphics.** This is a system with which a line, for example, is remembered by its location, direction, and length. Vector graphics are extraordinarily precise, since, unlike bit-mapped graphics, they do not depend on the capabilities of the display: a line is always drawn as a single string of dots, no matter how much you zoom in or out.

Drafting programs are primarily two-dimensional tools for constructing detailed drawings. They generally include sophisticated drawing and editing capabilities, as we will discuss in Chapters 3 through 5 (Figure 2-2). They may also include a projective three-dimensional drawing capability, as we will see in Chapter 6.

simply **pixel graphics.** This system is used by **paint** software and is sometimes used to "render" images that have been created by drafting and modeling programs, after they are translated into a pixel-mapped image (Figure 2-1). Some painting programs can display a series of images in rapid succession to create animation effects.

FIGURE 2-2 An architectural plan, drawn with AutoCAD software. An on-screen menu of commands is located to the right: "line" has been chosen and is highlighted. Commands may also be typed with the keyboard; keystrokes appear on the "command line" at the bottom. Buday–Wells, Architects.

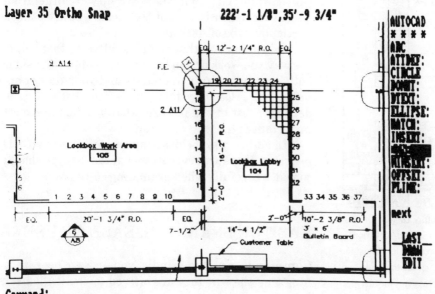

Modeling programs allow you to "draw" in three-dimensional space, then extract two-dimensional drawings from your model. Some modeling programs send these two-dimensional drawings to a separate drafting program, while others include their own integrated drafting capabilities (Figure 2-3).

Among all the available computer-aided drawing programs, only some are **architecture oriented.** Of those that aren't, some are designed specifically for other professions and are not appropriate for architecture. Others are adaptable enough to be used by architects, though usually with extra effort or expense. Some general-purpose CAD programs have been adapted for architecture by the addition of customizing software packages, some of which can transform a general-purpose program dramatically. Programs that are specifically architecture oriented often include drawing tools and symbol libraries that are targeted specifically toward building design.

Adaptable programs have two important advantages over software that can only be used "as is." A program that can be modified or added to is likely to support a thriving market for add-on packages that enable you to do things that the original software designer may never have thought about. Secondly, an adaptable program can usually be modified in-house with a bit of simple programming, if necessary. This may not be a capability you will use frequently, but it's nice to know it's there. Thus, a program that seems underfeatured by itself may be a powerhouse when

built up with add-ons and modification. The catch is that you must be able and willing to put some effort into building up the system.

TRY IT OUT

No two CAD programs work exactly alike, and the capabilities and ease of use can vary greatly from one to another. However, you will find that as you become familiar with one, others will be easier to understand. This book should help you become acquainted with the general principles of CAD and to understand the importance of various features.

The best way to learn about different programs is to spend time using one, then compare the features of alternative programs by reading reviews, manufacturers literature, and especially by talking to experienced users. There are three inexpensive ways to try out some CAD programs. If you know other people who are using CAD, arrange to use their system on nights or weekends. If you have the appropriate hardware available, you can sometimes obtain a "demonstration" version of a program from its publisher. These are generally limited versions of the actual program, with no ability to save or plot drawings. Some programs are available in low-budget, "entry level" versions, which you can purchase to try out. This is not recommended, because these versions often belie the capabilities of their bigger siblings. Also, avoid "canned" dealer demonstrations; they can be easily set up to show only the flashiest features of a program, completely bypassing problematic areas. If you can, arrange for an experienced user to create a simple drawing, start to finish, while you watch. The best help you can get from a software dealer is a list of architects who are using a particular type of software.

It is important that you find software that works the way you work or can be adapted to do so. Consider both your organizational habits and your design approaches: a CAD system will affect both. Try to develop a list of the features that you feel are most important to the way you want to work.

In addition to the drawing capabilities of a CAD program, there are several other areas that you should consider carefully when evaluating software.

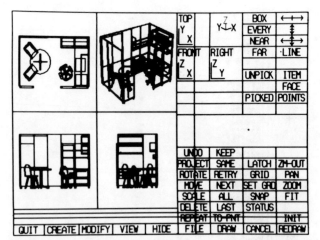

FIGURE 2-3   A three-dimensional model of an office cubicle. On the left side are three orthogonal views (plan and two section/elevations) and a perspective view. On the upper right are boxes for locating and selecting elements of the model; the lower right includes the commands for manipulating the model. Note the cursor, or crosshair, located at "repeat." Courtesy of MegaCADD, Inc.

EASE OF LEARNING, EASE OF USE

Commands are the handle you use to operate a program; the way they are offered to you is the **user interface.** The interface is what you see on the screen as you work; it is also the way you give commands to the computer. Some interfaces make a program easy to learn, others are easy to use only *after* you have learned. (Some, unfortunately, are neither.) Ideally, a user interface should be easy to learn and to use.

When you sit down to draw with a computer, you can give it commands in one (or more) of three ways. (Some programs allow only one method, others allow you to choose from several different interfaces.)

First, you can enter commands by typing them in English on a **keyboard** (Figure 2-4). You must, of course, know what the commands are to do this, either by memorizing them or posting a list nearby. You may also be able to abbreviate commands with single-letter codes, for speed, if you prefer.

Second, you can pick commands from on-screen lists called **menus**. (Menus are illustrated in Figures 2-2 and 2-3.) Usually a program will offer a series of menus that you may step through, from one to another. Since all the commands are displayed in front of you, this is the easiest system to learn, but, as you learn the commands, it will seem somewhat slow, since you must move the **cursor** (generally crosshairs on the screen) away from your drawing to pick a command, then move from one menu to another. It also takes up valuable screen space, making your drawing smaller.

Third, you can use a **digitizing tablet**, a sort of electronic notepad, which can also be set up with a menu of commands. The commands are laid out, generally on a grid, and mapped out by a paper or plastic overlay (Figure 2-5). On even a small tablet, a large number of commands can be placed on the menu. Each command can be picked by pointing at it on the tablet with a stylus.

FIGURE 2-5 A digitizing tablet with stylus. The lower left rectangle is used to move the cursor on the screen; the remaining area is divided into a grid, with each small rectangle representing a command. Tablet courtesy of Computervision, Inc.

Each of these interfaces has advantages and disadvantages, so the best system lets you choose among them. Thus, different people within the same workplace can choose their own way of working. Beginners, for example, usually prefer on-screen menus, while veterans often choose to type commands or codes. Even the most typewriter-phobic users tend to use the keyboard frequently, since commands can be entered with the nondrawing hand, without taking it away from the drawing to pick a command.

Easy-to-learn programs are *intuitive:* the commands and command sequences are logical and consistent. Using an intuitive program, you can often figure out how new commands work on the basis of the ones you already know. *Counter-intuitive* programs are inconsistent, and the commands are structured in unrelated or contradictory ways. Some have too many commands or use different names for commands that seem to do the same thing in different situations. Unfortunately, some of the most sophisticated (and expensive) programs are designed with difficult interfaces.

Documentation, the user's manuals and references that are supplied with a program, is also important. Manuals should be readable and organized well enough that, when you are working and need to know something, you can find it quickly. These too are sometimes badly written and can be a tremendous impediment to using an otherwise excellent program. When you are evaluating software, see if the manual is easily understandable: if it sounds like it was written

FIGURE 2-4 A typical (IBM) keyboard. Note that the cursor (arrow) keys are combined with the numeric keypad on the right, forcing you to toggle to one or the other. A better arrangement provides separate keys for these two functions.

by someone who does not understand your needs or capabilities, it probably was. Don't blame yourself for being a nonexpert with software you have yet to learn. Be sure that you have some reliable source of information for any software you use, be it the manual, other references or tutorials, a well-staffed user-support phone line, or experienced users who will answer questions.

SPEED

CAD programs vary greatly in the speed with which they can draw images on the screen. Given a very large drawing, some will seem very sluggish when you call for a new screen view, while others are relatively rapid. Since displaying images is often a bottleneck, let's look at the factors involved.

There are two ways a computer can perform the myriad of calculations that are required by a CAD program. Most programs use *floating* (decimal) *point* calculation, which has the advantage of being accurate enough to permit almost unlimited magnification of a drawing but can be relatively slow. A few programs use *integer-based* calculations, which can be performed much faster. However, integer-based programs are inherently less accurate. They can only support a limited amount of magnification, and a user must be prepared to limit the use of a drawing to a range of scales that might go from $\frac{1}{16}$ in=1 ft to $\frac{1}{2}$ in=1 ft.

When you wish to *refresh* a screen that has become cluttered with layout lines or erasures, you can do so very quickly, since the image has been calculated previously and is stored in the computer's memory. However, when a program must recalculate all the information in the drawing, the screen must be *regenerated*, which can take more time. With some programs, this takes place whenever you change the viewpoint by moving in, out, or around the display. Some programs keep a copy of a large portion of the drawing in memory, so that when you change the viewpoint within an area that has been calculated and drawn, the redisplay is very quick, like a simple screen refresh.

A program can speed regenerations in several other ways. First, drawing elements that are outside the display can be *clipped* from the redrawing process, reducing the number of calculations the program has to do. Secondly, the number of drawing layers that must be redrawn can be reduced, usually by eliminating those that are currently hidden, a process sometimes referred to as *freezing* layers. You can determine whether a program uses either or both of these tech-

niques by timing screen regenerations, comparing redisplay times when you move in and out of a drawing, and when you turn layers on and off.

COMPATIBILITY

Before you can use a CAD program, you must start with a "foundation" program called an **operating system.** The operating system tells the computer how to coordinate the machine with your various programs, and it manages the use of the computer's memory, data storage media, and peripheral equipment. Each program you use must be written to be used with a specific operating system. Some computers, though, allow the user to choose from several operating systems, according to the desired software. Many microcomputers use an operating system called MS-DOS, its descendant OS/2, or a more powerful system called Unix. (Some versions of Unix can run MS-DOS *within* them.) For the most part, graphics software is written to work with a specific operating system, but a few programs are becoming available in versions that will work on different operating systems.

Chances are you will not use your computer only for drawing, and you may want to use more than one drawing program. Any time you want two or more programs to work together, you have to consider whether or not they are compatible with each other.

Exchanging Drawings . . .

Programs that run on the same computer, using the same operating system, do not necessarily produce compatible files. In fact, most CAD programs are not directly compatible with each other. Some, however, include utility programs for translating drawings and data into intermediate formats that can be read by other programs. There are several formats that can be used to share graphic information; the most widely recognized is the *IGES* (Initial Graphics Exchange Specification) format. Another widely adopted standard is the AutoCAD *DXF* interchange file format, which numerous other programs can read and write. Unfortunately, only custom-written translation systems can transfer *all* of the information between programs that are inherently different. Data regarding layers and symbols, for example, is sometimes dropped or simplified in translation. It is not always practical to use a system like IGES to link several CAD programs, swapping information every day, unless you are aware of *exactly* what data may be compromised. With this qualification, it is possible, if awkward, to use these interchange capabilities to design a project on two different CAD systems. The primary reason for considering this is cost: an inexpensive microcomputer-based system might be used as a cheap workstation for a more powerful (and more expensive) minicomputer.

... and Data

You may also want to write notes on a word processor and import them into your drawings or export lists of materials to a spreadsheet or database management program. A CAD program must either include these capabilities internally (this software is said to be "integrated") or make allowances for you to transfer such information to and from other programs. Data must, again, be imported or exported in a format that is recognized by other software.

HARDWARE FOR GRAPHICS

In order to use a computer, you need to know very little about the machine itself. Your biggest concern, once it's purchased and hooked up, is how to turn it on and adjust the video display. However, the more you know about what goes on inside, the more you can optimize it to get the most out of your software. As time passes, you may wish to add new hardware to your system. Since only certain combinations of computers and add-on *peripheral equipment* will work together, it is important to be familiar with different types of computers and peripherals.

INFORMATION PROCESSORS

The first "small" computers were the so-called minicomputers: by today's standards they were physically not so small and only moderately powerful. They were made possible by printed circuit boards that could hold a complete **central processing unit** (CPU), the "brain" of the computer. Previously, the CPUs of mainframe computers had been housed in large cabinets of individual transistors; earlier still (the 1950s), mainframe CPUs had been contained in entire rooms full of vacuum-tube assemblies.

In the early 1970s, the first silicon chips were developed to house computer CPUs. These **microprocessors,** pocket-sized wafers, could process and store information far more efficiently and quickly than their

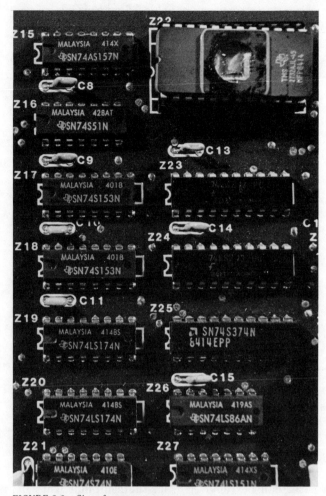

FIGURE 2-6   Chips from a microcomputer.

predecessors. Silicon memory chips were also developed, as well as numerous other specialized chips. Eventually, in the late 1970s, these chips were used to create an even smaller type of computer, dubbed microcomputers or personal computers (Figure 2-6).

The first microcomputers had relatively small processing chips that could handle 8 pieces of information ("bits") at once. Small-capacity processors mean slow computers, since it takes more time to squeeze data through a small processor than a big one. Before long, 16-bit chips were introduced, such as Intel Corporation's 8088, the processor that went into the IBM-PC. Since then, improved 16-bit chips were introduced, followed by 32-bit chips. Specialized chips called *math coprocessors* and *graphics coprocessors* were created to handle the intensive calculations required by engineering and graphics programs.

Minicomputers, too, became smaller and less expensive. They retained major advantages over microcomputers: they are capable of supporting several graphic workstations from a single central processor, enabling users to easily share information from the centralized source. They are also powerful enough to enable a user to do more than one operation at once, such as drawing, plotting, and database sorting. (This is called **multitasking**.) The CAD systems that were originally developed for these machines became more efficient and affordable. Using the first 32-bit microprocessors, they remained capable of handling larger projects at a greater rate of speed than the microcomputers.

Now, however, the distinctions are breaking down. Powerful 32-bit microprocessors, such as the Motorola 68020 and the Intel 80386, are bringing tremendous capacity and speed to small, affordable computers. They can also offer multiuser and multitasking capabilities. More efficiently designed computers like *reduced instruction set computers* (RISC) are further speeding up the hardware. In the future, even advanced computers will be relatively small, and many will be affordable for even small architectural firms.

REMEMBERING AND STORING INFORMATION

Most computers use two primary ways of storing information—on silicon chips, which reside within the computer, and on media such as disks, which in some cases can be removed from the computer. Internal chip-based memory, called **random access memory** (RAM) due to its quickly accessible nature, depends on uninterrupted electric power. It is used primarily for *working* memory: when the machine is turned off, it loses its information. Permanent storage media, such as **diskettes** and **hard disks,** can be used to save your work periodically, as you work, in case of power failure, and to archive drawings indefinitely.

Diskettes are an inexpensive, easily transportable medium. They can be carried from one computer to another, and they can be erased and used repeatedly. These *floppy disks* or *microdisks* come in several sizes and capacities, varying with the computer model (Figure 2-7). Typically, a disk can carry anywhere from one very large architectural drawing to a dozen medium-size drawings. You can also place a very large library of symbols or small drawings on a single disk. Unfortunately, reading from and writing on diskettes is slow. Many programs send information back and forth to a disk, so storing the program or drawing on which you are working on diskettes can slow a CAD program down unacceptably.

FIGURE 2-7 Floppy disks (left) and microdisks (right) can store dozens of small drawings or single drawings that are very large. For example, all the text for this book can easily fit on one 1.2 megabyte-capacity disk, while the illustrations for Chapter 1 fit on another.

Mass storage media such as hard disks are a necessity for computer-aided drawing. They are faster and have a greater capacity, 10 to 100 times greater, than diskettes. A hard disk is a complete mechanism, not a removable medium. Since they are very delicate they are not as portable and are often fixed inside the computer. Since they hold so much information, they must be organized very carefully. Typically, a single hard disk will contain your CAD program, your drawings, various "utility" programs, and, perhaps, additional software for cost estimating or word processing. Groups of *files* (drawings, programs, and other data) can be organized into *directories* and *subdirectories*, so that you can manage them more easily. Since hard disks are prone to disastrous breakdowns, all important information must be *backed up* onto diskettes or onto tape cassettes. The importance of this cannot be overemphasized: an entire project, or more, can evaporate in an instant if a hard disk fails.

Several alternatives for data storage exist. Large-capacity disks on removable cartridges are like portable hard disks. They are ideal for a situation in which large drawing files may be passed around between workstations, and when it is useful to file a large project on a single disk that can be stored safely. Laser disks are another alternative, with important advantages and limitations. *Compact-disk, read-only memory* (CD-ROM) systems offer vast amounts of storage capacity but cannot be written on directly. They are most appropriate for storing prepackaged, mass-marketed drawing libraries, standard specifications and cost-estimating information. An alternative, CD-WORM (*write once read mostly*) allows you to store information on a disk, once, that can be read back at any time. You could, perhaps, place a firm's entire drawing output for a year on one of these disks. Laser disks that can be written and erased like floppy disks are also under development.

SHARING INFORMATION

Sometimes you will want to transfer information from one computer to another: there are several ways to do so. The simplest is to copy a file onto a disk, then put the disk in the second machine. This is not the fastest method, nor is it very convenient if the second computer is on the other side of town. If your two computers are compatible with each other and are using compatible software, there are several electronic means to transfer information.

Computers can be linked over telephone lines, or over do-it-yourself internal telephone lines, by using a device called a **modem**. Since these devices send information in a one-bit-at-a-time stream and since they must check for errors, they tend to be slow in sending large files like drawings. Newer models are appearing that operate at relatively high rates of speed, and improvements in the quality of telephone lines are improving the quality of modem links. Modems are relatively easy to use, although they require compatible communications software at both ends.

Within a single building or workplace, computers can be linked directly in a **network**, (or *local area network*). There are various kinds of networks, some very complex, most of which use a single computer as a central storage point and "traffic cop." In addition to being able to share data, such a network can be used to ensure that a single "master" copy of each file is maintained at a central point. Each user at a peripheral workstation can "borrow" the original, updating it at the end of each session. Since each workstation is itself a microcomputer, files can be stored locally, as well. Networks usually require special hardware and cabling, and sophisticated software for managing the demands placed on a single CPU by several machines.

The predecessor to the microcomputer network is the single large computer with peripheral "dumb" workstations, which cannot function on their own. With a sufficiently powerful computer, this setup has the advantage of strict control over the central database. Many of the early CAD systems were written to take advantage of this centralization, allowing several workstations access to a project at the same time. This is difficult to implement in a decentralized network.

SEEING CLEARLY

Most of your computer-drawing time will be spent watching a display screen, so it ought to be as comfortable to look at as possible. Although displays using liquid crystal diodes (LCDs, commonly used in wristwatches) and electroluminescent screens may eventually produce flat, portable, comfortable viewing, most computer-aided drawing is done on video displays.

A video display is really a two-part system. First, it includes a **monitor**, the box that houses a cathode ray tube, better known as the screen. It also includes an electronic **graphic adapter**, often located in the computer itself, that interprets the signals sent out by the program, translating them into graphic images for the monitor. A monitor must be capable of displaying the images as they are sent out by the adapter: not all adapters and monitors are compatible, nor, for that matter, do all CAD programs work with all graphic adapters. You must be particularly careful in matching these.

Many CAD programs give you a choice of several different display options. In choosing a graphics display, the most crucial variable is **resolution**. Resolution is measured by the number of dots displayed, horizontally and vertically, on the screen. The available range runs from 640×350 (the absolute minimum acceptable for CAD: many people find this too low) to about 1000×1000 or even higher. High-resolution displays are not only more comfortable to look at, but they allow you to see, accurately, *more* of your work at once. Using a low-resolution display forces you to "zoom" in and out of a drawing frequently, a time-consuming process, while higher resolution lets you work at greater levels of detail on a large drawing area (Figure 2-8). (While higher resolution is generally better, some high-resolution systems tend to be slower to redraw their screens, somewhat offsetting the advantages.)

High resolution displays are also well suited to displaying several *windows* at once, dividing the screen into different areas to display different kinds of information. This becomes increasingly important as multitasking becomes more common: you may wish to work on a database management program to edit a finish schedule while you work on a drawing, or you may wish to display two drawings at once, in different windows. If you want to view a large schedule or two complex drawings, you'll need high resolution to squeeze them onto the screen area.

The *size* of the monitor is independent of the

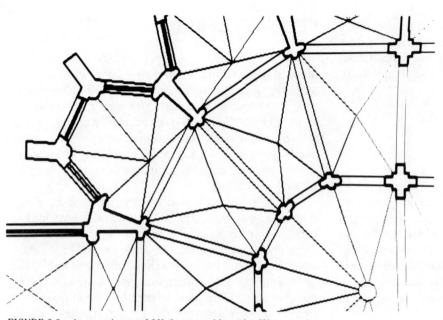

FIGURE 2-8   At a resolution of 640 (horizontal lines) by 480 (vertical lines) on a 13″ monitor, diagonal lines and curves are somewhat jagged.

capabilities of the graphic adapter, just as any size TV can display broadcast signals. However, a large monitor is largely wasted on low-resolution output, so monitors of about 13-inch (measured diagonally) are usually used for medium- and low-resolution displays. With high-resolution adapters, most people prefer 19-inch or even 25-inch monitors.

Color displays are an important factor in computer-aided drawing. CAD software is designed to let you display groups of drawing elements in different colors to aid in editing and plotting them: this capability is wasted with anything less than a color display. Rainbows of hundreds of colors are not needed for drafting, but a palette of sixteen or more colors is very useful. If you will be using three-dimensional software that allows surface shading, or image-capture software that offers multicolor rendering capabilities, a large palette can be a valuable design and presentation tool.

Monochrome monitors are useful for displaying text on a CAD system that lets you use separate monitors for graphics and textual information. Not all CAD programs allow this arrangement, but it can be very useful, since it allows the entire graphics screen to be used for graphics. High-resolution monochrome monitors, which display a single color on a black, white, or green background, are less expensive than multicolor monitors. Monochrome is not well suited to layered drawing, since it is difficult to see on which layer an element is located.

HANDWARE

Drawing is a manual activity. Just as a straightedge guides your pencil, the computer assists in putting lines where they belong. But like a pencil or straightedge, computer tools must be comfortable for your hands, and they must allow good hand and eye coordination. As we mentioned above, there are several different kinds of user interfaces available for computer-aided drawing. Each uses a particular type of hardware (handware?).

Typing and Cursoring

Many architects are not accomplished typists and use the "hunt and peck" method, which is hardly a pleasant way to *type*, much less draw. Although it is probably a good idea for anyone to learn to type proficiently in the computer age, typing skills are not required to use the keyboard effectively for drawing. Touch-typing is not necessary to type one- or two-key codes.

Since a keyboard can be used to write drawing notations and perform numeric calculations, it is more than a means to enter commands. Typed notes and dimensions, which are displayed and plotted according to the typeface you choose, are one means by which you can produce extremely readable drawings. The arrow keys can also be used to move the on-screen drawing cursor, or crosshairs, more precisely over short distances than a hand-held pointing device.

Talking to the Machine

An alternative to typing commands is *speaking* them: **voice recognition** systems are available that enable you to talk to your computer instead of typing to it. They consist of a microphone, an electronic board that usually is placed in the computer, and special software that translates voice patterns into words. You can "teach" the computer to recognize a limited set of spoken sounds, generally from one person's voice, and treat each word as if it had been typed. These systems are far from foolproof—a chance remark may have unpredictable consequences—but the idea of drawing without manually entering commands is certainly attractive. While the notion of a studio full of people talking to machines is almost comical, we may see the day when our voices take over many of the functions of handware, leaving the hands free for drawing.

Mousing Around

Several kinds of devices can be used as electronic pencils. Each is used to move the crosshairs around on your screen. Since they are all used to point to on-screen graphics, they are also a means of picking items from on-screen menus.

A **mouse** is a hand-held box with several buttons and a tail linking it to the computer (Figure 2-9). By sliding it around on a pad or on the desktop, you can move the crosshairs on the screen. At first, drawing with a mouse feels odd, because you watch the screen, not the drawing tool, as you work, and because the

FIGURE 2-9   An "optical" mouse, which registers movement by reflecting a light onto a small pad with a reflective grid imbedded.

distance the mouse moves does not correlate exactly to the distance the crosshairs move on the screen. You will get used to these contradictions very quickly; most drafters find mice fairly comfortable for drafting. They are somewhat less ideal for freehand drawing, since they are awkward to move rapidly.

There are two species of electronic mice: *optical* and *mechanical.* The only effective difference is that an optical mouse must be used on a reflective pad, onto which a small light is bounced, while a mechanical mouse can be used on any flat surface. This distinction is inconsequential.

The evolutionary ancestor of the mouse is a stationary directional pointer called a **joystick,** which is used by a few CAD programs. This stationary device can be pointed in any direction, and the crosshairs move in that direction. Since it is difficult to control the speed of movement, a joystick is not a comfortable drawing tool.

Screen Pointing

A **light pen** is a pen-sized pointer that is held to the display screen to pick menu items and move the crosshairs around a drawing. In theory, it is the most direct pointing device. In practice, however, light pens have several serious disadvantages. A light pen requires that the user be within a comfortable arm's length, under sixteen inches, from the video screen. However, most video screens are best viewed from about two feet away: any closer can be very tiring for the eyes. Also, holding a light pen on a vertical surface can be tiring over long periods of time. If the screen is tilted or laid flat, the user may be even closer to the screen.

Light pens may become more popular when more mobile, less eye-straining screens become available. High-resolution, low-flicker video screens and other alternatives may make this possible.

Digitizing

Mice are *relative* pointers: they indicate direction but do not measure distance accurately, hence they cannot be used for tracing. In order to copy a paper drawing, you need a **digitizing tablet,** an *absolute* pointing device.

A tablet is used with either an electronic stylus or a box with buttons (and a tail) that looks, at first, like a mouse. This box, called a cursor, has a pair of crosshairs that travel over the drawing surface, as does the point of the stylus. Since the stylus is much like a pencil, it is favored by many architects (Figure 2-5). Either of these two pointers can be used like a mouse, to indicate direction and to point to drawing elements and menu items on the screen. They can also be used, however, to trace with a very high level of accuracy, as well as to pick commands and symbols from a menu that is overlaid on the tablet.

When you trace a drawing on a digitizing tablet, you use the same drawing procedures that you use in normal computer-aided drawing. To copy a line, for example, you pick the endpoints. You can use the built-in accuracy of the CAD program to actually improve the accuracy of the original, by making lines and objects conform to dimensional requirements. A good tablet is accurate to about 0.001 inch. If your drawing is bigger than the tablet, you can shift the drawing across the tablet, then, give the computer two reference points from an overlapping area: the drawing will be automatically aligned. Even a small 12-inch × 12-inch tablet can be used effectively this way, although the larger the tablet, the less shifting you must do. If your work involves large amounts of tracing, a large tablet may be a good investment.

Tablet menus can be purchased with some architectural software, and many programs allow you to create your own menus. The surface is divided into a grid of boxes, and each box is assigned a meaning, which is invoked when you point to it. A box may contain a command, a sequence of commands, or a graphic image that you can insert into your drawing. A 12-inch × 12-inch menu can contain most of the commands used by a program, with room for a number of special boxes for command sequences (*macros*) or graphics. A small area, usually about one-fourth of the surface, is reserved for a blank space on which the stylus or cursor can be used in "mouse" mode, dragging the on-screen crosshairs.

HARD COPY

Once you create an electronic drawing, you usually need to find a way to get it onto paper, velum, or mylar. In architectural practice, you need to be able to reproduce your drawings at large size, reasonably fast, and with great accuracy. It doesn't hurt if they're beautiful, too.

Printing

Graphic printers are the quickest way to reproduce a drawing. Images are produced by printing dots onto paper, very small and very close together, one of three

ways. A printhead with 8 to 24 pins can be used to strike a ribbon; an ink jet can squirt patterns onto the paper directly, or an electrostatic process, using a laser or LCDs, can produce images in a manner similar to photocopiers. In each case, the software must translate the vector graphics into a matrix of dots, a process called *rasterizing*.

Pin *impact* printers are limited in resolution by the mechanics of the tiny pins. When you need a quick record of a drawing, and you are not concerned with detail, a mechanical dot-matrix printer will often suffice. Since they are also good for printing text, such as lists that are created while you draw, it's a good idea to have a basic dot printer handy. Although some can print in color by using multicolored ribbons, they are inherently too small and too low-resolution to produce high-quality architectural drawings.

Ink jet printers share most of the advantages and problems of pin printers. They are generally used for text and medium-resolution graphics. However, jet printers have the potential for producing higher resolution drawings at large sizes, and they may find a greater role in architectural graphics than they currently play (Figure 2-10).

Electrostatic dot-matrix printers are relatively expensive, but they are both fast and accurate. Small, desktop laser printers have sufficient resolution to produce architectural details and small presentation drawings, while doubling as letter-quality printers. Large electrostatic plotters, which are essentially huge dot printers, can be used for most architectural drawings. Because they are extremely costly, they may

FIGURE 2-10   An inkjet printer, capable of very quiet operation and able to produce medium-resolution graphics (192 dots per inch, compared to 300 dots per inch for a typical laser printer).

be available only to large firms or through reprographic services in the near future.

Plotting

Pen plotters are the kind of tool that you curse when something goes wrong and brag about when everything works. A good pen plot, using several pens to create different line weights and colors, can be strikingly attractive. The quality of diagonal lines and curves that are produced by a good pen plotter is vastly superior to any dot-matrix medium. (Most of the drawings in this book were produced on a pen plotter.) (Figure 2-11)

Large plotters move a sheet of paper under the pen in one direction, while the pen is moved in the other direction. (Smaller plotters move the pen, on a bar, both directions.) Low-cost plotters often move the pen in short, visible "jumps," making diagonal lines into

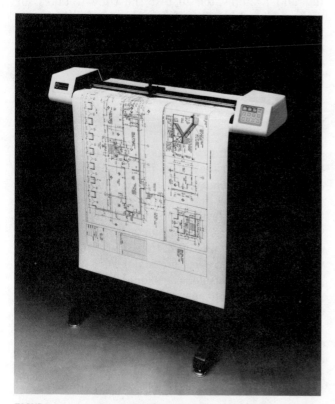

FIGURE 2-11 A single-pen "C" and "D" sheet-size plotter, also available in "E" size. This is a plotter that most small firms can afford, yet it plots without the visible "steps" that some low-end plotters produce when drawing diagonal lines and curves. Most of the drawings in this book were plotted with this plotter. Courtesy of Houston Instrument Division of Ametek.

"stair steps," just like a dot printer. A good plotter will produce smooth diagonals and curves. Multipen plotters will automatically change pens according to your instructions, although single-pen plotters will stop to let you change pens manually. You can use either technical pens or inexpensive felt-tip pens.

Pen plotters have several distinct disadvantages. Most plotters operate at several speeds. At the highest speeds, the pens move at a blazing rate of speed, almost too fast for the eye to follow, but it still takes a long time (5 to 45 minutes) to plot an architectural drawing. They tend to be noisy, so that you will probably want to put them in a transparent soundproof enclosure. Why transparent? Once in a while, usually when you are in a hurry, a pen will clog or run out of ink, usually necessitating a new plot. Thus, you will want to check on the progress of a plot as it proceeds. Still, when it comes out right, you will usually be pleased.

HARDWARE COMPATIBILITY

Computers and peripheral equipment such as displays, plotters, and printers suffer from an unfortunate lack of complete compatibility that must be resolved by programs. As a result, a program that produces beautiful results on one plotter may produce incomprehensible garbage or nothing at all on another, so programs thus must include *drivers*, subprograms that tell specific peripherals what to do.

Since it is difficult to write drivers and since so many peripherals are available, some software writers have chosen to support only a few pieces of equipment, in essence endorsing a "required" workstation. Some of these companies sell "all or nothing" software-hardware packages: if you want the software, you must buy a specific hardware configuration. Others support a wide range of peripherals, allowing you to "mix and match" to design your own workstation. Given the price competition that exists among hardware manufacturers, the advantages of this approach to the user are obvious.

Sometimes the most popular hardware becomes a "standard," as has happened with IBM-compatible computers. Unfortunately, the standards are not always the best solution, as in the case of the popular medium-resolution IBM Enhanced Graphic Adapter. A better solution is a multipurpose hardware-software link that allows any program to communicate with any piece of equipment. Several of these standards have been proposed, and some are in use in various forms. Until such standards gain wide acceptance, software that supports a variety of peripherals is a good choice.

CHOOSING AND USING CAD

HOW MUCH ... AND WHEN?

The rapid development of computer-aided drafting and design can be expected to continue in the near future. Why, then, begin using something that will be "obsolete" in a year or two?

Most important, as we explained in Chapter 1, CAD is a tool that is already useful, even if you buy a system and never upgrade it. The *payback* time, the period in which your costs can be recovered through labor savings, is relatively short for PC-based systems.

Also, if you choose carefully, you can pick both hardware and software that will evolve as standards and capabilities change. Today's state-of-the-art computer can be tomorrow's training and plotting workstation; usually your software can be upgraded to newer versions at less than full cost.

What kind of criteria should you use when you choose or upgrade a CAD system? Here are some suggestions:

Cost and Style

"Cost" is an elusive issue in architectural computer systems. Prices for hardware and software may vary widely from one system to another, but these capital costs will eventually seem almost trivial compared to the investments you make in training and in building up libraries of drawings and data. Architecture is labor-intensive work, even when you use computers, and the ease with which people in a firm can learn and use a system will determine its ultimate cost. Many architects have made the mistake of buying low-budget hardware or software, only to find themselves spending great amounts of time making up for shortcomings. Once you know what your needs are, try to fulfill them: if you go halfway you will probably end up going the rest of the way sooner or later, possibly at a greater overall expense.

Pick your software before you pick your computer. Find a program that will do the kind of work you want to do and is easy to learn and use. Ease of use requires that the computer help you to work in a way that feels comfortable and suits your "style" of working. Plan on doing some self-analysis as well as software analysis: try to sort out which working habits you want to keep and which you would like to get rid of. (More on this in Chapter 8.) If you are choosing CAD software for a design office, consider whether or not your firm will be able to hire people who have used a particular software package. Experienced people can not only save you training time, but they can help set up your system.

After you find the right software, then find a computer on which it will operate. Some programs are designed for *dedicated* systems, which are specifically assembled for the software. This is becoming less common, and chances are that any program will operate on several different computers.

Speed is essential. A slow CAD program will make you feel like you are drawing in molasses. It is impossible to overstate the importance of a speedy CAD system: if you find yourself waiting every time a drawing is displayed on the screen, you will eventually begin to lose your concentration and become frustrated. The rate at which a drawing appears on the screen is a function of both the hardware and the software, as we explained. In order to evaluate both, learn a little about what makes the machines different, then try the same program on several computers. Try different programs on the same machine. Use a complex drawing and a stopwatch to test the time it takes for different combinations of hardware and software to perform simple operations, especially tasks that require a drawing to be redisplayed from scratch. You will **always** want a faster system, so start with the fastest you can possibly afford.

Growing

Plan strategies for growth. Assume that you will want to purchase upgrades of your software and budget accordingly. If you expect that, as you become more experienced, you will want to move up to more sophisticated software, develop criteria so that you will know when you are ready. Most important, if you foresee this sort of growth, get an idea of the software to which you will want to upgrade and make sure your initial purchase is compatible. You should be able to transfer your drawings from one to the other, so you don't lose all the work you put into developing libraries of drawings. Then, either plan to move to a system that can use your hardware, or plan to sell the hardware. Remember that hardware too can be upgraded, by installing add-on options and switching peripherals like plotters and video displays.

Shopping Around

One of the benefits of PC-based CAD systems is the ability to mix and match computer hardware. While most minicomputer systems force you to use a predetermined setup with a predetermined price, micro-computers are available with many options for both price and performance. Unfortunately, the number of options can be bewildering.

The best way to shop is with a shopping list, and a computer shopping list can serve as a specification for comparing and purchasing hardware. It can be used to ensure that your system meets specific standards, and that, if you visit different dealers, you aren't comparing apples and oranges.

Buying computer hardware is difficult because, like automobiles, there are many models available that look the same and accomplish more or less the same function, but do it at different levels of efficiency. There are also different levels of prices, and they don't always correlate to quality. It's always tempting to buy well-known brand names, but even IBM, often considered the safest choice of all, has marketed mediocre hardware at premium prices. If you're careful, it's possible to buy "no-name" brands that work as well as or better than their more familiar competitors. But since it's also possible to buy defective hardware from companies that may be out of business when you call for help, caution is in order.

There are three things to look for when you put together a computer shopping list: *compatibility, reliability*, and *numbers*. Each of these can be written into your shopping list.

There are three ways to ensure compatibility: read the documentation for each element; try out the specific combination before buying it, and, finally, write an agreement with the dealer guaranteeing compatibility of specific elements. If you can't do all three, be sure to do the latter; it can be part of your shopping list/specification.

Reliability is often hard to evaluate; often hearsay and magazine reviews are all you have to go by. However, if you can't ensure reliability, you can ensure that you're not helpless when your computer breaks down. First, make sure you have a reasonable warranty and run your hardware hard during the warranty period. Second, be sure you can get prompt, *local* service, even after the warranty expires. Finally, if you have any reason to doubt that the manufacturer will be in business in a year or two, be sure that service and parts are available from another source.

Numbers are the exact specifications of the hardware, and they should be the centerpiece of your shopping list. Each component of a computer system can be evaluated in terms such as speed, capacity, resolution, size and options, and you can use these ratings to specify the minimum performance that is acceptable to you.

Performance Specs

The concept of **performance specifications** is familiar to most architects and engineers. Essentially, it is a list of criteria that defines standards to which a product must measure up. A supplier can sell you any brand of merchandise, as long as it meets or exceeds the specifications. Applied to computer purchases, performance specs can enable you to submit a detailed shopping list of hardware and receive a price bid for equipment that meets your needs while allowing the dealer to assemble the lowest cost system.

Performance specs can be applied to a long list of CAD hardware, including the computer (CPU), memory-expansion boards, floppy disk drives, graphics adapters, monitors, pointing devices, modems, plotters, and printers. Each of these items has several crucial variables that can be used to describe what you need, without specifying a specific brand.

Just as in writing specs for a building, the completeness and accuracy of hardware specifications is vital. Processor speed, data storage capacity, display resolution, and other similar concepts are crucial to assembling a good CAD system. There is no fixed set of criteria, since standards are generally improving all the time. You may want to write specs for several systems, from the best you could hope for to the minimum you can accept, and compare prices. If you do your homework, you can write computer specs yourself without becoming an electrical engineer, but if you don't have the time or inclination, you can get help from an experienced CAD-user or a knowledgeable consultant, just as you might go to a professional specification writer for building specs.

If you spend some time reading the computer magazines, you can do a pretty good job of putting computer specs together by yourself. Most magazines review hardware frequently, often publishing charts with which you can compare features. You can get an idea of current discount prices by reading the ads. Since you have (presumably) selected your CAD software *before* picking the hardware, pay close attention to the requirements and recommendations that come with the program. Try not to include brand names in your specs, except in reference to standards, such as "Hayes compatible," "includes Postscript capability," or "AutoCAD driver available."

Making Decisions

After you receive bids from dealers, compare both prices and whatever "extras" are included. For example, if two price bids are equal, one might offer, say, better repair service than you specified. Also, once you get a bid, check the specific brand names very carefully: if you (or your consultant) aren't comfortable with a manufacturer's reputation, or with magazine reviews of their products, think twice. It's also a good idea to try out items like keyboards (their "feel" varies tremendously), monitors (are the colors OK?), and plotters (how noisy is it?) before buying.

MAKING THE SYSTEM FIT

If you are going to draw and design effectively, you should not have to worry about distractions. Using a computer, you should make sure *before you start working* that all the mundane software setups are taken care of, and that your hardware is ready to use. When everything is organized, get comfortable!

Setting Up

Computers can hold vast amounts of information, but they can also lose vast amounts of information. Short of disastrous breakdowns, it's possible to simply lose track of important files or even to forget how to start up your CAD program. In a firm in which more than one person is using the CAD system, staying organized is especially important.

Start by making sure your hard disks are organized in a clear, efficient manner. When you create directories and subdirectories, think of them as a *tree* structure, starting from the *root* directory, with each directory containing related subdirectories. For example, your CAD directory might contain a subdirectory for each project you are working on (Figure 2-12). Draw a map of the directories and post it so that everyone who uses the machine can see it. Also, be sure that each individual graphics workstation is set up in a similar way, if people will be moving from one to another.

Personalizing the Operating System

When you turn on a computer, you are greeted by the operating system, unless the machine has been set up

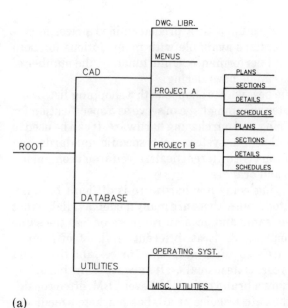

(a)

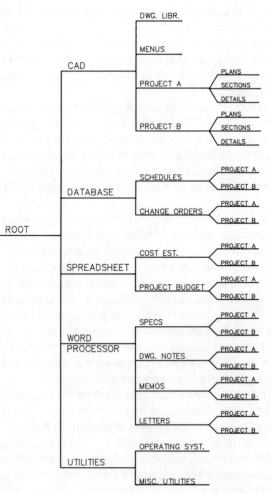

(b)

FIGURE 2-12   Two alternative directory structures: the first *(a)* stores the CAD program and a database management program in the first level subdirectories, then places each project in its own CAD subdirectory, with further subdirectories for each drawing type. The second *(b)*, which is more appropriate to a very large hard disk, contains four primary program directories, and subdirectories for each type of task for the nongraphic programs.

to take you straight into a program. The operating system may present something as uninformative as "A>" or "C>," referring to the current disk drive, leaving you to give it the appropriate commands. There are two ways to deal with this situation.

First, you should learn to use the operating system. Even if you have an aversion to using codes and seemingly arcane procedures, an understanding of the ins and outs of the operating system will enable you to manage your programs and files much more effectively. You will also be able to set up automatic sequences (called *batch* files) that simplify starting programs and backing up files. Not *every* user needs to be an expert, so you can write batch files that insulate novices and computerphobics from the operating system.

There is a reasonable alternative (or supplement) to learning all about operating systems. "Front-end" programs are available to give you an intuitive, visually oriented handle on the operating system. Typically, a front end gives you menus of commands to choose from and will list the directories and their contents for you. The more sophisticated front ends add new commands that go beyond the capabilities of the operating system; some enable you to operate several programs, on screen, at once. These utility programs are useful for even a computer veteran, to simplify necessary computer housekeeping.

Configuration

Once your computer is set up, make sure that your CAD system is ready to use. Peripheral hardware should be in place, and your program should be *configured* so that it knows what it is attached to. Most programs are set up so that you can configure them by responding to a set of on-screen queries regarding your peripherals. Get connected: you should not have to hook up or configure tablets, printers, or plotters while you work.

During the configuration process, you may also be given a choice of different menu and display options. Drawing and designing are very personal processes, and you should set up the system to suit your own working style. If different people will be using the same machine, you can write macro "scripts" that will automatically reconfigure the system to the liking of each user.

A Comfortable Environment

Most important of all, make sure your working environment is comfortable. Don't just place a computer on the nearest drafting table: put the screen at a comfortable

FIGURE 2-13   This workstation reserves plenty of space for drawings. If space was a problem, the computer could have been placed on its end under the table, and the monitor placed on a swivel arm, which would make it accessible from the drafting tables, as well. Neeley/Lofrano Inc, Architects, San Francisco.

viewing height, preferably on an adjustable arm, and make sure there are no lights or windows reflecting on it. If the monitor is moveable, you can adjust it to changing light conditions and reorient it as you move around at your desk. A simple nonreflective glare shield can prevent headaches where overhead lighting is a problem.

Leave enough desk space for a mouse or tablet, keyboard, and large paper drawings (Figure 2-13). If you can, keep the computer itself out of the way: you only need to reach it to occasionally insert and withdraw diskettes, so don't put it in the middle of your work area.

Moving around and taking breaks is important when you're working at a computer. Try to take short breaks when the computer is busy saving files or redrawing the screen: rest your eyes and walk around. Muscle fatigue can result from sitting too long in one position. If you are using a small digitizing tablet or mouse, you have more mobility than you do when you work on paper drawings: as long as you can see the monitor, you can move around at your desk or sit back, put your feet on the desk, and draw with the tablet or mouse in your lap.

Finally, treat yourself to a comfortable chair that supports your lower back and posterior. A computer program is not the only soft ware that needs support.

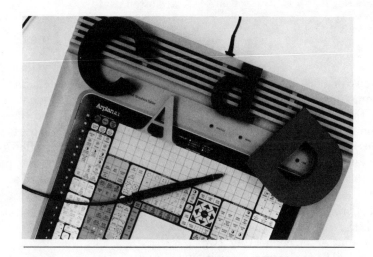

THE CAD
TOOLBOX

CHAPTER 3

Architectural computer programs provide you with a set of tools that help you to perform repetitious tasks and organize your work. Each of these tools can help you carry out complex operations in a few steps. You can draw with multiple lines, copy elements that are repeated, then edit your work and enhance it with other multiple-task tools.

Computers are ideally suited to carrying out sequences of tasks; indeed, this is essentially what

a *program* is. A well-designed program allows you to give a command, then let the machine do the dirty work. To the architect, this means freedom from many repetitive drawing, lettering, and reporting operations.

The tools that are available for multiple operations can be classified as drawing, editing, enhancing, and data-handling aids. In this chapter, we will examine some of the features that are commonly offered by drawing and design software.

DRAWING TOOLS

LINES AND WALLS

The simplest elements you can draw are lines, circles, and arcs. These are sometimes called **primitives**, since they are so basic. In the coordinate world of CAD, these are stored in the computer as vectors, or entities with locations, directions, and lengths. You will be seeing them on the display screen as graphics and need not concern yourself with the numbers, unless you would like to pinpoint the exact location or angle of an element. In this case, many programs enable you to see the pertinent data, as it is shown in Table 3-1.

Drawing a line is a matter of connecting two points, whether you use a pencil or an electronic mouse. However, drawing a *wall* is not so simple by hand: you must make several parallel lines, properly spaced, and perhaps hatch or poché between them. The computer will let you connect two points with a wall, essentially drawing a linear *object*. There are several ways of doing this, and you can use them for a variety of tasks, in addition to drawing walls in plan.

All *architecturally oriented* software allows you to draw multiple parallel lines. Minimally, you need to be able to draw two lines to indicate the sides of a wall; you should also be able to set four or more lines to represent wall surfaces over studs and other kinds of assemblies (Figure 3-1). Another common tool is the ability to *offset* a single line (or curve), automatically creating a copy a certain distance from the original. Beyond this,

there are several special tools for drawing lines that are often useful.

Special Kinds of Lines

Connected lines and walls are very useful. When you draw a many-segmented line, it's convenient to be able to "pick" the entire sequence of lines for modification or erasure. These linked lines can be thought of as a single object, saving you the trouble of working on each segment. **Curve fitting** allows you to transform a set of connected lines into a curve, producing smooth curves without resorting to linked arcs or to a manual french

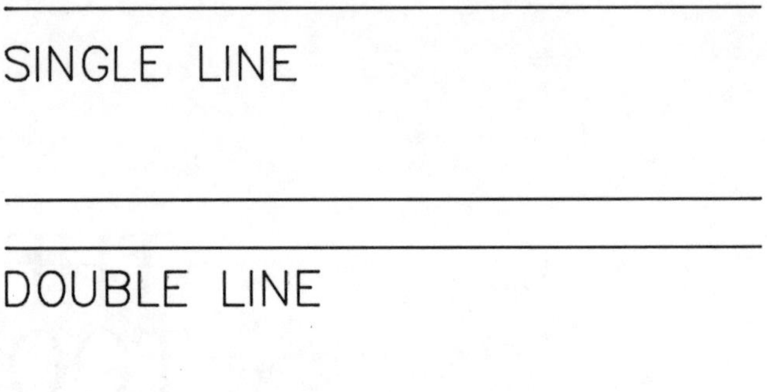

SINGLE LINE

DOUBLE LINE

WALL SURFACES

SOLID LINE

WALL DETAIL

FIGURE 3-1 Architectural CAD software should enable you to draw double lines and solid lines as easily as single lines, and it should also allow you to draw more complex walls, such as multiple lines and insulated walls, without too much difficulty. The wall detail shown here was created with a simple user-written program that automatically repeats the stud/insulation/wall surface assembly between two points.

TABLE 3-1

```
      LINE       LAYER: 1FL-WALL-F
  from point, X=   59'-1"   Y=   30'-8"
    to point, X=   59'-1"   Y=   -3'-4"
       Length =   34'-0",  Angle =  270.1
       Delta X =    0'-0",  Delta Y =   -34'-0"


      CIRCLE     LAYER: 1FL-WALL-F
center point, X=  47'-10"   Y=  -8'-10"
radius      4'-4"
Circumference =   27'-3",  Area = 8494.8665


      ARC        LAYER: 1FL-WALL-H
center point, X=   49'-4"   Y=   -8'-0"
radius     12'-0"
 start angle  180.0
   end angle  270.0
```

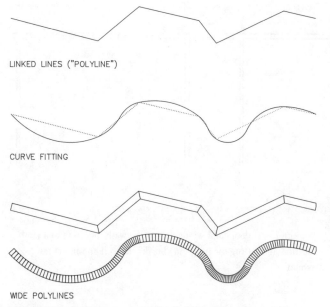

FIGURE 3-2   Polylines: a special kind of linked-line that can be changed in width or fitted to a curve.

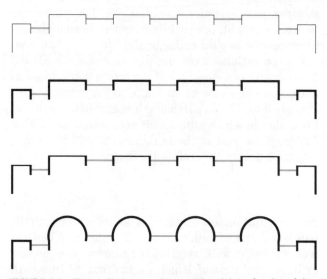

FIGURE 3-3   This wall plan was drawn with polylines for the solid walls; the variations include, top to bottom, single lines, wall-lines of constant width, wall-lines of two widths, and wall-lines with fitted curves. No redrawing was required to produce these variations: the polyline widths were changed with one command.

curve. Fitted curves are particularly appropriate for contours and other landscape forms (Figure 3-2).

A special kind of connected line, offered by a few programs, is called a **polyline.** These can be fitted to a curve, changed in width, or *varied* in width from one end to the other. Wide polylines can be filled, as well, to be drawn as solids (Figure 3-3).

Solid lines, composed of double lines with a solid fill, are an obvious choice for pochéd walls. Like double wall lines, you can set the width of a solid line, but some other tools for drawing walls, such as "cleaning up" intersections, may not be available. Remember, two computer functions that look alike may behave very differently; some programs have developed solid lines for circuit board designers and do not allow neat intersections or window insertions. Nevertheless, you may be able to take advantage of such a limited feature for a task like wall sections or for drawing pochéd columns in plan.

Architecturally oriented programs (or architectural add-ons to general-purpose programs) may enable you to draw walls with symbols embedded in them, such as those for insulation or studs. You may also be able to create these wall types yourself, by using a relatively simple do-it-yourself program, which we will examine later.

If it sounds like there are too many ways to draw a wall, remember that any CAD program will have one technique that suits most architectural situations. It's a good idea, though, to know what other methods are available, so that you can deal with special situations effectively. Also, remember that you can use parallel lines for more than drawing plans of walls.

Intersections and Openings

Unlike simple lines, walls do not intersect at a point, and walls are not allowed to overlap each other, by architectural convention. In order to free you from erasing and joining lines at every corner and intersection, architectural software will "clean up" wall intersections by automatically eliminating the superfluous lines (Figure 3-4).

When you draw a wall, you may not know where you want to place windows and doors. Instead of leaving openings, you can automatically "break" a wall and insert the appropriate symbols, and the computer will take care of the mundane work of "casing" or ending the walls (Figure 3-4).

Like most CAD tools, these can be used for purposes other than those for which they are intended. In particular, you can use double lines and intersection-cleanups for drawing in section and for drawing large-

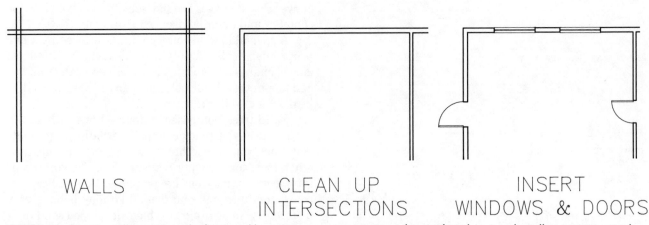

WALLS

CLEAN UP
INTERSECTIONS

INSERT
WINDOWS & DOORS

FIGURE 3-4   Drawing walls: architectural software enables you to first draw double-line walls, then "clean-up" their intersections by simply pointing to each and invoking a cleanup command. Afterward, you can insert doors and windows into the walls, pointing to a jamb location and letting the program "break" the wall and insert the symbol.

scale details. In section, floors, roofs, and walls can all be drawn using these same techniques. Any time you draw with parallel lines, try to make use of these techniques.

Automatic Assistance

One of the most useful tools available for drawing walls in plan is the ability to *automatically* transform a number of single lines into double lines, spaced according to wall thickness. Some of these wall-drawing tools will clean up intersections as they create double lines, and some will open up walls for door and window symbols, as well. These capabilities are particularly helpful in schematic design, when you want to quickly outline spaces without taking time to carefully detail wall widths and intersections.

ACCURACY

Drawing with a computer can be mindlessly accurate. You must decide what level of detail is appropriate and consciously limit yourself to that level.

A plan, for example, can be developed at "full scale" by zooming in (enlarging the screen display) on a detail (Figure 3-5). In fact, you can easily work on details to be magnified larger than life, assuming there's a reason to do so. Yet zooming in and out of a drawing can be time consuming, so you want to make use of three drawing tools that ensure whatever level of accuracy you choose to maintain.

Orthogonal Drawing

Orthogonal drawing modes serve the function of T-squares, parallel rules, and triangles. They allow you to draw straight, parallel lines, in two perpendicular directions. When the orthogonal mode is "on," all lines will align with two axes, usually the x (horizontal) and y (vertical) axes. However, if you rotate the orthogonal axes, you can draw at an angle to the x and y axes (Figure 3-6). This is particularly useful in an architectural plan in which some forms are rotated, say, 30° or 45° from the rest of the building. Pitched roofs, too, might be drawn on a rotated orthogonal.

Snap

Snap resolution sets up a grid of points to which all the points you "pick" with cursor will conform. When you pick a point, it will "snap" to the nearest point on this grid. A resolution of 1 inch means that all lines will start and end on even 1-inch increments; no two parallel lines could be closer than 1 inch. You can set the resolution as is appropriate to the level of detail of your work, and you can change it as you work, accordingly. (Note that the snap resolution may be different from the visible grid of dots that you may display as a reference.)

Snap lets you do two things quickly: you can draw with extreme accuracy, and you can draw in a "semi-orthogonal" mode. The latter means that you can pick orthogonal points easily, since two almost aligned points will snap to precisely aligned points. However,

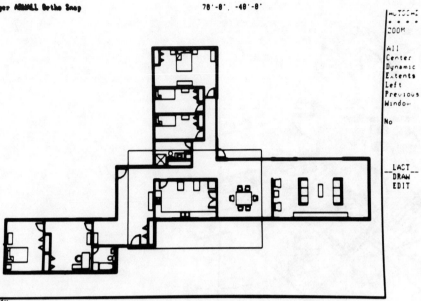

(a)

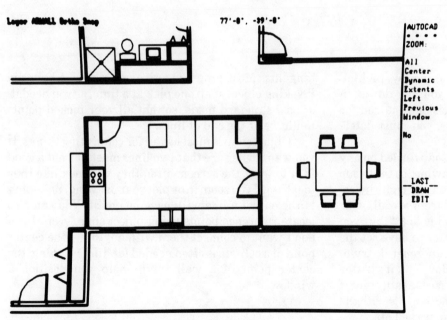

(b)

FIGURE 3-5   Zooming in: the window outlined in the first picture
defines the display extents after the zoom.

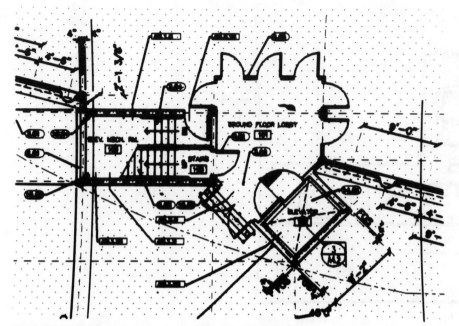

FIGURE 3-6 The displayed reference grid illustrates the rotated
orthogonal axis; in this case it has been rotated to facilitate drawing
the entry and elevator. It could be rotated again to match the angle
of the walls. David Baker and Associates.

when you want to draw at an angle by picking
unambiguously unaligned points, you can do so. In
effect, you can *sketch* with the precision required for
working drawings. First, of course, you must determine the right resolution.

It's usually a good idea to keep snap turned on any
time you will be dimensioning a drawing, so that your
dimensions will automatically fall on the right increments. If you locate a column $8\frac{23}{64}''$ from a wall, your
automatic dimensioning may round it to $8\frac{1}{4}''$ but you
may have intended it to be $8\frac{1}{2}''$. Better to have set the
snap to $\frac{1}{4}''$ resolution, or even to $\frac{1}{2}''$. In general, try to
pick the largest useful increment. However, it's better
to set the snap too small than not to use it at all, since it
is easier to draw at, say, precise $2''$ increments with the
snap set at $\frac{1}{2}''$ than it is with the snap turned off.

Object Snap

Object snap lets you pick specific points on your
drawing elements precisely. If you want to start a line
at the end of a previous line, the "endpoint" object snap
mode will pick it for you. All you have to do is pick a
spot nearby, and the software will "grab" the end of the
line. Other common modes include intersection points,
midpoints, perpendicular lines, and circle centers and
tangents. Most programs give you a choice between
invoking object snap one pick at a time, as you need it,
or as a standard mode, so that all your picked points
might be at the end of lines.

Object snap is most useful for connecting things. If
you want to be sure that two lines meet, it's not a good
idea to trust the screen: often they will look like they
touch until you zoom in or plot your drawing. Snapping
to the end of a line will leave no doubt. You can also
locate reference points using object snap, even if you
don't want to connect them with anything: the center
point of a column is often needed for dimensioning; the
center point of a wall might help you position a
window.

EDITING TOOLS

One of the most difficult manual drawing habits to
break is . . . drawing. Computers provide editing tools
that often make it easier to copy and adjust a previously drawn element than it is to draw a new one. Even
a simple line should be copied when you want to repeat
the exact length of the original.

REPETITION

Anything that you've drawn, you can **copy**. This includes lines, walls, symbols, objects, groups of objects, anything. If your work is repetitive, you can save time by drawing each element once, then reusing it as you put together your drawing. If your work has many similar-but-not-identical elements, it is often easier to copy similar elements and then modify them accordingly.

If copying and modifying something as simple as a line seems silly, remember that a line is more than it often appears to be. It has an *exact* length that is sometimes difficult to duplicate without resetting the snap resolution or zooming in. Lines are drawn on specific layers, and resetting your current layer is often more work than copying a line that's on the appropriate layer, then modifying it. The same holds true if a line has three-dimensional coordinates.

Copying is a design tool too, not just a drafting tool. When you design, try to reuse as many drawing elements as you can, even if you change them to suit a specific situation each time. Save yourself the distraction of putting together, piece by piece, each part of your drawing. Remember: *never draw anything twice!*

Multiple Copies

When you want multiple copies of an element, you can **array** them in a line, a grid, or a circle. In a rectangular or linear array, simply specify the horizontal and vertical spacing of the copies. You might use this to repeat a series of parallel walls, a grid of columns, or layout lines when you begin a drawing (Figure 3-7). A circular (or *polar*) array is specified by the center point of the array and either the spacing (in degrees) of the objects, the number of objects, or the number of degrees of the array. The objects may be either rotated as they are arrayed or remain orthogonal. You can create circular layout grids, fan-shaped patterns, such as bricks in an arch or branches on a tree, or you can place objects, such as a semicircle of columns or chairs around a circular table.

A special kind of copying, using *symbols* and *blocks*, is covered in Chapter 5. You will use these when you want exact duplicates of elements that you can thereafter treat as single objects.

Modifying Your Drawing

The traditional tool for editing is the eraser. Erasing on the computer has three advantages over erasing by hand: it's more accurate, because you erase only what

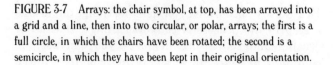

FIGURE 3-7 Arrays: the chair symbol, at top, has been arrayed into a grid and a line, then into two circular, or polar, arrays; the first is a full circle, in which the chairs have been rotated; the second is a semicircle, in which they have been kept in their original orientation.

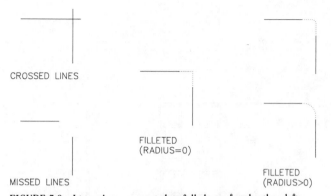

CROSSED LINES

MISSED LINES

FILLETED
(RADIUS=0)

FILLETED
(RADIUS>0)

FIGURE 3-8   Lines that are crossed or fall short of each other, left,
can be filleted to an angle or a curve, as illustrated by the dotted lines.

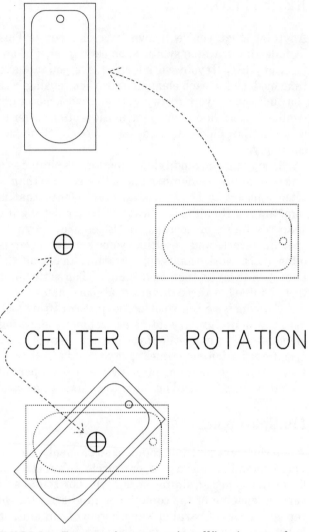

CENTER OF ROTATION

FIGURE 3-9   Two ways of rotating an object: When the center of
rotation is outside the object itself, it will move and turn, simultaneously;
when the center is inside the object, it simply turns.

you want to erase; it's quicker, and it's neater, since it doesn't leave a trace and doesn't leave holes in your paper or matte. (Don't laugh: it happens!)

Erasing accuracy is no small matter. Whenever lines are close together or intersect, manual erasing risks ruining neighboring lines, which then have to be redrawn. Not only does the computer let you pick single, discrete items to erase (or, of course, groups of items), but it lets you pick overlapping elements according to the layers they are drawn on. (More on this in Chapter 5.) You also get a second chance: if you've erased something accidentally, you can usually call it back from the grave.

CAD software offers several unique editing tools. Just as intersecting walls can be "cleaned up," intersecting lines can be neatly intersected, or "filleted." A fillet can make any two nonparallel lines meet in either an angle or a curve of a specified radius (Figure 3-8). When you are drawing lines, you can concentrate on the direction and location, without taking the time to be sure that intersections are drawn precisely. Draw them so that they overlap and be sure they cross at the right place. Then, fillet them and you will get a perfect intersection. You will find that this can "loosen up" your drawing process, without sacrificing accuracy.

Individual lines can also be **broken** into segments (which can be treated independently) or into separate lines with space in between. This too can be done with great precision.

Moving Parts

Erasers are not only used for deleting things but also as a step in the process of *changing* things. Instead of erasing and redrawing elements, you can use the computer to "copy and erase" or more simply, **move** elements in a single operation. It's almost always

easier to move parts of your drawing than to erase and redraw them.

The ability to move elements around is extraordinarily useful. If you want to position a line more accurately, it's simple. You can "cut and paste" one part of a drawing into another, "dragging" it across the screen into position. Elements may also be moved and copied with great precision by specifying numeric distances or coordinate targets. It is particularly helpful to be able to choose a group of objects and to move them all the same amount. You may, for example, move a number of elements that are spread across your drawing, such as columns, a few inches in one direction.

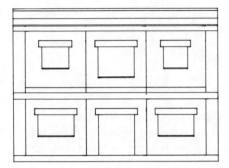

Rotation is another technique for moving elements or groups of elements. By specifying a point around which a rotation will occur, you can either pivot it in place or move it as it rotates (Figure 3-9).

When you want to move an object that is attached to other drawing elements, many CAD programs let you **stretch** the attached elements to the new location. For example, if you wanted to move a window to another location in a wall, the wall lines would move at their points of attachment to the window casing, stretching as if they were stuck to the window. This can save much redrawing effort and is yet another way that CAD can spare you from mundane graphic tasks as you design.

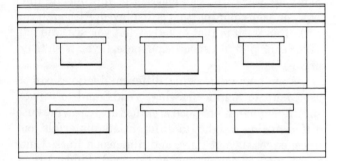

Another useful editing tool is the ability to **scale** parts of your drawing. An element or group of elements can be stretched or shrunk in one direction or two. You can adjust the size of building parts or change the width-to-length proportions. Design studies of proportion can be carried out on a window or an entire building. Some programs allow you to scale the *spacing* between objects, which is particularly useful for changing the spacing between column lines and other building elements (Figure 3-10).

Most of the tools for editing your work can be used to great advantage with snap, object snap, and orthogonal modes. When you copy or move an element, these modes let you choose new locations that are precisely located according to the snap grid, on an orthogonal line, or in a specific relationship with another drawing element.

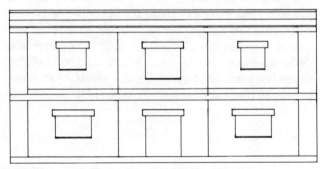

FIGURE 3-10   The top facade is scaled, horizontally, in two ways. The first, middle, stretches all elements equally. The second, bottom, is stretched leaving the windows, which were previously defined as objects, intact.

ENHANCING YOUR DRAWINGS

A third set of tools helps you to enhance a drawing by adding information, making it more readable or more attractive. These aids include different line types and colors, hatching patterns, solid fills, text, and dimensions.

LINES

You may control the appearance of a line two different ways: on the computer display and on paper. When you are working on a drawing, you will want to make full use of the color display to differentiate lines. Line types such as dashed or dotted lines are not as easy or fast to work with, so you will generally use different colors to represent different kinds of lines. When you prepare to

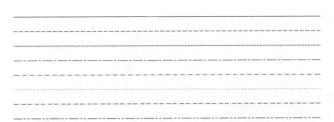

FIGURE 3-11   Eight different CAD linetypes. Most programs allow the spacing between dots and dashes, and the length of dashes, to be adjusted, as well as allowing users to design new linetypes.

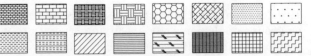

FIGURE 3-12   Hatching patterns: the two brick-like patterns are the same pattern at different scales.

plot your work, you can choose the appropriate linetype for each color line that is displayed. Although you will often wish to plot exactly what you see, you can tailor each plot to a specific purpose, if you wish (Figure 3-11).

As in manual drawing, different linetypes can be used both to help a drawing "read," and to convey specific information. Good architectural drawings use different line weights to differentiate materials, cut lines, edges, layout lines, and dimension lines. Linetypes such as centerlines and dashed (hidden) lines have conventional meanings, of course. Since the computer allows you to change linetypes at will, at plotting time you can choose the appropriate type: a roof outline might be plotted solid for a roof plan and dotted for the plan of the floor below. You can also designate line weights and colors as you plot, by assigning each displayed color to a specific pen number. Even if you are using a single-pen plotter, you may

substitute pens to use a variety of line weights and colors. You can use these to emphasize, say, an elevation outline or to differentiate a particular material.

Although multicolored plots are not generally acceptable for construction documents, colored lines are very useful for displaying and studying different kinds of information on a single plot. You can compare overlapping structural or mechanical systems by plotting them in different colors, for example. Of course, you can also plot attractive multicolor presentation drawings, either diagrammatic or realistic.

HATCHING AND FILLING

Patterns and solid "fills" are useful in many different circumstances. If you have a broad range of hatches available and the ability to scale them, you can render surfaces realistically or schematically (Figure 3-12). Walls or floors (in section cuts) can be pochéd with either a pattern or solid; often hatching is preferable because of plotting considerations. Since it is relatively

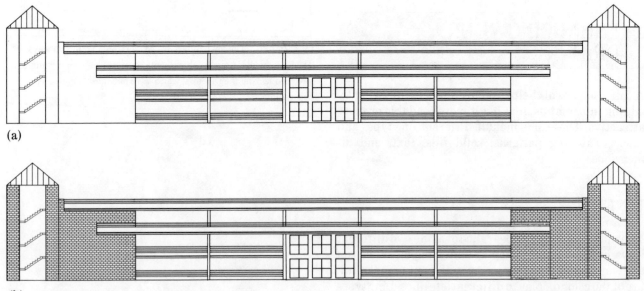

(a)

(b)

FIGURE 3-13   The brick hatching was applied by outlining the areas to be hatched, then filling them with bricks. Arch.1 Architects.

simple to hatch an area (and then hide the hatching on a turned-off layer), it can be used more liberally than is possible with manual drawing. Hatching can also be drawn around objects or text, for drawing clarity.

For renderings or design studies, consider using hatching to delineate circulation paths, paving patterns, siding or other wall surfaces, roofing, or shadows (Figure 3-13). For working drawings, CAD software generally includes hatches for many material conventions. Most software also allows you to create new hatching patterns as you need them. If you want a particular project to include a special surface pattern, for example, it's worth the effort to draw it, especially since you'll have it available the next time you want it.

LETTERING AND DIMENSIONING

Titles, notes, and dimensions can be printed on your drawings, clearly and precisely. If you wish, you can annotate drawings just as you do by hand, typing notes from the keyboard, or you can insert blocks of text that have been typed on a word processor and translated into graphic form.

Text

Fonts, or type styles, can be chosen according to the situation: most software offers you a choice of fonts. The simplest fonts are made up of many short lines and aren't particularly attractive. However, they can be drawn on the screen or plotted rapidly, and they take up relatively little computer memory. Better-looking fonts are made up of arcs and multiple lines and eat up significantly more time and memory. They can be very useful for presentation purposes: with a good plotter they can be used to reduce or eliminate the need for press-on lettering (Figure 3-14).

When initially drawn, text can be modified in a number of ways. In addition to being able to stretch lettering in either direction, a font may be slanted to simulate italic lettering. Special software instructions can allow you to use a font vertically, so that you can type columns of letters. A computer-generated font can, of course, be plotted at virtually any size, but the larger a letter is plotted, the more its imperfections show. Furthermore, good typographic practice requires somewhat different proportions for very large letters, and a high-quality font set should accommodate this.

Since it's easy to choose and change type fonts and sizes in your drawings, you can adapt text to specific situations. Each text "style" that you set up can be changed at any time, giving you the ability to replace all the text in your drawing with new sizes or fonts. When a drawing is plotted at different sizes, different size notes (relative to the graphics) are required. You can also substitute a fancy font when you use a drawing for presentation purposes, then replace it with a simple font for working drawings.

This is a basic lettering font ("TXT") by AutoCAD

Note the simple character construction:

A 6 m

"SIMPLEX" is a smoother font

Look closely...the curves are made with lines:

S 5 g

Letters may be STRETCHED, RAISED

or they may be *SLANTED* at any angle

AutoCAD's 'COMPLEX' font is better-suited for presentations

An 'ITALIC' version is also available

THIS IS A HELVETICA FONT

NOTE THAT THESE CHARACTERS ARE FORMED WITH ARCS, RATHER THAN LINES.
(FONT BY TURBO DESIGNER)

G 2 &

This is a VERTICAL font

FIGURE 3-14

Dimensions

Semiautomatic dimensioning is one of the most valuable drafting tools available. Once you specify the size and type style for your dimensions, you can pick two or more points and the computer will draw the appropriate numbers, arrows, and witness lines (Figure 3-15). (Fully automatic dimensioning can provide dimensions for an entire drawing without requiring the user to select starting and ending points. This capability is less common in microcomputer CAD.) In order to be certain of the legibility of your dimensions (and notes), you must consider the size at which the dimensions and arrows are *plotted*. It's up to you to choose the level of detail you wish to show in your dimensions. Most programs allow you to change dimension sizes, like other text, by changing text styles.

Another extremely useful dimensioning tool is **associative dimensioning,** in which a dimension witness line is attached, or associated, with a particular drawing element. If the element is moved, the witness line is automatically moved with it, and the dimension text is updated to note the new distance between the witness lines. This capability can enable you to dimension a drawing relatively early in the design process, with the knowledge that you won't have to redraw the dimensions every time you make a change. Even in schematic design, you can use associative dimensioning to note the actual locations of walls, columns, doors, and windows, as you place and move them visually.

Dimensioning aids can be dangerous if not used thoughtfully (it's easy to specify construction dimensions at absurd levels of detail) but used carefully they can be some of the greatest drafting time savers.

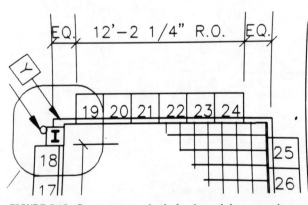

FIGURE 3-15 Dimensions: as the drafter located the witness lines in this drawing, the option of recording the exact distance was offered; on the ends "EQ" was typed in, and in the center R.O. was added to the correct dimension. Then the dimension lines were added automatically.

CUSTOM TOOLS

WRITING SCRIPTS

With many CAD programs, you can create your own drawing tools by writing **macros,** or linked sequences of commands. A simple macro is like a script that will repeat a predefined set of keystrokes. For example, a macro for writing a specific, prepared note on a drawing might do the following tasks.

- Change the current drawing layer from "walls" to "notes."
- Request that the user pick a location for the text.
- Specify a specific font and font size.
- Automatically type, say, "Verify dimensions in the field."
- Change the current layer back to "walls."

This series of operations could be invoked by a single new command, or it could be assigned a position on a digitizing tablet.

Any frequently used series of commands can be linked, with pauses for data input, by a *keyboard customizer* utility, which enables you to assign series of keystrokes, including commands and text, to a key on your keyboard. These are so easy to use that it frequently makes sense to "record" your commands for a replay any time you expect to do a series of operations more than a few times.

DO-IT-YOURSELF PROGRAMS

Some CAD software is *open,* allowing users to make modifications or additions to the program itself, while other software is *closed,* and does not allow customization. A **user programming language,** such as Auto-CAD's *AutoLISP* or Versacad's *CAD Programming Language,* opens a program to many kinds of user interaction. In addition to helping to write simple macros, a user-accessible programming language can be used to write sophisticated new commands. This is true *programming.* Although the mere thought often strikes fear into faint hearts, a familiarity with simple programming techniques can help you to modify the commands you are using or to write new ones.

When you buy a CAD program, you might expect that you would not have to write any further programs yourself. This expectation is reasonable: any software that you *have* to program yourself is a dubious value for an architect. However, a good user programming language adds so much power and flexibility to a CAD system that you may want to at least learn a few basic tricks. Fortunately, a user language often requires only an understanding of a few rules (the language *syntax*) and whatever commands you need.

What sort of programs can you write? In order to demystify the process a bit, let's look at an example you can use as you work. AutoLISP can be used as a calculator by typing the following.

$$(+ 37.3\ 15)$$

which will result in the statement

$$52.3$$

A number may be remembered as a constant, by giving it a designation, such as the letter *K*.

$$(SETQ\ K\ *(3\ 52.3))$$

will result in K being equal to 3×52.36, or 156.9. Any time you refer to *K* as you draw, the computer will use "156.9." Many other functions are available and may be used as you work or in stored scripts.

Short custom programs can be tremendously useful as you draw. For example, you can write a program that calculates and draws stairs, in plan or section. Such a program requests the user to point to the top and bottom riser locations, then calculates the number of risers and treads based on specified maximum and minimum dimensions, and finally draws them. This entire process can be written in an 18-line AutoLISP program. Other programs can be used to draw wall assemblies (such as the insulated wall plan in Figure 3-2), to calculate dimensions based on structural criteria, to lay out seating plans or parking lots, and so on.

A market has developed for add-on programs that use these languages to provide advanced capabilities for CAD software. Architectural firms can buy (and sell) programs that help them automate difficult or repetitious problems. With some programming knowledge, a purchased add-on program can be customized to better suit a firm's need or to meet the needs of a particular project.

Mastering a programming language is not a trivial undertaking, but it is not so difficult that you would have to become a programming specialist. Indeed, it is worthwhile (though by no means essential) for any firm to have at least one in-house designer or drafter who can write simple programs in the midst of a project, as they are needed.

HANDLING INFORMATION

Some of the most helpful tools for computer-aided architecture are not drawing tools, but accessories for linking drawings to nongraphic information. Data management tools can help you keep track of the numbers and types of objects you place in your drawings. They enable you to make lists, in table form, automating a process that is otherwise time consuming and error prone.

KEEPING TRACK WITH ATTRIBUTES

Attributes are words or numbers that you can attach to objects when you place them in a drawing. Although the term "attribute" is applied to *all* the characteristics of a drawn element (such as size, direction, and color), here we refer to *nongraphic* data that you attach to graphic elements. Various CAD programs have different attribute capabilities; some only allow a single tag to be applied to an object while others enable you attach as many as you choose.

An attribute can be a *label* that applies to an individual object being inserted or to all similar objects; it can also be a *description* of a characteristic of an object (such as size, quantity, color or cost). An object may have one attribute or many (or none). Attributes are primarily used for counting and describing building parts. They can be displayed graphically as part of your drawing, they can be printed out as lists, or they can be *extracted* and processed by a database management program.

When you assign an attribute to an object (either when you first draw it or when you place it in your drawing), you can decide whether you want the attribute to be displayed or plotted. If an attribute is a label, you may want it displayed; if it's a description that you will feed to a database manager, you may want it hidden. Either way, you can turn attributes on and off as you wish.

Listing and Counting

In architecture, the most common use of attributes is in generating lists for tables ("schedules") of windows, doors, finishes, and so on (Table 3-2). A door symbol, for example, can include attributes regarding door type, dimensions, thickness, surfaces, hardware, hinge side, and fire rating. You might choose to display the dimensions and a key number on the drawing (accord-

TABLE 3-2

DOOR SCHEDULE

NO	ROOM	WIDTH	HEIGHT	TYP	HDW	RAT'G	CONS	GLASS	FIN	THICK	FCON	FFIN	HEAD	JAMB	SILL	RMRKS
101	ENTRY	[2]3-0	6-8	FG	1	NON-RA	AL	TEM	AL	1-3/4	AL	AN	1/A8.1	2/A8.1	3/A8.1	-
103	COURT 1	3-0	6-8	-	2	20MIN	WD-SC	-	LAM.	1-3/4	ST	PG	4/A8.1	5/A8.1	6/A8.1	-
104	COURT 3	3-0	6-8	G	3	NON-RA	-	TEM	AL	1-3/4	AL	AN	7/A8.1	8/A8.1	9/A8.1	-
105	COURT 5	3-0	6-8	G	3	NON-RA	-	TEM	AL	1-3/4	AL	AN	7/A8.1	8/A8.1	9/A8.1	-
106	COURT 7	3-0	6-8	G	3	NON-RA	-	TEM	AL	1-3/4	AL	AN	7/A8.1	8/A8.1	9/A8.1	-
107	COURT 9	3-0	6-8	-	2	20MIN	WD-SC	-	LAM.	1-3/4	ST	PG	4/A8.1	5/A8.1	6/A8.1	-
108	COURT 11	3-0	6-8	-	2	20MIN	WD-SC	-	LAM.	1-3/4	ST	PG	4/A8.1	5/A8.1	6/A8.1	-
109	COURT 13	3-0	6-8	-	2	20MIN	WD-SC	-	LAM.	1-3/4	ST	PG	4/A8.1	5/A8.1	6/A8.1	-
111	COURT 15	3-0	6-8	-	2	20MIN	WD-SC	-	LAM.	1-3/4	ST	PG	4/A8.1	5/A8.1	6/A8.1	-
112	COURT 16	3-0	6-8	-	2	20MIN	WD-SC	-	LAM.	1-3/4	ST	PG	4/A8.1	5/A8.1	6/A8.1	-
113	COURT 14	3-0	6-8	-	2	20MIN	WD-SC	-	LAM.	1-3/4	ST	PG	4/A8.1	5/A.81	6/A8.1	-
114	COURT 12	3-0	6-8	-	2	20MIN	WD-SC	-	LAM.	1-3/4	ST	PG	4/A8.1	5/A8.1	6/A8.1	-
115	COURT 10	3-0	6-8	-	2	20MIN	WD-SC	-	LAM.	1-3/4	ST	PG	4/A8.1	5/A8.1	6/A8.1	-
116	COURT 8	3-0	6-8	-	2	20MIN	WD-SC	-	LAM.	1-3/4	ST	PG	4/A8.1	5/A8.1	6/A8.1	-
117	COURT 6	3-0	6-8	-	2	20MIN	WD-SC	-	LAM.	1-3/4	ST	PG	4/A8.1	5/A8.1	6/A8.1	-
118	COURT 4	3-0	6-8	-	2	20MIN	WD-SC	-	LAM.	1-3/4	ST	PG	4/A8.1	5/A8.1	6/A8.1	-
119	COURT 2	3-0	6-8	-	2	20MIN	WD-SC	-	LAM.	1-3/4	ST	PG	4/A8.1	5/A8.1	6/A8.1	-
120	PROGRAM	3-0	6-8	-	4	20MIN	WD-SC	-	PG	1-3/4	ST	PG	4/A8.1	5/A8.1	6/A8.1	-
121	PROGRAM	[2]3-0	6-8	-	4	20MIN	WD-SC	-	PG	1-3/4	ST	PG	4/A8.1	5/A8.1	6/A8.1	-
122	BUSINESS OFF	3-0	6-8	-	5	20MIN	WD-SC	-	PG	1-3/4	ST	PG	4/A8.1	5/A8.1	6/A8.1	-
123	CHECK IN	3-0	3-0	-	6	NON-RA	WD-SC	N/A	LAM.	1-3/4	N/A	N/A	-	-	-	-
124	WOMENS WEIGH	[2]3-0	6-8	-	7	60MIN	WD-SC	-	PG	1-3/4	ST	PG	10/A8.1	11/A8.1	12/A8.1	-
125	WOMENS WEIGH	3-0	6-8	-	8	60MIN	ST	-	PG	1-3/4	ST	PG	10/A8.1	11/A8.1	12/A8.1	PANIC
126	POOL	[2]3-0	6-8	F	8	NON-RA	ST	N/A	PG	1-3/4	ST	PG	13/A8.1	14/A8.1	15/A8.1	PANIC
127	EQUIPMENT	10-0	8-0	-	10	NON-RA	ST	N/A	PG	1-3/4	-	-	-	-	-	-
128	DOCK	[2]3-0	6-8	F	9	NON-RA	ST	N/A	PG	1-3/4	ST	PG	16/A8.1	17/A8.1	18/A8.1	PANIC
126	POOL	[2]3-0	6-8	-	9	60MIN	ST	-	PG	1-3/4	ST	PG	19/A8.1	20/A8.1	21/A8.1	-
130	MASSAGE-105	3-0	6-8	-	4	20MIN	WD-SC	-	PG	1-3/4	ST	PG	4/A8.1	5/A8.1	6/A8.1	-
131	MASSAGE-104	3-0	6-8	-	4	20MIN	WD-SC	-	PG	1-3/4	ST	PG	4/A8.1	5/A8.1	6/A8.1	-
132	LAUNDRY	3-0	6-8	-	4	20MIN	WD-SC	-	PG	1-3/4	ST	PG	4/A8.1	5/A8.1	6/A8.1	-
134	MEN'S LOCKER	[2]3-0	6-8	-	12	60MIN	WD-SC	-	PG	1-3/4	ST	PG	4/A8.1	5/A8.1	6/A8.1	-
134	MENS LOCKER	3-0	6-8	-	12	60MIN	WD-SC	-	PG	1-3/4	ST	PG	4/A8.1	5/A8.1	6/A8.1	-
135	EXIT	[2]2-8	6-8	-	1	NON-RA	ST	-	PG	1-3/4	ST	PG	19/A8.1	20/A8.1	21/A8.1	-
136	BASKETBALL C	3-0	6-8	-	14	60MIN	ST	-	PG	1-3/4	ST	PG	19/A8.1	20/A8.1	21/A8.1	-
137	BASKETBALL	3-0	6-8	-	14	60 MIN	ST	-	PG	1-3/4	ST	PG	22/A8.1	23/A8.1	24/A8.1	PANIC
138	BASKETBALL	[2]3-0	6-8	F	21	60MIN	ST	N/A	PG	1-3/4	ST	PG	22/A8.1	23/A8.1	24/A8.1	PANIC
139	STAIRS	[2]3-0	6-8	F	9	60MIN	ST	N/A	PG	1-3/4	ST	PG	22/A8.1	23/A8.1	24/A8.1	PANIC
140	AEROBICS	3-0	6-8	F	14	60MIN	ST	N/A	PG	1-3/4	ST	PG	22/A8.1	23/A8.1	24/A8.1	PANIC

ing to standard drafting practice) and hide the remaining data.

In order to keep track of the number of objects in your drawing, you can display or print a list of all objects with a given type of attribute. If there are too many to count manually, you can use database management software. If you know how to write very simple programs in a computer language like BASIC, you can use this to total them.

Attributes as Symbols

Some sets of attributes are not associated with specific objects. For example, in order to create a wall finish schedule, you can attach attributes to the segmented "diamond" symbol that is usually placed in the center of a room as a finish schedule key. As you place a number in each segment of the diamond, you can assign attributes for wall surfaces and baseboards, as well as ceiling and floor finishes (Figure 3-16). If you choose, you can set these up in a format that can be displayed next to the symbol, providing an easy way to note finishes directly on the drawing.

Attributes can also be used to help you set up predesigned formats like title blocks for your drawings. When you design a standard title block, include "fill-in-the-blank" attributes such as the project name, drawing title and number, scale, and so on (Figure 3-17). When you place this block into your drawing, the program will prompt you to fill in each of these and then will display them wherever you have specified. You may hide the lettering while you work, to speed up screen redrawing, then you can display it when you are ready to plot.

DATA MANAGEMENT

Some CAD programs have built-in database programs, while others let you use your own. A built-in program will tend to be more architecture specific and may be preformatted to accept notes for whatever symbols that are supplied with the program; an add-on, however, may be much easier to customize to your own way of working and adapt to your own symbol library. Either way, study the manuals, work by trial and

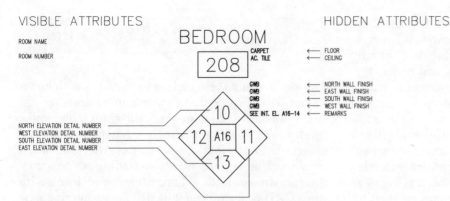

VISIBLE ATTRIBUTES   HIDDEN ATTRIBUTES

ROOM NAME

ROOM NUMBER

BEDROOM

208

CARPET   ←   FLOOR
AC. TILE   ←   CEILING

GWB   ←   NORTH WALL FINISH
GWB   ←   EAST WALL FINISH
GWB   ←   SOUTH WALL FINISH
GWB   ←   WEST WALL FINISH
SEE INT. EL. A16-14   ←   REMARKS

NORTH ELEVATION DETAIL NUMBER
WEST ELEVATION DETAIL NUMBER
SOUTH ELEVATION DETAIL NUMBER
EAST ELEVATION DETAIL NUMBER

10

12 A16 11

13

FIGURE 3-16   Attributes have been used to add text, hidden and visible, to this room symbol. When the symbol is inserted into a drawing, the drafter is prompted to supply the room name, number, and detail reference numbers, which are lettered visibly, and the types of finish for each surface, which are normally not displayed (although they may be displayed as plotted here, in order to refer to them). Any of these attributes can be written to a data table and printed as a finish schedule by a database management program. (When the symbol is inserted, any attributes can be skipped and entered later, either as attributes or simply typed into the database.)

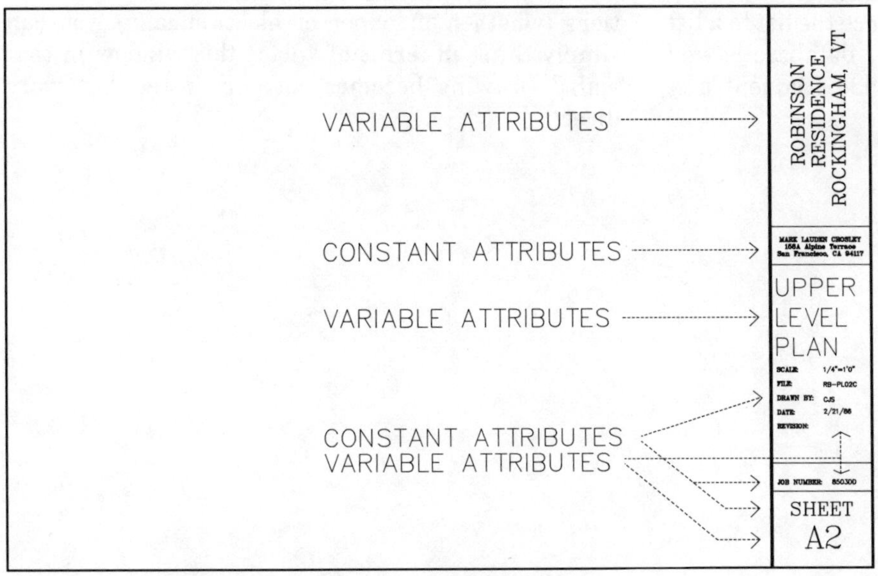

VARIABLE ATTRIBUTES ------------→

CONSTANT ATTRIBUTES ------------→

VARIABLE ATTRIBUTES ------------→

CONSTANT ATTRIBUTES ------------→
VARIABLE ATTRIBUTES ------------→

ROBINSON
RESIDENCE
ROCKINGHAM, VT

MARK LAUREN CROSLEY
106A Alpine Terrace
San Francisco, CA 94117

UPPER
LEVEL
PLAN

SCALE: 1/4"=1'0"
FILE: RB-PL02C
DRAWN BY: CJS
DATE: 2/21/86
REVISION:

JOB NUMBER: 850300

SHEET
A2

FIGURE 3-17   Attributes were used to add text to this title block. Those labeled constant would be automatically printed each time the block was inserted; the variable attributes are filled in by the drafter each time a new title block is created.

error, or hire someone who is familiar with database programs. Learn to use them: they can save tremendous amounts of repetitive work when you initially enter data and when you manipulate and revise it.

Many CAD systems permit you to transfer text, such as that produced by a database program, and insert it into a drawing. Thus, you can use the traditional practice of placing schedules on full-sized drawing sheets, included in the construction document drawing set. However, this can require extended periods of plotter time for information that is essentially nongraphic. Furthermore, changes must either be made manually, which wastes the power of a database management program, or replotted. Increasingly, architects are producing material schedules in notebook format, in order to speed the process of printing and updating them.

In setting up a database program to accept attributes, you can usually follow your standard schedule formats fairly closely. You should make sure that the program is set up to do the specific tasks you require as conveniently as possible. Consider which attributes you will want to count, and which you might want to sort into a specific order or into groups. Plan any links you might want to make to other databases. For example, if you want to use a list of materials to develop cost estimates, you can cross-reference the list to a list of material and labor costs. If your database is well organized, you can use it to provide frequent cost updates as your project progresses.

PUTTING IT ALL TOGETHER

The key to using these tools is to learn to use them together. It's possible that in a minute of drawing you could use half a dozen or more different tools: walls, lines, fillets, copying, mirroring, hatching, inserting objects with attributes, and so on. After you learn what's available, concentrate on finding out how they interact with each other. Long after you've "learned" to use a CAD program you will still be discovering new tricks.

Practice on work that interests you and don't be afraid to try outlandish things. One advantage of CAD is that you are always working on a copy of an original, so no matter what you do, the original is unharmed. By letting loose now and then, you may find an undiscovered use for a drawing tool. Eventually, you should develop your own ways of working, as if you had assembled a toolbox full of personalized tools.

The ability to work with groups of operations, custom-designed to an individual's working method, is one of the reasons that CAD can approximate a person's way of *thinking* about design. When you are freed from the need to draw and edit as individual actions (whether on paper or electronically), you can simply think in terms of "place this window in that wall." Drawing becomes not only faster, but more direct.

DRAWING
AND
DESIGNING

PART 2

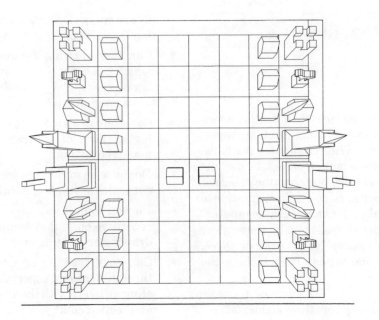

OPENING MOVES

CHAPTER 4

Computer-aided design systems come in all sizes, shapes, and colors, but rarely do they come ready to start drawing your own way. Although most programs arrive "ready to use" and add-on programs are available to adapt others to the requirements of architectural practice, you will probably want to set up a CAD program to work the way *you* work, as much as possible. Many design and drafting software packages are remarkably easy to adapt to suit your needs. By setting up your software and beginning a drawing with a clear strategy in mind, you can get the most out of your electronic assistant.

Drawing with a computer is a little like driving: if you plan your destination and route, your trip will be more pleasant and efficient. Planning might result in the fastest possible trip, or it might leave opportunities for scenic side trips. Likewise, successful computer-aided drawing requires a certain amount of preparation; you can define both the objectives and the basic structure of a drawing, much as you would map out the goal and intermediate points of a trip. If your schedule permits side trips, you can use the time for additional drawing or for exploration of alternative designs.

BEFORE YOU BEGIN

BY HAND OR BY CAD?

One of the first decisions you face when starting a new drawing is usually between using tracing paper, velum, mylar, or whatever. With a computer available, you now have to decide whether or not to use the computer. (You can, however, postpone the choice of media until you are ready to plot.) The first question to ask is: can a drawing take advantage of the computer?

There are a number of reasons why the answer might be "yes"; if you answer "yes" to two or three, that's a pretty strong indication. They include the following.

- Do you plan to use many repetitive elements?
- Do you want to create variations of a basic drawing by changing elements, moving elements, or changing the relationships between elements?
- Can your drawing use graphics drawn in layers, which can be worked with independently, viewed simultaneously when desired, and plotted in various combinations?
- Can your drawing (as you plot it) make use of a higher level of accuracy than is possible with manual drafting?
- Do you wish to view or plot your drawing at different scales or levels of detail?
- Do you expect to make revisions, particularly repetitive ones, that would require extensive re-drawing or starting over?
- Can your drawing be developed and viewed in three dimensions, especially if you are using modeling software with the ability to create new views and section cuts?
- Would you like to compile numeric or textual

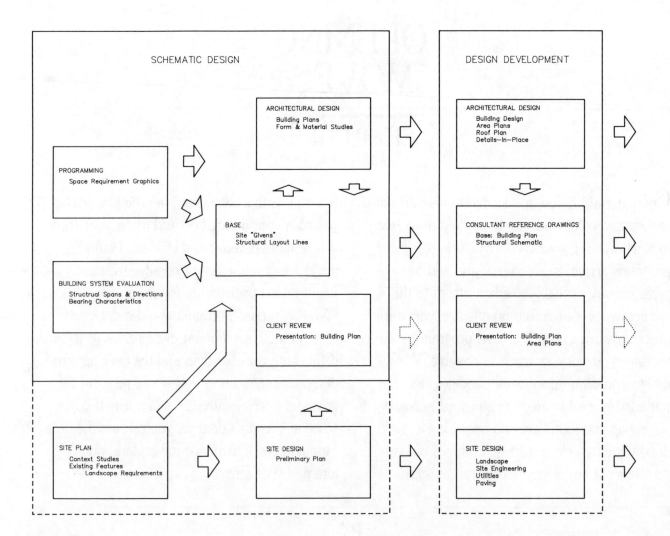

information (*attributes*) in association with specific forms, for purposes of identification, counting, or keeping track of data for cost estimating and specifications?

There are, of course, still good reasons for sticking with manual drawing. These include:

- You would rather sketch with a pad and pencil than sit at a video screen.
- Your drawing could be done more attractively by hand.
- Your drawing is very simple and is not worth the time to set up the computer and plot your drawing.
- Few or none of the first set of factors apply.

It should also be mentioned that many drawings, most in some types of work, will be taken off the CAD system and worked on by hand, at some point. This is particularly true for the following.

- Design or detail studies where plots will be used as a base for further study, using manual methods.
- Working drawings that require minor changes that are too insignificant to justify replotting a drawing. Sometimes these changes will be added at a later date on the computer; in other cases a drawing will be taken off the equipment completely.

DRAWING OBJECTIVES

The ultimate purpose of a drawing may be the description of a building design to a construction crew, or it may only be a quick trial of a new idea; its destination may be a museum wall or a trash can. In general, architectural drawings can be classified as *study/design drawings*, *presentation drawings*, and *technical/construction drawings*. Each has its own graphic requirements; whether you are using a pencil or a

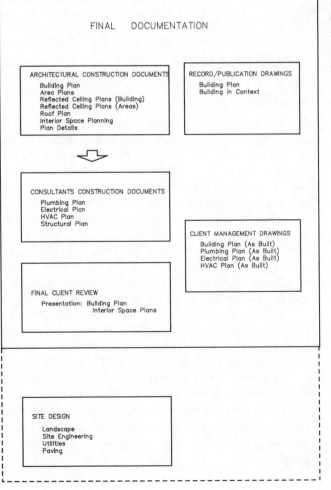

FIGURE 4-1   This chart illustrates the many incarnations of a plan drawing as a project evolves. Beginning with schematic diagrams and site information, a drawing file will become more complex, periodically producing offshoots for presentation, consultants, or new, related drawings.

computer, it's a good idea to think about who will be looking at a drawing and what kind of information they need from it.

Consider also that a single drawing may serve multiple purposes. In fact, one way that CAD can make your work more efficient is by allowing one drawing to become many different drawings. For example, a "site plan" might contain landscape, paving, utility, grading, and roof plans, all able to be plotted independently or in combination. (This technique is similar to overlay drafting, except that you may view all layers as a single drawing, whenever you wish.) As you consider the purpose of a drawing, be sure to think about its siblings and cousins. Not only will this make your work more efficient, but it can help you see the whole scope of a project more effectively.

Families of Drawings

When you expect to use CAD through more than one stage of a project, things become a bit more complex . . . and interesting. Your drawing must be flexible enough to accommodate very different techniques, and some of the requirements of the later stages may not be apparent as you begin.

Using CAD, a single "drawing" can evolve through many lives, or it can serve as the "parent" of numerous offspring. At the start of a project, it is often helpful to chart this evolution and note the characteristics at various points. For example, the plan of a single-level building might evolve like the chart in Figure 4-1.

There are differences in the way that you would work on, say, a design study and a working drawing. For example, in an early design stage, precision may be unimportant, but when you reach working drawings, a specific level of accuracy is required. Furthermore, in the design stage, you may want to try out many variations of a plan and set up your drawing in modules (say, rooms or building masses) that can be moved around. Drafting a construction document, on the other hand, is sometimes a matter of recording previous decisions or designing new details within a rigidly defined base.

Generally, the amount of detail and level of precision required for a drawing grows finer as a project progresses. If you can determine, from the start, how much detail and precision will ultimately be required, you can draw with an appropriate snap resolution and develop details according to your objective.

Phases

In schematic design, programming and information gathering often take graphic form. Space sizes and proximities can be simulated by moving, stretching, and shrinking enclosed areas. This initial space planning is assembled, along with site requirements and dimensions based on construction systems, into a diagrammatic design, which can be placed on the site plan to become a base drawing. From this point on, all the plan drawings will be "descendents" of the base drawing.

As the architectural design progresses, various plan drawings are developed. The architectural plans may all be located in a single drawing file, or, in the case of a larger project, they may each be developed from a common base. When alternative designs are studied, there may be several sets of drawings; eventually, the preferred alternative becomes the new base.

Other drawings, such as the consultant base drawings, can be extracted from the architectural plans; if the design changes, the revisions can be passed on to the consultants. Presentation drawings, simplified versions of the architectural plans, may be "spun off" and rendered at any point.

By mapping out this sequence ahead of time, with specific information like plotting scales and target dates, you can significantly reduce duplicated efforts. The door that you place in your schematic design drawing may still be in your as-built drawing after the building is finished.

DRAWING CRITERIA

Accuracy

The *level of accuracy* to be pursued in a drawing is especially important, because drawing is done on an infinitely expandable and contractible display that is like drawing with real dimensions. If a drawing is to be used at a scale of, say, $\frac{1}{8}''=1'\text{-}0''$, then drawing to an accuracy appropriate to a $\frac{1}{4}''=1'\text{-}0''$ drawing is probably unnecessary. Much time can be spent making extraordinarily precise drawings, but, in reality, builders usually work from written dimensions rather than carefully scaled measurements. Common sense based on experience is the best guide for determining this and most other drawing requirements.

Although accuracy is most important for construction drawings, schematic work may also benefit from precision. In work in which elements of predetermined size are being used, CAD can allow very realistic studies of different combinations and assemblages. When column spacings or ceiling heights are known accurately early in a project, engineering studies, area/volume calculations and materials estimates can be conducted with precision that may serve to inform subsequent design decisions.

Detail

Consider, also, the *amount of detail* that will be useful. In traditional terms, the scale at which drawings will be plotted will provide a good reference, since scales are chosen to best convey certain types of information. However, even when you decide to use a certain scale for one drawing, areas of the drawing may be developed and plotted at a larger scale (Figure 4-2). This *nesting* of drawings within drawings is extremely useful, but without carefully mapping out the most useful areas to be developed, much effort can be wasted.

It is also important to select *which* parts of a drawing will be developed in detail. Most designers have a natural tendency to focus on interesting or familiar details and often change scales in order to work on a particular area or form. One of the greatest advantages of computer-aided drawing is the ability to change "scale" (or viewpoint) effortlessly. While zooming in and out of a drawing can be enormously useful, it can also lead to much unnecessary drawing if done impulsively, with no clear strategy. Since details are often developed *in place*, it is important to pick the *right* place to work.

As in manual drafting, you must draw whatever is necessary to describe a design, first to yourself, then to a builder, with a minimum of redundant effort. You will often want to draw the details that are *most difficult* or have the *closest tolerances*. The computer can help to minimize redundant drawing, if you study the relationships between different areas and details in advance, then reuse parts of one detail in the next. For example, in a building section, each wall might be slightly different, but, by copying or mirroring the elements that repeat, you can eliminate much redrawing. In this manner, moving from one variation of a form to another, you can plan a *sequence* of drawings

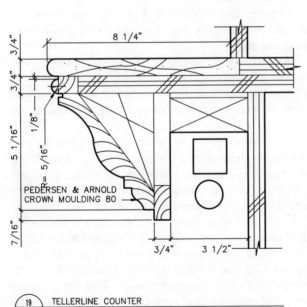

19 | TELLERLINE COUNTER
A9.3 | HALF SIZE

(a)

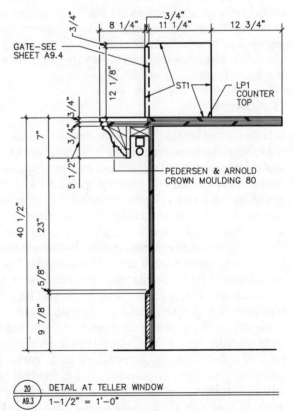

20 | DETAIL AT TELLER WINDOW
A9.3 | 1-1/2" = 1'-0"

(b)

FIGURE 4-2   The molding detail *(a)* may be used in a number of larger sections, such as *(b)*, ensuring consistency without the effort of redrawing the detail. This principle applies to many types of drawings at all scales, large and small. Neeley/Lofrano Inc, Architects, San Francisco.

that cover all the conditions you must design and document, while reducing repetitive work.

Drawing Type

The *type of information* that will go into a single-phase drawing is often easily defined. A design study may include physical forms and dimensional criteria, period. A presentation drawing might include forms and text, while a working drawing generally includes a long list of information types. Listing this range in advance enables you to avoid conflicts between different orders of graphics that may be added at different stages or by different people. In the case of a drawing that will go through multiple phases, it is usually best to structure a drawing for maximum flexibility.

Layers

The ultimate objective of a drawing is usually a plot, and a multilayered drawing can be plotted in many forms. By preplanning the *combinations of layers to be plotted*, you can make one drawing into many different drawings with a minimum of effort. The consequence of not mapping out a strategy can be a drawing that is impossible to plot in more than one or two combinations. We will examine layering strategies in detail in the next chapter.

Handwork

It is also important to consider the *amount of handwork* to be done on a drawing. A layering of handwork over a plotted base can be attractive and very productive, but thoughtless mixing of machine graphics and hand graphics can be ugly. If you are using the computer to lay out a base for sketching or rendering, adding unnecessary details is not only a waste of time but can clutter up a drawing. A good rule of thumb is that each type of information (such as walls, dimension lines, or notes) should be predominantly hand-drawn or computer-drawn. This is particularly important for lettering, since few drafters can copy a plotter-drawn font successfully. A common compromise on lettering is to do large titles via CAD, and small notes, which tend to be changed frequently, by hand, or to do peripheral notes in text blocks by machine, and individual notes within a drawing by hand. Similar techniques can be used for graphics when you can anticipate the need to mix techniques.

Changes

The real test of any drawing process is how well it accommodates *changes*, since few of us ever "get it right" completely the first time. Again, planning helps. Some CAD programs can require labyrinthine contortions to accomplish simple changes, and some knowledge of the idiosyncrasies of a particular system is essential. Knowing exactly what steps you might go through to, say, change a column design throughout a drawing can save a lot of pain when you actually need to do it.

If you can determine in advance what sort of alterations you are likely to want to make as you work, you can draw accordingly. Any change can take place at a particular place (locally) or it can be repeated throughout the drawing (globally). Local and global changes usually require very different techniques, but they are not, fortunately, exclusive of each other. There are four kinds of changes you can make to a drawing, as illustrated in Figure 4-3.

Modification refers to adding or subtracting elements like lines, symbols, objects or, for that matter, data attributes. Local modifications are the kind of work we do in revising a manual drawing. Global modifications, meaning changes that take place in all identical objects, are impossible with manual drafting, as are all the types of changes that follow.

Replacement (or substitution) is, obviously, taking away something and inserting something else. The organization of a drawing can facilitate replacement at one scale, while constraining it at another. Automatic search and replacement of numerous identical elements is one of the most useful functions of a good CAD program.

Movement is simply a matter of transferring something from one place to another. The relationships that you establish within a drawing will determine which elements can be moved easily in relation to others.

Scaling refers to the process of changing dimensions, by stretching or shrinking drawing elements in one or two directions. Knowing in advance which elements might be compressed or spread apart can make the process relatively easy.

Each kind of change is fundamental to the evolution of an architectural design and drawing. Design is sometimes described as a process akin to changing a tire, in which you tighten one nut, go on to the others, then come back and retighten each. Tracing paper is the logical outgrowth of such a process, allowing each successive try to be better, without having to start from scratch. The computer allows you to draw a series of studies as a single drawing or make multiple copies of a drawing and develop each differently. You can keep parts of an early study and throw away the rest, but you don't have to redraw the parts you are keeping. You can transform a whole drawing by changing a few

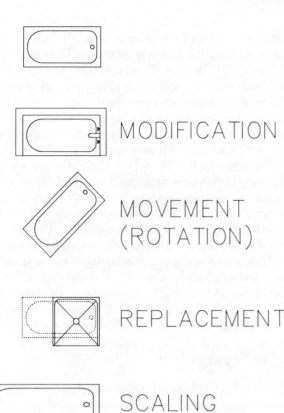

MODIFICATION

MOVEMENT
(ROTATION)

REPLACEMENT

SCALING

FIGURE 4-3   Changing a drawing.

work as you proceed: if there are enough appropriately sized niches, you can practically forget about the framework; if there are not, you may have to change either your work or the framework.

A drawing framework is based on the number and size of elements in a drawing and the relationships between them. Thus, a drawing that is composed of individual lines on a single layer will behave differently than a multilayered drawing assembled from predrawn objects and symbols. Often a simple structure, like the first, is sufficient, but a more complex framework, like the latter, will open up the real power of computer-aided drawing.

The key to making a really useful drawing framework is letting it grow out of your project and out of your own (or your firm's) way of working. If your drawing reflects your thinking about spatial relationships, building systems, and ways of using materials, then the process is much less likely to get in the way. The decisions you make about the relationships of drawing parts can be virtually the same decisions that you make as you design. Most kinds of design involve hierarchies; if you draw in a manner that reflects these patterns that are present in your work, you may find that the results become clearer.

GETTING STARTED

After you know what you want to do, think about how you're going to do it. When you begin any drawing you are confronted with some decisions to make about formats and drawing techniques. The list of issues can be fairly long if you include every possible item, such as scale, units, snap resolution, layer names, 3-D coordinates, linetypes, color, and other display-related issues. However, you don't want to have to go set up these working parameters every time you start a drawing.

CONVENTIONS

Most programs come with a set of default values that take effect if you make no decisions yourself. Of course, these are not necessarily the *right* values, and they don't cover a number of important items. Therefore, it's a good idea to save a record of the drawing parameters that you set up when you work on any drawing; the next time that you do a similar drawing you will be ready to go. Eventually, you will arrive at a set of **conventions** that will simplify the start-up process.

elements, or you can change a set of column lines by a few inches without having to redraw columns or anything else. The only catch is that the more you plan ahead, the more effectively you can work.

SETTING UP A FRAMEWORK

The "structure" of a drawing is not something that you can always see. A CAD drawing that looks identical to a manual line-drawing may have a tremendously complex internal structure. In fact, the way a drawing is organized is often completely invisible, just the way musical time signatures and keys may not be readily apparent to the uninitiated listener. Much as a composer sets out with a structure in mind, you should plan a CAD drawing's hidden organization.

The invisible structure of an architectural drawing is like a **framework** on which you will hang your

You can purchase software modules that will set up specific kinds of drawings for you; these can be very helpful in avoiding some of the trial-and-error process of developing drawing conventions. If you can adapt a set-up package to suit your own needs, then it will save you work; if, on the other hand, it is difficult to modify, it will inevitably force you to work in uncomfortable and inefficient ways.

Convenience and Consistency

Conventions are not only timesavers, of course. They are a method by which different people can produce consistent, synchronized drawings. When more than one person is working on a CAD project, such standards are essential. The complexity of a CAD drawing's organization simply requires such agreements, and they are best defined beforehand. Table 4-1 is a "status report" from an AutoCAD drawing, illustrating some of the variables that are set for each drawing.

Some parameters are largely matters of convenience and can even be changed in the course of a drawing. *Units* of measurement, for example, must not only be set up as metric or English but also be given levels of precision, in decimal places or fractions. Such a decision can be deceptively important. If you have not carefully considered the desirable level of accuracy, you may draw a site plan full of dimensions accurate to $\frac{1}{16}$th inch, which is unnecessary and inconvenient when you, say, want to dimension paving and utilities.

In a CAD drawing, the one format decision that you don't really need to make at first is setting the *scale* of your drawing. Remember, you are not drawing to scale, only plotting to scale. If you need to be concerned about a certain scale plot on a certain size sheet, then it's sometimes helpful to draw a rectangle representing the area of your plot on your drawing. You can drag it around to "fit" the plot, if you like. The only other time that scale really matters at first is when you are using text or dimensions, and you want them to plot at the proper size. Most software allows you to change sizes, some does so automatically, but sometimes it's nice to have text read properly as you work.

On a computer display, *colors* and *linetypes* affect your perception of a drawing so strongly that it is a good idea to have standard sets for each type of drawing. Again, it is particularly important that if different people are to work on a drawing they use the same conventions. The colors and linetypes that you see on the screen are not necessarily those you will plot—they can be chosen for maximum visual clarity. Later, when you plot your work, you can select linetypes that are appropriate to a specific plot. These may be plotted with linetypes and weights for different purposes.

Layer Organization

The most important parameters concern the assembly of a drawing. **Layer organization**, in particular, is an important factor in keeping a large drawing manageable and making any drawing as useful as possible.

A systematic set of layers can streamline the drawing process and allow you to view your work in ways that are impossible using traditional methods. By displaying or plotting selected layers, you can compare different systems like structure, mechanicals, and finishes. Drawings can be custom plotted by individual trade, for both estimating and construction, in ways that are impossible to produce manually. (More on this in Chapter 5.)

TABLE 4-1

```
2988 entities in \ACAD\HOUSE\PLAN
Limits are       X:  -100'-0"   1000'-0"  (Off)
                 Y:  -100'-0"   1000'-0"
Drawing uses     X:     7'-4"     69'-10"
                 Y:   -41'-10"     30'-8"
Display shows    X:     7'-4"    112'-10"
                 Y:   -41'-10"     30'-8"

Insertion base is  X:   0'-0"  Y:   0'-0"  Z:    0'-0"
Snap resolution is X:   0'-2"  Y:   0'-2"
Grid spacing is    X:   1'-0"  Y:   1'-0"

Current layer: 1FL-WALL-F
        Color: 2 (yellow) Linetype: CONTINUOUS
Current elevation:    0'-0"  thickness:    0'-0"
Axis off  Fill off  Grid off  Ortho on  Qtext off  Snap on  Tablet off
Object snap modes: None
Free RAM: 20221 bytes.  Free disk: 3565568 bytes
I/O page space:  82K bytes
```

It is particularly important that you develop a consistent layer organization that you use in all your work. While each project will have its idiosyncrasies, you do not want to have to create and name layers as you work. A good system will allow you to add occasional special layers as they are needed, with names that will be easy to remember and manipulate. Furthermore, it is crucial that different people who work on a project know exactly how a drawing is organized: ideally they should be able to tell at a glance which drawing elements are on which layers.

MENUS

Another key to comfortable computer-aided drawing is having whatever you need at hand. If you have to shuffle disks while you are working, you'll feel like a computer operator, not a designer or drafter. The most important thing you can set up in advance is a menu that suits your working style well.

Many programs allow you to design menus to place on a digitizing tablet or to adapt menus that are supplied with the software. Some also allow you to reconfigure on-screen menus. Many PC-based systems allow you to redefine the keyboard as you please (Figure 4-4). Like developing a set of conventions, you don't want to have to design a menu each time you start drawing, so you should design (and continue to evolve) a basic menu that suits you.

On-screen menus can be designed hierarchically, so that one menu will lead into other more specific menus. Thus, menus that you only use occasionally are out of sight but are available when you need them. Custom menus within menus let you make specific drawing libraries and layer organizations available

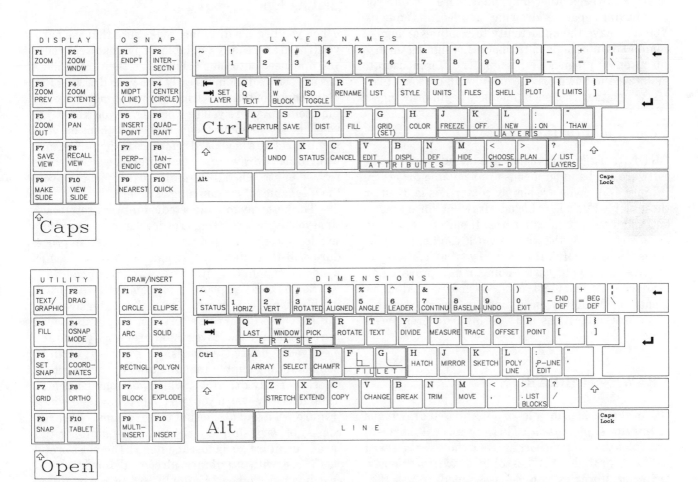

FIGURE 4-4   Using a keyboard modification utility program, a command (or set of commands) can be assigned to each key on the keyboard. This map illustrates AutoCAD commands assigned to keys in combination with the "alternate" and "control" keys. This allows you to quickly enter commands with one hand, while drawing with the other. The keys for "layer names" can be assigned by the user to suit a specific drawing, so that appropriate groups of layers may be turned on and off with a single keystroke.

for each type of drawing you do. Likewise, specialized sets of commands, like those for dimensioning or working with attributes, can be collected into specialized menus and called up when needed.

Personalizing Menus

Every user of your CAD system should learn how to set up and adapt menus. When commands are personalized, the system is able to "fit" an individual better. For example, some people like to use a keyboard with one hand while drawing with the other; conversely, non-typists are often terrified of keyboards. There's no reason that everyone should have to use the same setup.

When you lay out a menu, especially a detailed, specialized one, you can set up an arrangement of commands in a manner that reflects the way you work, not the way a software designer thinks you should work. Simply placing two commands like "line" and "copy" near each other may make more sense to you than having separate "drawing" and "editing" menus. You also have the opportunity to combine strings of commands into single-entry macros, assigning them to spaces on your menu. It is possible for different users to maintain their own private menu, with personal macros, which they load each time they begin drawing.

Front-End Programs

"Ready to use" tablet menus are included with some software, and add-on menus are available for others (Figure 4-5). Some are simply commands laid out on the tablet, while others include drawing library references and sophisticated macros. If one of these *front-ends* is set up for the kind of work you do, it can be tremendously useful. However, if you can't adapt it to the type of drawing you are doing, it may prove to be a headache. A front-end menu system should allow plenty of flexibility in setting up layers, drawing elevations and sections, and working at different levels of detail.

DRAWING LIBRARIES

One of the basic principles of object-based drawing is *never draw anything twice*. This is based on **libraries** of drawings that you can borrow from whenever you need to use a graphic that has been drawn previously. Drawing libraries can be assembled from other sources, or you can create them yourself.

A drawing library can be a constantly evolving, growing collection. Although you might occasionally sit down and work specifically on developing library drawings, it is much easier to create them as you work on projects. Any time you even *think* you might ever want to reuse what you've drawn, no matter how simple or complex, save it outside your drawing. Sometimes, it makes sense to save your whole drawing, for instance, if you have drawn a bathroom layout that might be useful in the future. If you do this prodigiously, you will very soon have a wealth of graphics (and, in some case, database information) ready to use when you start a drawing.

Give your library files clearly identifiable names, and organize them carefully. You can save a lot of images on a single floppy disk, so it's a good idea to put them into separate directories, according to type of project and type of drawing. Keep a list of names with any notes that might be helpful, and try to keep a notebook of plots of your available graphics.

Setting Up

When you begin a drawing, make sure that the parts you'll need are readily available. Copy whatever groups you may need onto your hard disk, if they aren't there already, or load them directly into your drawing file. Make copies of the plots from the master notebook and pin them up where you're working. If you know that you'll be using some frequently, load them on your menu or set up a keyboard reference to them. You may want to load a drawing several different ways, perhaps rotated or stretched differently, so that you can avoid the mechanics of customizing each insertion.

The best way to avoid a tedious library setup each time you begin a drawing is to develop your own menu sets for specific types of work. A single set-up procedure will then allow you to place a library, such as windows or plumbing fixtures, at your command.

Some CAD programs come complete with drawing libraries, some of which are fairly extensive. You can purchase library sets for most programs, and if you can find any that cover the kind of work you do and meet your quality standards, it's probably worth it. Some building supply manufacturers provide sets of insertion-ready drawings, which you may be able to use and modify even if you don't plan to buy their wares (Figure 4-6 *a* and *b*). Most of these "canned" libraries consist of very simple elements, like plumbing fixtures, furniture, or landscape items. The most useful sets come with attributes already defined, or 3-D coordinates attached. Minimally, you should be able to modify the drawings as you need to, as well as add your own drawings. Be sure that a library can be adapted to the requirements of your layering scheme: many are

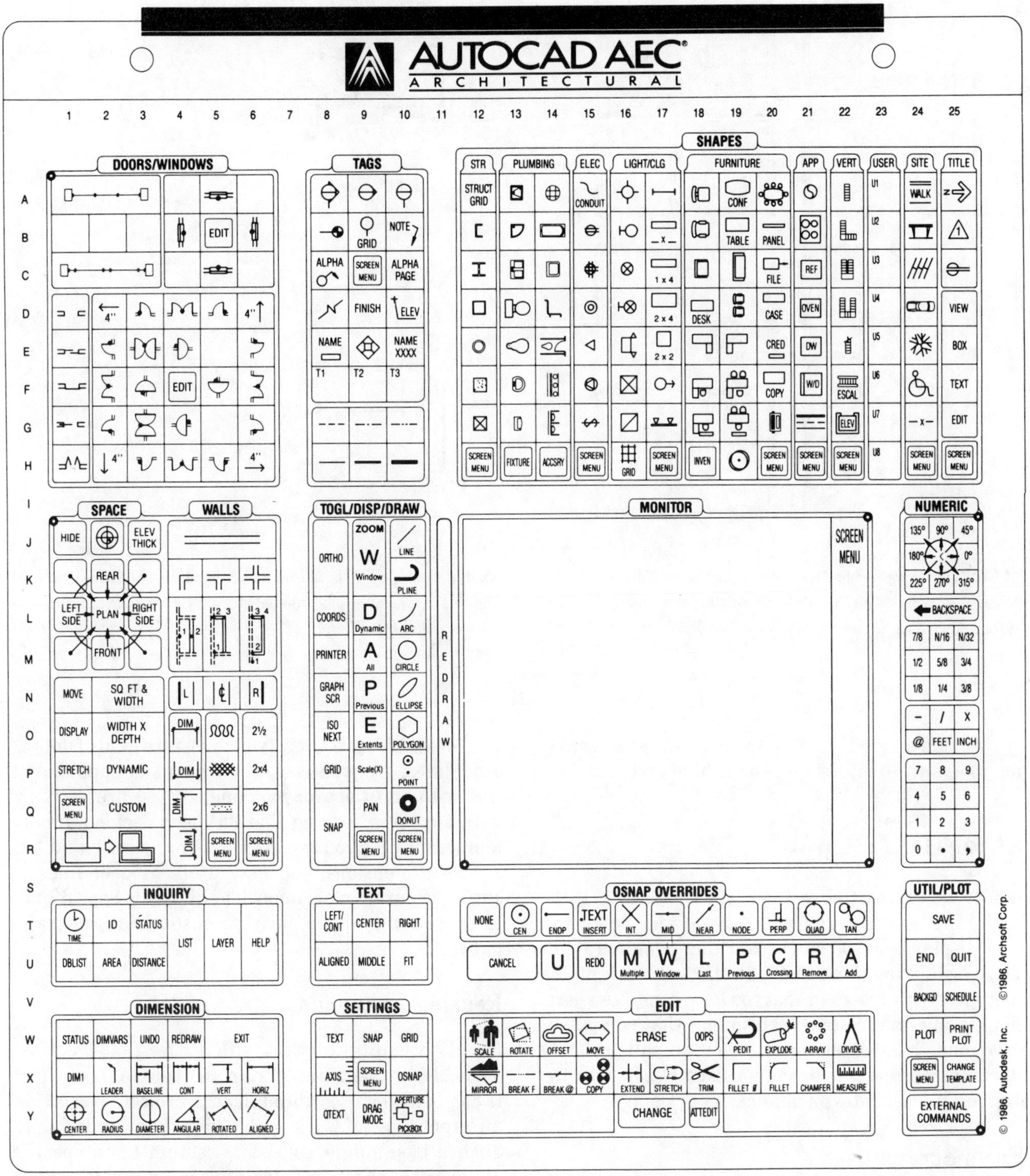

FIGURE 4-5 This tablet menu is part of an AutoCAD add-on program that is specifically oriented toward drawing architectural plans; it is limited to a very specific layering system. Rather than adapt your working method to these kinds of limitations, you might decide to use different "ready to use" menus for different tasks, you could modify a purchased menu package, or you could write your own. Autodesk, Inc.

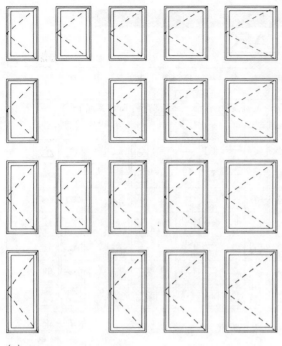

(a)

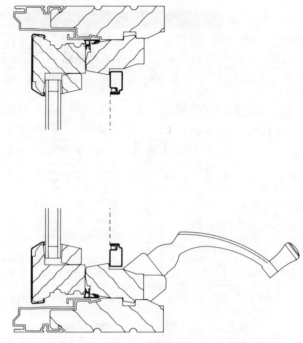

(b)

FIGURE 4-6 Some building materials manufacturers offer their catalogs on floppy disks in common drawing formats. Shown here are a group of window-elevation symbols and two details from the Pella window catalog-on-disk, which includes hundreds of other symbols and details, available to be inserted into drawings by their catalog numbers. Rollscreen Corp.

drawn on a single layer and must be edited to enable you to use different linetypes or to hide text.

LAYING OUT A BASE

What are you starting with? If you're starting at the beginning, you've got a blank slate on your desk or on your display, and you will be working "from scratch." You may, on the other hand, be starting work on the computer with drawings that you have done elsewhere. Don't make the mistake of thinking that computers have made hand drawing obsolete: you will probably start many projects with manual sketches, base drawings, or at least notes on dimensions or details.

From Scratch

If you are starting from scratch on the computer, sometimes the easiest way to begin is by sketching a first pass of your work, then going back and working more carefully on a separate layer. This is particularly useful if you are sketching volumes in a three dimensional mode: a rough massing study will provide a good base for developing plans, elevations, and sections.

Most software allows you to set up a grid of dots as guidelines; frequently you will want to supplement this with additional layout lines. If you are working with a column spacing that has been decided, if only temporarily, or you are assembling anything that has known dimensions, you may use a grid of lines to ensure accurate placement. The ability to repeat lines gives you the opportunity to custom-design graph paper.

Reusing Drawings

It's often helpful to start with a base that has been derived from sketches or from another CAD drawing. It can often be used throughout a project, overlaying different types of work on it, and perhaps updating it. Such a base might consist of column lines, specific dimensions, or site constraints. Or, you may want to start, instead, with forms or objects from your drawing library that provide a dimensional and formal reference as you work (Figure 4-7).

A part of a previous drawing can serve as a base for a new drawing. After you have drawn a floor plan, you can often copy and reuse much of it for subsequent plans. Elevations and sections may be selectively

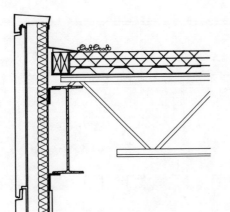

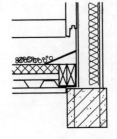

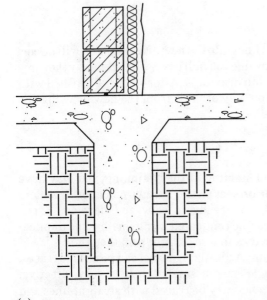

(a)

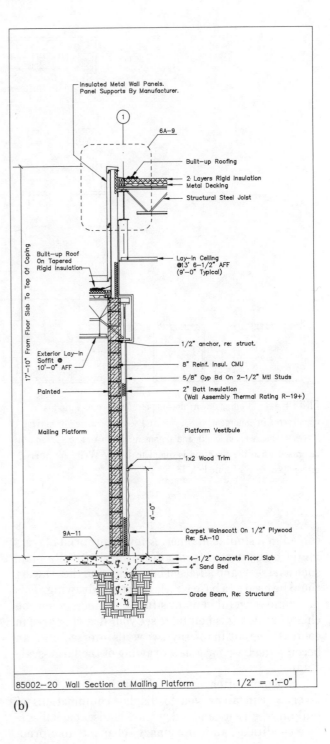

Insulated Metal Wall Panels.
Panel Supports By Manufacturer.

6A—9

Built-up Roofing

2 Layers Rigid Insulation
Metal Decking

Structural Steel Joist

Built-up Roof
On Tapered
Rigid Insulation

Lay-in Ceiling
@13' 6—1/2" AFF
(9'—0" Typical)

17'—10" From Floor Slab To Top Of Coping

1/2" anchor, re: struct.

8" Reinf. Insul. CMU

5/8" Gyp Bd On 2—1/2" Mtl Studs

Exterior Lay-in
Soffit @
10'—0" AFF

2" Batt Insulation
(Wall Assembly Thermal Rating R—19+)

Painted

Mailing Platform

Platform Vestibule

1x2 Wood Trim

4'—0"

9A—11

Carpet Wainscott On 1/2" Plywood
Re: 5A—10

4—1/2" Concrete Floor Slab
4" Sand Bed

Grade Beam, Re: Structural

85002—20 Wall Section at Mailing Platform   1/2" = 1'—0"

(b)

FIGURE 4-7 Several individual details (a) were assembled to produce
the wall section (b). The details could have been retrieved from an
electronic drawing library or traced from paper drawings or sketches,
perhaps from originals that were drawn at different scales. Buday
Wells, Architects; drawing (b) property of US Postal Service.

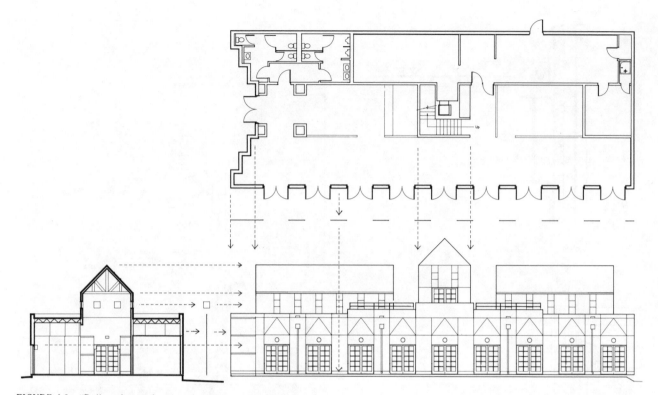

FIGURE 4-8 "Pulling down" drawing elements: an elevation is constructed in alignment with a plan and section, copying or moving pieces to ensure exact length and alignment. The plan and section can be erased when the elevation is complete. Buday Wells, Architects, drawing courtesy of Autodesk, Inc.

copied in a similar manner. A few appropriate layers might be extracted from a fully developed site plan, such as streets and adjacent buildings, and these layers could be used as a base for a larger scale drawing. This principle is useful in many situations, since, when you change scales, it is helpful to see your drawing area in context. The outline of, say, two walls intersecting, can become the base for a new drawing of the large-scale detail.

Site plans often make good base drawings. Careful layering can allow you to display combinations of buildings, streets and sidewalks, landscape, subsurface conditions, and "imaginary" elements like property lines. Frequently you can adapt parts of your base into a final drawing, editing out parts where you have placed buildings.

In manual drafting, different drawing types are often developed adjacent to each other, to facilitate direct transfers of dimensions. In a similar manner, you can begin drawing a section or elevation by starting with a plan and actually "pulling down" (moving

or copying) lines into the new drawing. You will be certain that any line you pull down will be exactly the same length on both drawings. After you have finished with the plan, you may erase it from the new drawing file (Figure 4-8).

From Paper to CAD

If you're not starting at the beginning, you may have part of your project already drawn on paper, freehand or drafted, and ready to copy and develop. Paper drawings can be replicated using line-by-line duplication with, say, a mouse or light pen, though this is not very efficient. A digitizing tablet can be used to trace a drawing, and even a small tablet is very effective. Rough sketches may be traced with straight lines and accurate dimensions, using the computer to produce orthogonal lines at an appropriate snap resolution.

The easiest method of copying paper drawings is with a digitizing scanner or camera, but (in addition to being expensive) this often produces a drawing with all information on one layer, in "primitive" (i.e., line, arc, and circle, rather than object) form. Some scanners can differentiate text and symbols, placing them on separate layers; nevertheless, most scanned drawings must be edited, often extensively, to take full advantage of CAD.

A useful copying technique is to assemble a new CAD drawing from several paper drawings, perhaps sketches or details. This is similar to tracing from several originals onto a single sheet, except that you can change scales, make multiple copies, or "drag" a form around a drawing. This kind of *assemblage* is, in fact, basic to computer-aided design, whether you are copying paper drawings or combining electronic file drawings. It is a technique that gives you the ability to develop libraries of building parts and use them in various projects, modifying them as each situation requires.

Software is also available that can transfer an image from a video camera or recording into computer-aided drawing programs. Although you cannot use these images in a CAD vector-graphics drawing, you can use it as a base for "tracing" on the screen. A video image of a facade, for example, could be traced with lines, using CAD, then erased, leaving a facade line drawing.

CAD to CAD

If you are using two semicompatible CAD programs, such as high- and low-end drafting systems or separate three-dimensional modeling and two-dimensional draft-

ing, you may only be able to translate part of your work. In the transfer between drafting programs, for example, layer and block information may not be transferred precisely. Nevertheless, a not-quite-perfect translation will often provide a good base for building new drawings, even if it is eventually replaced by your new work.

A base can be anything that helps you get started. If you use graphics that you have previously created, you can assemble a base that, just like a drawing library, helps you "never draw anything twice."

DRAW!

If it seems like there are too many things to think about before you start a drawing, don't let it stop you. Get started anyway. Most of the issues discussed in this chapter will either become second nature very quickly, or you will, by necessity, standardize them as conventions.

Only by designing and drawing will you figure out what works best for you and for your software. You may discover that different setups work better for different kinds of work: different phases or different kinds of projects. You may find that improvising a drawing takes little preparation, or you may find that a particular setup makes improvisation easier. Make notes: you don't want to have to reinvent the wheel each time you start. Before long, the wheels will turn by themselves, and you can concentrate on your destination.

BUILDING A DRAWING

CHAPTER 5

In architectural drawing, each building element must be set into its proper place, just as it is when you build a structure. Complex elements are built up of simpler ones, just as walls are built of bricks and wood and glass. Designing and drawing manually, each line is added as if each brick was being hand cast, as if each window was being assembled on-site piece by piece. Computer assistance allows you not only to place the bricks without having to make them first, but also to place the whole wall at once, as if it was prefabricated.

The computer's ability to remember information and then process it according to your instructions gives you two special tools for handling your drawing parts. First, you can identify *groups* of elements that can be controlled simultaneously. Second, you can create *symbols* or *blocks*, complex objects that you can treat as single elements. These two tricks allow you to *build* a drawing as if you were constantly assembling and refining a "kit of parts." A computer is also well-equipped to handle the often mundane tasks of *changing* or *replacing* parts of a drawing; in ▸

fact it can even take over some of the work of assembling a drawing in the first place. A CAD program that *automatically* follows your

instructions for drawing assembly is like having an entire construction crew at your command.

COLLECTIONS OF DRAWING PARTS

Every computer-aided drawing program provides several different ways to handle groups of drawing parts. Individually, each method can be a useful tool; they can also be used together to give you tremendous control over a drawing.

Whenever you pick elements by making a *window* (or *box* or *fence*) around them, you have defined a group of objects, even if they are on different layers. After choosing them, you might copy them, stretch them, or erase them. Some CAD programs will "remember" the group, so that whenever you want to, say, copy or move the group you can point to it or refer to it by name.

Some software includes unusual or unique ways of collecting groups of elements. A program might let you refer to, say, all green circles in your drawing. A three-dimensional program might allow you to manipulate elements according to their elevation. We will examine several of the most common grouping tools and look at ways to use them effectively. If you encounter different techniques, try to use some of the ideas outlined here to get the most out of them. Many of the methods we describe are applicable to any system for collecting drawing elements.

By far the most common method of grouping elements is called **layer** (or *level*) **organization**.

LAYERS

Layers are an easily understood way of grouping elements. Think of a drawing as a stack of transparent, interchangeable sheets of film; each group of related elements can be thought of as overlays. This is very similar to overlay drafting, a widely used technique for drawing on highly transparent plastic sheets. Layering lets the computer take care of juggling the sheets; it also lets you use many more layers, and thus control more groups, than overlay drafting.

Electronic Overlays

In overlay drafting, each sheet represents a specific type of work, such as framing or plumbing, and a location, such as a roof or a particular floor. These distinctions make a good starting point for structuring a drawing using CAD. Often, however, it is useful to create very specific layers, so that a drawing might be structured as shown in Figure 5-1.

Note, first, that the term "drawing" has a new meaning here. You may wish to break up a project into the "sets of layers" that you will be working with at one time: each of these sets can be called a "drawing." However, when they are combined, the entire set of plans for an architectural project can be considered a single drawing. The benefits of having all the information, top to bottom, siting to lighting, available, in correct position, for an entire project, at a moment's notice, are enormous. It also assures that proximities and alignments will always be shown correctly. It allows floor-to-floor comparisons and easy floor-to-floor copying of repeated elements.

The "set of layers" column is a list of what would traditionally be the plan drawings for a building, and, indeed, these may be the drawings that would finally be plotted. Each of these drawings, though, will be made up of many layers. If "area plans" are to be developed at a larger scale, these may be drawn "in place," adding special sets of layers for elements and text that should not appear on small scale plots. An area plan can be plotted, large-scale, with the overall plan as a base, or it may be hidden when plotting the full plan (Figure 5-2, *a* and *b*).

Even though you can keep all these drawings in a single drawing file, you may wish to divide a set of drawings into groups to work on separately. In fact, you may *have* to divide up large drawings: the practicality of maintaining a single, comprehensive drawing file for a project is subject to the realities of project management and computer speed and capacity. (The means of sharing data, as discussed in Chapter 8, is particularly important.) A very large drawing can be split into several drawings by areas, which is particularly useful if different people are working on different areas of the building. However, if work is divided according to *types* of work (say, writing notes, detailing exterior walls and developing ceiling plans), groups of layers can be assigned to people working at different workstations. In this manner, a project can be developed by consultants using different drawings sharing a common base, so that layers from one set may be inserted into another.

But why build a drawing with so many layers?

Seeing through Your Work

If you are making a set of drawings, you will want to be able to use repeated elements in different combinations. In the example of Figure 5-1, the base floor plan is reused in most of the individual drawings. However, in a reflected ceiling plan, windows and doors will be dashed or will not be shown. If they have been drawn on a separate layer, there is no need to erase them: instead, the layers containing the window and door symbols can be plotted with a dashed linetype or turned off. If the walls are redesigned in the floor plan, they are automatically revised in the ceiling plan too; since they are really the same drawing. In addition, layers from the engineering drawings are used in the architectural reflected ceiling plan. Light fixtures and air diffusers, for example, can also be used in two different kinds of drawings (Figure 5-3).

Elements like columns and bearing walls often repeat from floor to floor in a multistory building. You will want to be able to change them on all floors,

LEVEL	DISCIPLINE	SET OF LAYERS	LAYERS
	Landscape	Overall	
		Planting	
	Site Engineering	Drainage	
		Paving	
		Floor Plan	Walls/Bearing Walls/Nonbearing Windows Doors Plumbing (Fixtures) Partitions Surfaces Overhead Symbols Notes Dimensions
Floor #1	Architecture	Reflected Ceiling	Walls/Bearing Walls/Nonbearing Fill—in (Door, window openings) Lighting (Fixtures) HVAC (Diffusers) Sprinklers Tiles Symbols Notes Dimensions
	Structural	Framing	
		Fabrication Drawings	
	Mechanical	Plumbing	
		HVAC	
	Electrical	Lighting	
		Wiring	

FIGURE 5-1 The chart represents the organization of a multiple-disciplinary set of drawings that have been meshed into a single multilayer drawing. Each set of layers would share several common "base" layers, such as walls.

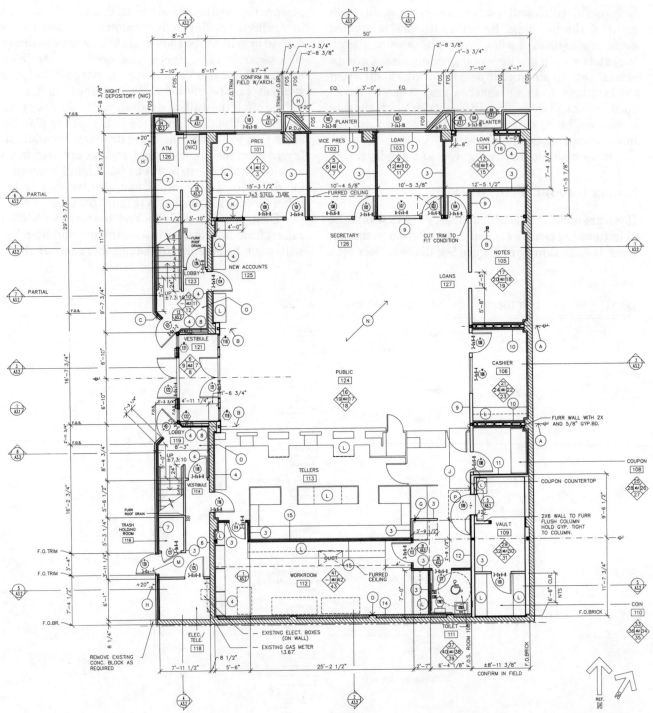

(a)

FIGURE 5-2 The full plan of a bank *(a)* was used as a starting point for the area plan *(b)*. Details and notes were drawn over the original plan on new layers: the entire area plan with details could be viewed and plotted in context, as well as in the two ways shown. Neeley/Lofrano Inc, Architects, San Francisco.

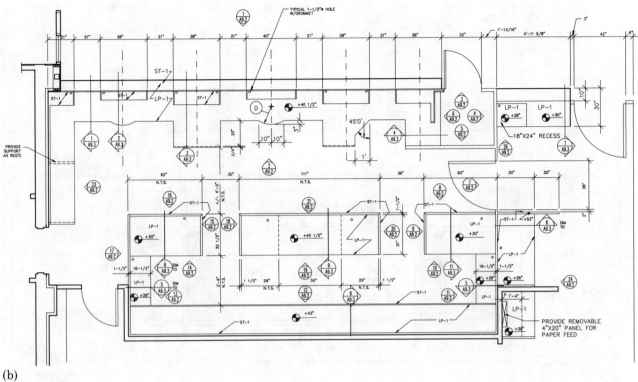

(b)

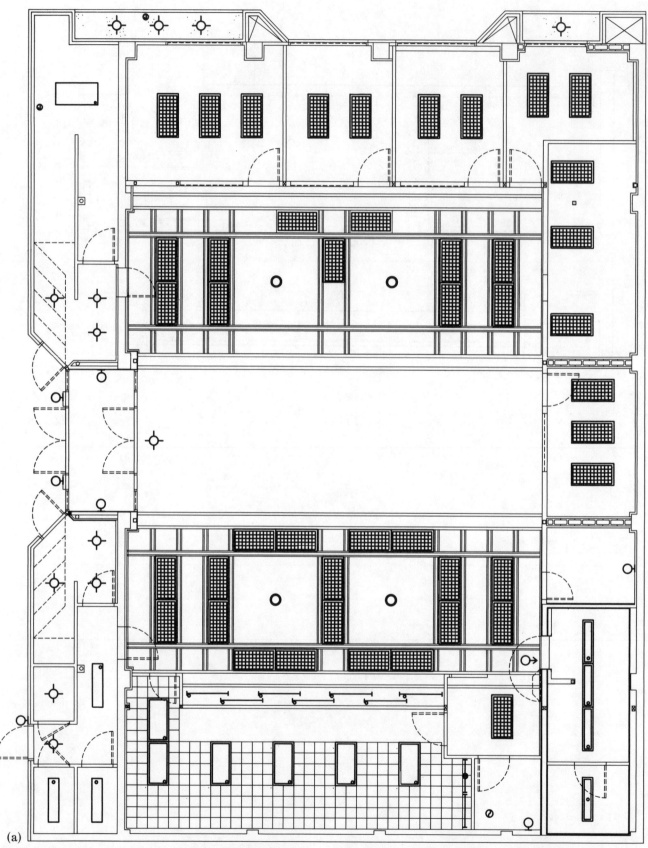

(a)

FIGURE 5-3   The reflected ceiling plan of the bank (a) uses the wall layers of the floor plan, as well as the door symbols, which are dashed for reference. Note that the heads over the doors are drawn in: these were automatically included on a hidden layer when the door symbols were placed. The electrical ceiling plan (b), adapted by a consultant using the same software, is identical with the addition of wiring and fixture symbols on their own layers. Neeley/Lofrano Inc, Architects, San Francisco.

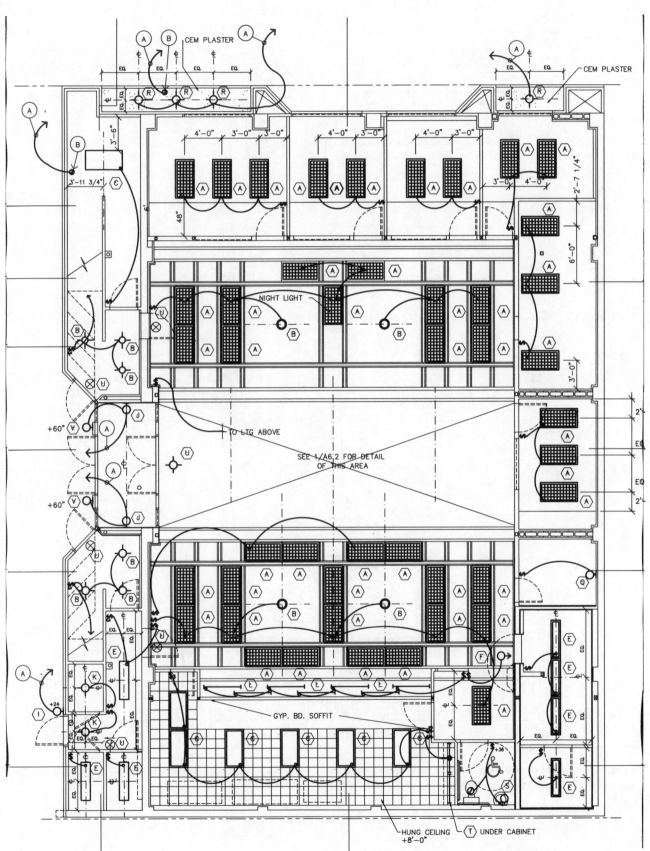

(b)

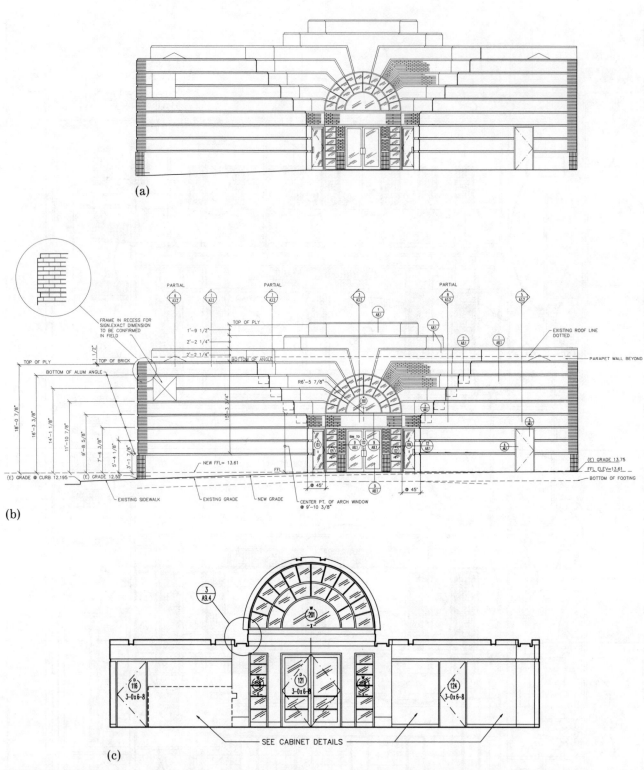

FIGURE 5-4 The bank elevation was used for a working drawing *(b)*, without notes as a presentation drawing *(a)*, and the central doors and windows were used again for the interior elevation *(c)*. Neeley/Lofrano Inc, Architects, San Francisco.

simultaneously, while partitions may vary from floor to floor and would not be repeated. Therefore, whatever elements appear on all floors can be drawn on base layers, then displayed with a different set of layers for each floor.

Sections and elevations too can be drawn in a single multilayered drawing, just as you would use a building section to lay out an elevation on a tracing paper overlay. Each section or elevation consists of a group of layers within the larger drawing file, like floor layers in a plan. Again, you gain the advantage of being able to easily check the alignment of the different drawings, and, if you are drawing multiple sections, you can copy parts that repeat from one set of section layers to another set. Interior elevations can be produced very efficiently by drawing them within the section: often an object that is cut by one section will be seen in elevation in another. It may be drawn in outline on the "cut" layer of the first, then copied to the "elevation" layer of the second (Figure 5-5).

After you lay out a section/elevation, you can develop various parts to different levels of detail, as you might in a plan. An elevation might be drawn on one set of layers to a level of detail equivalent to $\frac{1}{4}''=1'$, while a wall section, on other layers, might be developed to be plotted at $\frac{3}{4}''=1'$.

Displaying and Plotting

By grouping similar elements by layer, you gain control over both display and plotting of your work. In order to use large files of interrelated drawings, as outlined above, many layers must be turned off, or hidden. When too many layers are displayed at once, a drawing may become illegible. Some CAD programs enable you to *freeze* layers which are hidden, which allows the computer to draw the displayed portion without taking time to sort through the layers that are not displayed. (This capability is crucial to building large, multilevel drawings.) If your drawing is well organized, you may view the layers that you are interested in, at any time, and no others. Furthermore, you may assign colors and linetypes to different layers that indicate either their importance or the type of material. Thus, layout lines might read faintly; glass might be drawn in blue, and the outline of an overhead projection might be dotted.

When plotting, you will again be able to choose line weights, types, and colors according to your layering scheme. If your drawing is well-organized, you should be able to plot visually effective drawings with a minimum of effort. You *don't* want to turn on the plotter and discover that your walls and floor surfaces

are on the same layer if you want to plot them using different line weights.

Many CAD programs enable you to display elements that are drawn on one layer in different colors and, thus, plot them using different line weights and types. Though this increases your plotting flexibility, it can also cause confusion, since you have no way of knowing, at a glance, whether or not two different-colored elements are on the same layer. It is best to only use this capability as an exception, such as when you need to change the linetype of a few elements but don't want to create a new layer for them. In this case, try to use related colors, such as cyan and blue, or red and magenta, so that you can easily see that the two elements are on the same layer.

Custom Work

By carefully choosing combinations of layers to plot, you can create customized drawings for different purposes. Here are some examples.

An elevation might be plotted twice, without notes, for a presentation drawing, then again, with notes, for a working drawing (Figure 5-4). Windows and doors can then be used for interior elevations, in this case, drawn into the section.

Likewise, a section can be plotted with the windows from the associated elevation dotted in for reference (Figure 5-6).

A electrical plan may be plotted with a reflected ceiling plan, in order to assist the electrical contractor in wiring fixtures (Figure 5-3b).

When a drawing contains notes for a number of different trades, individual plots may be made with notes for each discipline or trade; a contract/bid set would, of course, include all notes. In situations in which two trades have special coordination requirements, drawings for those two trades can be plotted on a single sheet, helping to clarify the interrelationships between the two.

MANAGING LAYERS

A large number of layers can be difficult to handle unless you have a way to manage them in groups. One layer can be a member of several different sets of layers, giving you different "handles" for manipulating it. For example, the bearing walls and columns of a multistory building would appear in different floor plans, ceiling plans, and engineering plans, so you need a convenient way to combine the base layer (walls and columns) with each set of plans.

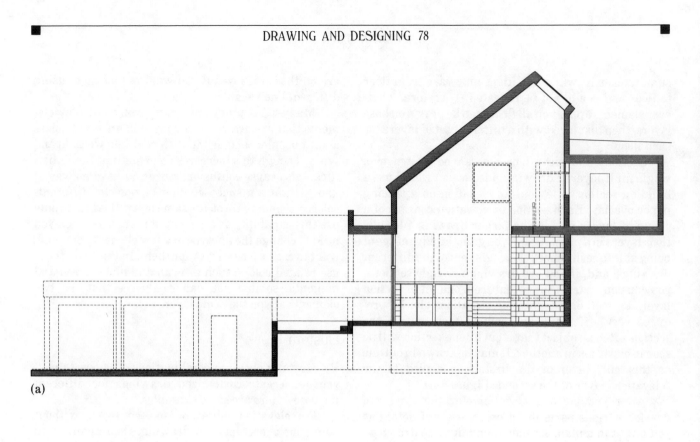

(a)

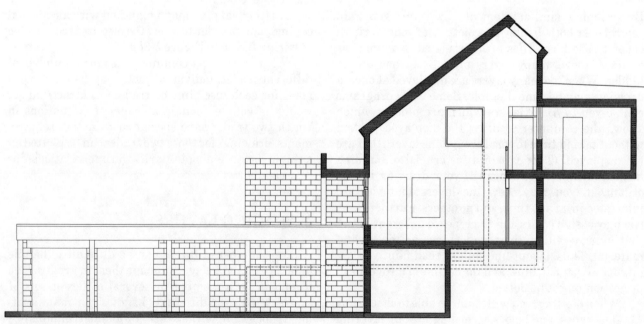

(b)

FIGURE 5-5 In the top section of a terraced house, near interior
elevations are plotted with light, solid lines, while background elevations
and section-cuts are dashed for reference. In the lower section (another
version of the same drawing), the section lines in front of the cut-plane
are dotted.

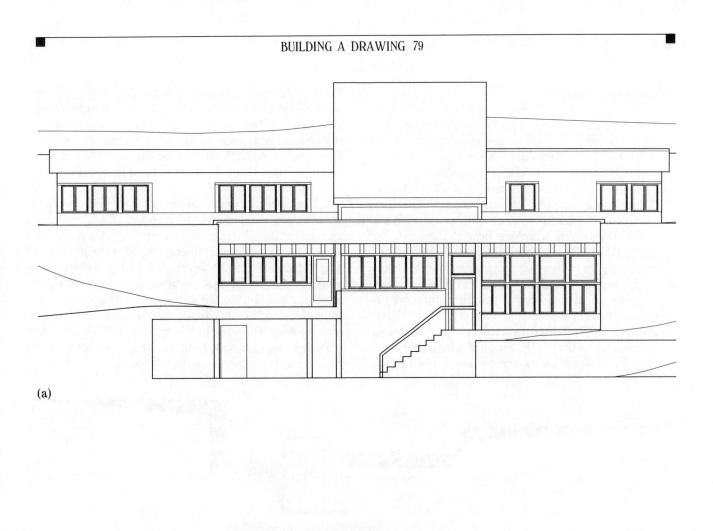

(a)

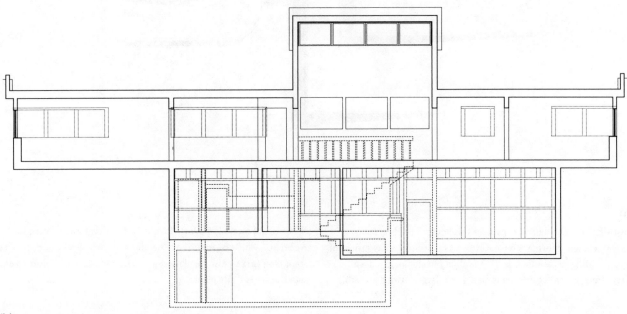

(b)

FIGURE 5-6 The elevation *(a)* and section *(b)* are different layers of
the same drawing: the windows are dotted on the section, for reference.
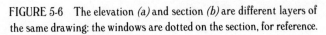

What's in a Name?

The ability to name or number layers and manage them in groups is, in itself, an important drawing tool. Give each layer a name that refers to all the sets to which it belongs. For example, the layers for Floor Number 1 can be referred to as FL1-Wall, FL1-Door, FL1-Mech(anical), FL1-Note, and so on. Not only can you turn on "all FL1," but you could display "all Wall," to check alignments from one floor to the next. You might further add FL1-Wall-Bearing and FL1-Wall-Partition to the names, and manage them the same way, by saying "all FL1-Wall." If walls will occur identically on each floor of a building, they may be drawn on (or copied to) a base layer called "Bas(e)-Wall" and displayed with each level. (Abbreviations are necessary so that each section of a layer name has the same number of characters. When you call for "all

Wall" you would actually ask for "???-Wall.") Even systems that number layers can be used effectively by developing a two- or three-digit code. The first digit may represent type or discipline, the second represents floor level, and the third represents specific layers that occur on each floor, with each discipline (Figure 5-7 and Table 5-1).

The most important criteria for naming layers is that they be convenient to turn on and off and that you can easily switch from one *current* layer (the one on which you are drawing) to another. To a great degree, this will depend on the degree to which you customize your system: it can become tiresome typing out layer names or numbers on the keyboard each time you want to change, so it is important to use macros to handle groups of layers and switch current layers. These tasks should be as easy as typing one or two keystrokes or making a single pick on a tablet menu.

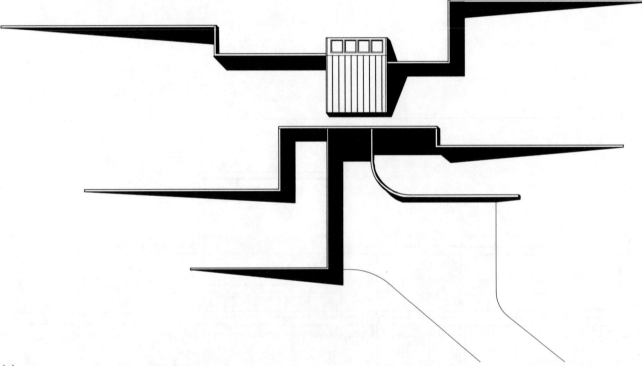

(a)

FIGURE 5-7   The four level plan for this house (3 levels are shown here) is a single drawing: simple macros were used to display groups of layers relating to each floor level. The ability to eliminate hidden layers from screen regenerations makes such large drawings possible.

The second level (*b*) is plotted with the first level walls dotted for reference, which is particularly helpful with this terraced design. The roof plan (*a*) can also be plotted without shadows, with contours and landscape, as a site plan.

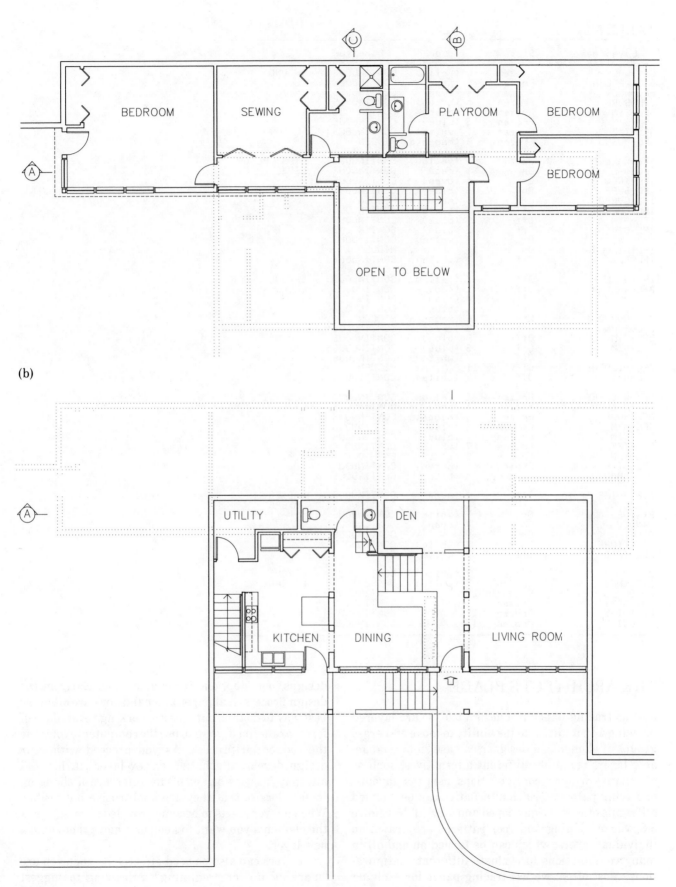

(b)

(c)

TABLE 5-1

Layer name	State	Color	Linetype	
GFL-WALL-F	Frozen	2 (yellow)	CONTINUOUS	GROUND
GFL-WALL-H	Frozen	1 (red)	CONTINUOUS	LEVEL
GFL-WNDW	Frozen	4 (cyan)	CONTINUOUS	
GFL-SURF	Frozen	3 (green)	CONTINUOUS	
GFL-SYM	Frozen	5 (blue)	CONTINUOUS	
GFL-DIM	Frozen	5 (blue)	CONTINUOUS	
GFL-TXT	Frozen	7 (white)	CONTINUOUS	
GFL-OVRHD	Frozen	6 (magenta)	HIDDEN	
1FL-WALL-F	On	2 (yellow)	CONTINUOUS	FIRST FLOOR
1FL-WALL-H	On	1 (red)	CONTINUOUS	LEVEL
1FL-WNDW	On	4 (cyan)	CONTINUOUS	
1FL-SURF	On	5 (blue)	CONTINUOUS	
1FL-OVRHD	On	6 (magenta)	HIDDEN	
1FL-FURN	Off	3 (green)	CONTINUOUS	
1FL-SYM	Off	5 (blue)	CONTINUOUS	
1FL-DIM	Off	5 (blue)	CONTINUOUS	
1FL-TXT	On	7 (white)	CONTINUOUS	
1FL-HIDDEN	On	11	HIDDEN	
1FL-ALT	Off	7 (white)	CONTINUOUS	
2FL-WALL-F	Off	2 (yellow)	CONTINUOUS	SECOND FLOOR
2FL-WALL-H	Off	1 (red)	CONTINUOUS	LEVEL
2FL-WNDW	Off	4 (cyan)	CONTINUOUS	
2FL-SURF	Off	5 (blue)	CONTINUOUS	
2FL-OVRHD	Off	6 (magenta)	HIDDEN	
2FL-FURN	Off	3 (green)	CONTINUOUS	
2FL-SYM	Off	5 (blue)	CONTINUOUS	
2FL-DIM	Off	5 (blue)	CONTINUOUS	
2FL-TXT	Off	7 (white)	CONTINUOUS	
2FL-HIDDEN	Off	11	HIDDEN	
2FL-ALT	Off	7 (white)	CONTINUOUS	
RFL-WALL-F	Frozen	2 (yellow)	CONTINUOUS	ROOF/SITE
RFL-WALL-H	Frozen	1 (red)	CONTINUOUS	LEVEL
RFL-SURF	Frozen	6 (magenta)	CONTINUOUS	
RFL-SYM	Frozen	5 (blue)	CONTINUOUS	
RFL-DIM	Frozen	5 (blue)	CONTINUOUS	
RFL-TXT	Frozen	7 (white)	CONTINUOUS	
RFL-HDN	Frozen	5 (blue)	DASHED	
RFL-SITE	Frozen	3 (green)	CONTINUOUS	
RFL-SHAD	Frozen	5 (blue)	CONTINUOUS	
ATRIBUTES	Off	1 (red)	CONTINUOUS	MASTER
PLUMBING	On	11	CONTINUOUS	LAYERS
FIXTURE	On	7 (white)	CONTINUOUS	
WINDOW	On	4 (cyan)	CONTINUOUS	
DOOR	On	9	CONTINUOUS	
FURNITURE	On	7 (white)	CONTINUOUS	
ELECTRIC	Off	7 (white)	CONTINUOUS	
0	Frozen	7 (white)	CONTINUOUS	LAYOUT
CTRLINES	Frozen	7 (white)	DASHDOT	LAYERS
LAYOUT-G	Frozen	20	CONTINUOUS	
LAYOUT-1	Frozen	11	CONTINUOUS	
LAYOUT-2	Frozen	22	CONTINUOUS	
LAYOUT-R	Frozen	13	CONTINUOUS	

THE ARCHITECT'S BLADE

Just as tracing paper is a design tool, so are layered drawings. In addition to the ability to move and erase groups of elements, a designer can use "interchangeable layers" to study different alternatives, such as alternative window configurations, partition layouts, or paving patterns. Each alternative can be "turned off" while others are developed and viewed. In Figure 5-8, various siding and roof patterns are drawn on individual layers, which can be turned on and off in many combinations to evaluate different configurations. Most often, we use tracing paper for evolving

designs, one step, one layer at a time. Early in the design process, real paper and handwork are often the best way to do this, but, after a working vocabulary of forms are defined, you can use the computer to continue the sequential process. As you proceed with your design, develop alternatives on new layers, turning old alternative layers on and off for reference or changing their colors so that they are unobtrusive but visible. When a layer starts to become crowded or messy, pick the elements you want to keep and move them onto a new layer.

Layers can also be used effectively when you are "marking up" or "redlining" a drawing to suggest

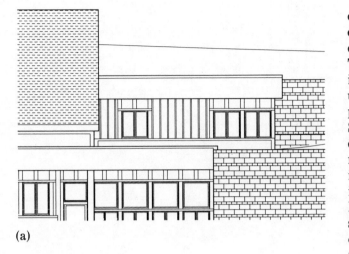

(a)

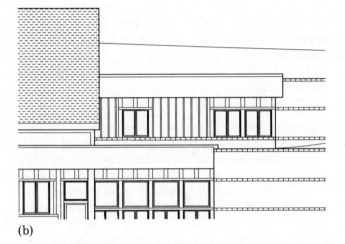

(b)

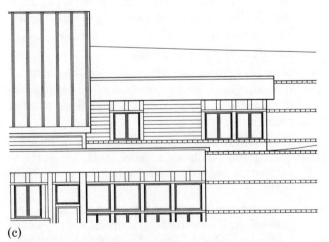

(c)

FIGURE 5-8 Studies of alternative wall and roof materials: each alternative was drawn on a separate layer, so that they could be interchanged in various combinations.

changes. Although you may sometimes prefer to make editing notes on a plot, by using an *editing layer* you can, essentially, make notes directly on the original. This enables you to see them as you make revisions, instead of having to refer to another drawing or underlay. You can use circles and arrows to point out problems, write notes, and sketch proposed changes. Some of your redline sketches may be transferred directly to the original layers, saving redrawing. You might want to develop a set of symbols that you can insert for "check this" or "replace this." As each change is made, the note can be transferred to another layer. Finally, the editing notes can be saved, perhaps as a separate drawing: each round of editing can be recorded on a separate layer and kept for future reference.

Into the Interstices

Layers—and other means of grouping drawing elements—provide a means of dissecting and reassembling drawings. By setting up layers according to the requirements of your design, you are able to *see* a project in ways that will increase your understanding of it. Think about the design issues that are important: if your layering system reflects this awareness, you will be able to effectively monitor them from schematic design through working drawings. Enclosure, for example, can be monitored by placing each type of wall—solid, transparent, half height, semiopen, and so on—on different layers and displaying them in ways that emphasize their space-making impact. The process of setting up a layer organization for a project (or the process of adapting a standard set) can help to clarify your thinking about a design problem by helping to identify the various families of forms that you will use in your design.

The philosopher Chuangtzu used the words of a butcher to explain the process of dissecting a problem:

A good cook changes his chopper once a year—because he cuts. An ordinary cook, once a month, because he hacks. But I have had this chopper nineteen years, and although I have cut up many thousand bullocks, its edge is as if fresh from the whetstone. For at the joints there are always interstices, and the edge of a chopper being without thickness, it remains only to insert that which is without thickness into such an interstice. By this means the interstice will be enlarged, and the blade will find plenty of room.[1]

[1]Christopher Alexander and Serge Chermayeff, *Community and Privacy*, Doubleday and Company, pp. 159–160.

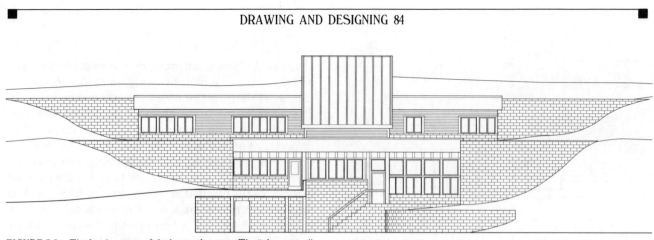

FIGURE 5-9   The final version of the house elevation. The "alternative" layers were stored, just in case . . .

Chermayeff and Alexander used the Taoist butcher's words in *Community and Privacy* to illustrate the need to carefully split design problems "at the interstices." This applies to computer-aided design nicely: layers and groups can be helpful in identifying a problem, then separating it into its constituent parts.

SYMBOLS AND BLOCKS: A WORKING SET OF FORMS

Object-based drawing, as we have called CAD, rests on the ability to place predrawn forms into a drawing. Various programs use different terms for graphic objects, including symbols, patterns, cells, templates, and blocks. The term **symbol** is often used to refer to objects, resulting in confusion between actual drawing symbols and other kinds of drawn objects. We will use the term *symbol* to refer to a specific kind of object: any drawing that is used as a graphic notation or a simplified graphic representation of an individual architectural form, such as a door, structural element, or plumbing fixture. We will use AutoCAD's term **block** as a general term for defined objects, because it serves as a good metaphor, and because this version is a particularly effective drawing tool. We will also continue to use the word *form* to refer to any group of drawing elements, whether they are blocks or are individual elements.

There are differences in the ways you use blocks in different programs. Some are intended primarily to serve as predefined symbol libraries, while others give you the option of easily creating blocks as you work. The most important capability is *replacement*, as we

will explain. Some CAD software does not include block replacement capabilities; since this function is crucial to effective CAD usage, we will assume it to be available.

BUILDING BLOCKS

Like layers, the concept of blocks is intuitively obvious, as simple as a child's building blocks. Yet there are many nuances in using blocks, which are important to learn.

A block is essentially any group of elements that can be treated as a single object. For example, blocks

- May be named and called for by their names.
- May be stored, recalled and used repeatedly, without leaving the drawing you are working on.
- May be treated as a single entity and moved, copied or erased accordingly.
- May be broken up into individual elements, if desired. This is usually necessary in order to make changes to a single insertion of a block without changing others.
- May carry nongraphic information (*attributes*) with them, such as a label, text, or numeric attributes regarding size, quantity, location, or cost.
- And, especially important, blocks may be "replaced" or "redefined." In other words, every occurrence of a block may be updated by changing the original.

A block may be a single line or an entire drawing. It may be drawn on one layer or a hundred. It may include other, smaller blocks, or it may be *nested* in a larger one. A drawing of a room may be inserted as a block into a drawing of a house, which may then be inserted into a drawing of a neighborhood, and so on. Making a block as you work is easy: simply select a group of elements in your drawing and give them a name. The real trick is learning *when* to make blocks and which parts of your drawing to "block."

TO BLOCK OR NOT TO BLOCK?

When you want to duplicate part of a drawing, it's often tempting to simply copy it instead of making a block out of it. Since you don't have to name or store the original, this is sometimes faster. When you do so, you are often missing a chance to give your drawing a structure that will save effort later.

When you begin a drawing, consider which parts of your drawing may be repeated. Think of it this way: you know that a building will have windows, but you don't know what size and you're not sure what kind. Fortunately, you don't need to decide right away. Just by knowing that you will be repeating a window, you can make a block, perhaps a simple rectangle, and come back later to change the size or add appropriate detail. When you change (*redefine*) the original, all the others will be replaced by the new window.

What if you want to use several different size windows? That complicates matters slightly. If you know beforehand that you are likely to want three sizes, then different blocks are called for. They may look similar at first, since you can always redefine them, but you should consider very carefully where you place each type. Although you can always go back and switch, it's nice to find, later, that all the corner windows are, in fact, on corners, or that all the bathroom windows are in bathrooms. These kinds of decisions are a part of any design process.

If an object is to be repeated, will you wish to change the individual elements of the repeated form? If so, you may wish to simply copy it in its elemental, "unblocked," form. For example, you might want to change the mullions on a particular window after you insert it. When an object is unblocked, or *exploded,* either as it is inserted or at a later time, it can be edited as a collection of individual parts, as it was before the original parts were defined as a block. However, you can no longer treat it as a single object, and it will no longer be revised or replaced if you change the original.

If an object or group of objects is not going to be repeated, you may still want to make it into a block if you anticipate moving it as a group, or you would like to be able to remove it completely and recall it later. An arrangement of furniture, for example, might be moved from room to room as a block in order to check dimensions. Since you can move it as a single object, it's easy to grab it and fit it in a room, or when you finish, erase it with a single pick.

DRAWING BLOCKS

Creating a block is often as simple as drawing or selecting a group of elements, though most CAD programs require a name and reference point for each block. However, when you later use the block—scaling, rotating or altering it—you will face the implications of some of the decisions you made when you first created the block. When you initially decide that an element or form should be made into a block, you can try to anticipate some issues that will come up when you next want to use the block, such as location, orientation, and scale.

Location

A block requires a reference point, called an **insertion point** (or *origin* or *handle*), with which you can place it accurately into a drawing. It should be easy to remember and easy to use. Many forms have a logical reference point, such as the intersection of two center-lines or the point of intersection with another form. If not, try to use one consistent reference for an insertion point, such as the lower left corner. (Figure 5-10)

If you are keeping a list or notebook of blocks, be sure to note the location of insertion points. Note them on your tablet menus, too. Any time you need to know where an insertion point is in your drawing, you may want to actually mark it with a point or *x* on a layer that you won't be plotting.

When you insert one drawing (as a block) into another, you can also assign a coordinate as an insertion point. A grid of layout lines, for example, may be defined as a block that is keyed to a corner of your drawing. The coordinate 0,0 is often used for this purpose.

Frequently used blocks, such as drafting symbols, can clutter up a drawing and add to screen redraw time. However, if you turn off/freeze the layer on which your symbols are drawn, you may lose track of them. If you draw a simple outline, or footprint, of your symbols on a different layer, you can turn off the layer that contains the symbols themselves, leaving the footprint layer displayed so that you know exactly where they are.

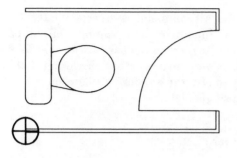

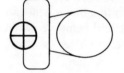

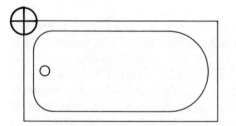

FIGURE 5-10   Typical insertion points for plumbing symbols.

Orientation

If a block is to be oriented consistently in one direction, draw it in the orientation in which it is to be used. If, however, it is to be used in several orientations, then you have two choices.

When you insert a block into a drawing, you have an opportunity to rotate it. This is simple enough, except that you must take care to rotate it correctly around its insertion point, aligning the form properly. If you must do this frequently, it can become tiresome or even mistake prone.

The alternative, if you will be using several orientations of the same block, is to make several versions of the same block, each rotated in a different direction. A 3-foot door can be used eight different ways (Figure 5-11). After drawing the door once, rotating it 90°, 180°, and 270°, then mirroring each, all eight can be named, then inserted in the right position. Remember to relocate the insertion points in a consistent manner, if necessary.

Another way to achieve the same results is to write a script of commands, a *macro* (see Chapter 3), to rotate a block appropriately, and place the macro on your menu or keyboard. This way, a single action (say, "rotate the block 90°") or several actions can be applied to different blocks.

Scale

You also may change the relative size of a block when you insert it, shrinking it, expanding it, or changing it in one direction only. Just as you may anticipate different orientations, you can create differently scaled versions of the same block in order to avoid scaling it each time you use it.

One especially useful trick for scaling blocks is the "1 × 1" block. A window-elevation symbol serves as a good example. Draw a single window so that its perimeter forms a 1 × 1 square, in whatever units you are using, let's say inches. When you want to make a 36″ × 44″ window, insert the 1 × 1 block with a scale factor of 36 for the x axis and 44 for the y axis (Figure 5-12). Some software lets you "drag" the size of the window, expanding and contracting it visually by moving the corners. Prepackaged drawing libraries are often set up to be used like this, so you may be using 1 × 1 blocks without even knowing it.

In another version of the 1 × 1 block, you may want to insert an object of a fixed width, such as a door symbol, at various lengths (Figure 5-13). Draw the original with a width of, say, $1\frac{5}{8}''$ on the y axis, and 1″ on the x axis. (In the illustration, we have used two doors, as a sliding unit.) When you insert it, give it an x scale

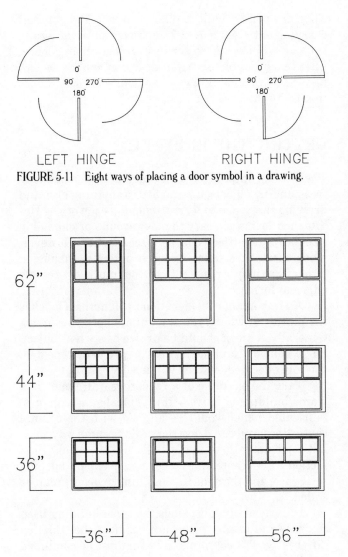

LEFT HINGE   RIGHT HINGE

FIGURE 5-11 Eight ways of placing a door symbol in a drawing.

62"

44"

36"

36"   48"   56"

WINDOWS FROM 1" x 1" BLOCK

FIGURE 5-12 The original window was drawn as a 1 × 1 square, with the same proportions as the 36″ × 36″ window. Each insertion is stretched accordingly; note the changing proportions of casings and mullions compared to the constant mullion dimensions produced by the symbol library in Figure 4-7.

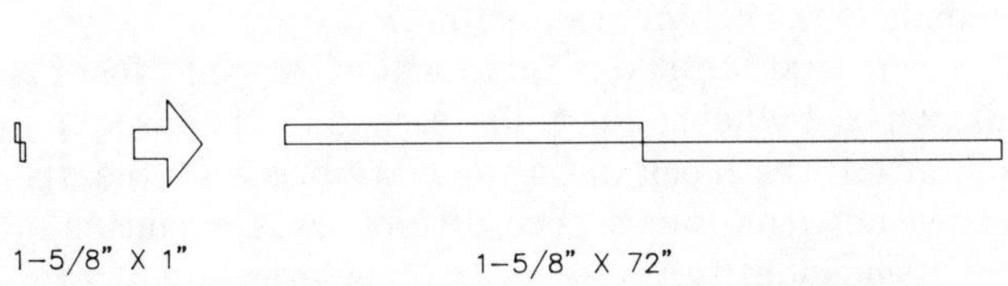

1-5/8″ X 1″   1-5/8″ X 72″

FIGURE 5-13 This symbol, representing two $1\frac{5}{8}$″ sliding doors, is drawn to be stretched in one direction only, according to the total width of the doors.

factor of, say, 36, and a y factor of 1. The door will be $1\frac{5}{8}″ \times 36″$.

The only disadvantage to using 1 × 1 blocks is that all parts of a form are scaled equally, so that a casing on a big window will be larger than a casing on a small one. When this is unacceptable, you may add detail to a block after you have scaled it, or you may draw two blocks, as we will explain.

PLANNING BLOCKS

Your design should rule your drawing structure, never the reverse. The blocks that you use to draw should be based on patterns that are inherent in the design of your project. As part of the framework you set up before you begin, sketch a plan of action that shows which building elements you expect to repeat. As you work, revise your sketch when you see the need for new repeating forms. Remember, you may have elements that repeat at different scales, some large, some small. You may find that large blocks contain other smaller (nested) blocks.

The kind of sketches you might use to plan blocks should be a part of, and not separate from, your normal design and drawing process. These sketches will help you with dimensions, orientation, and other important design and layout decisions. You can also use your preliminary sketches to pare down a block to its essentials. After you have placed it into your drawing, you can then go back and develop details on the original and update (replace) the copies.

Special Situations

Sometimes it will not immediately be clear *what* you should define as a block, even though you are using repeated forms. A plan drawing of a staircase, for example, seems like an obvious "object" that you would want to insert in one piece (Figure 5-14). Perhaps all the stairs in your drawing will be 14 risers high, but different widths, depending on the context. In this situation, you want to be able to change the width of the stair as you insert it into the drawing. However, when you change the width of the risers, you may not want to change the size of the railing, as well, so you can't simply scale the whole block.

There are several ways to cope with this dilemma. You can treat the stair as two blocks (or three if you have rail on each side), scaling the width of the stair as you insert it, then adding the rail. Alternatively, you can unblock the stair as you place it, then scale the risers without changing the rail.

Both of these solutions are two-step processes.

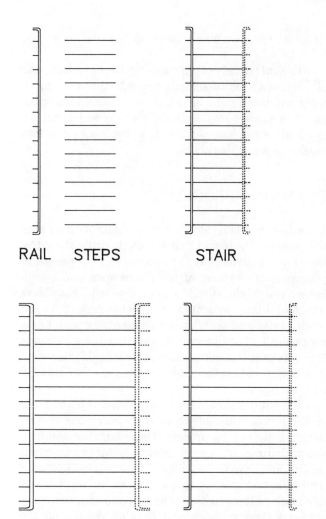

RAIL   STEPS   STAIR

STAIR x 2   RAIL x 1/STEPS x 2

FIGURE 5-14   The stair plan, top, is drawn as two separate blocks.
To double the width, the "stair" can be stretched, but the rail stretches,
too. Stretching only the steps leaves the rail intact.

They are not difficult to do, but, if you find yourself carrying out a sequence of steps over and over again, you can write a macro script to record them. Thereafter, each double or triple insertion can be accomplished by picking a few points, while the script does the rest of the work.

GETTING THE RIGHT FIT

There is an important difference between drawing freestanding objects, unattached to anything else, and drawing interrelated forms, touching each other. Unattached forms are easy to move around or change in size—all that is affected is the space between. However, when forms are touching each other, a change in dimension may require that you move or rescale adjacent forms.

An important consideration in planning a block is the matter of where you start and where you finish. Generally, a block should be drawn as a whole object, but, when you combine forms that are to be repeated, you must decide how they will meet.

Take the example of a repeating wall panel on a frame building (Figure 5-15). Typically, a large prefabricated panel would be aligned with the column centerlines; you can draw the wall the same way, even if it is not actually built of panels, like the brick/lintel section. The centerlines are a convenient spacing reference, and the ends (the building's corners) can be added.

If, instead of wall panels the same building used columns and beams, you might think of the situation differently. The column and beam must be combined into a form that can easily be repeated, but you may be reluctant to split a distinct form, such as a column, at the column line into two half forms.

There are two ways to combine the two forms; both are reasonable. First, you could draw a column and beam side by side, then add them together to build up the facade. Alternatively, you can split the column. Each block is identical, a self-defined unit that corresponds to the column centerlines.

The first method is **form oriented**: every form is drawn as a whole object. The second method is **space oriented**: the block definitions are based on the distance between forms. The difference is a matter of what you identify as your primary reference: a form or a space. Both can be thought of as "building blocks."

In the case of the split column and beam, the structural bay may be considered the primary reference. Another example—if you were drawing rooms (in plan) with which to assemble a building, you might draw only the interior wall surfaces, then define the walls by the space between the neighboring rooms

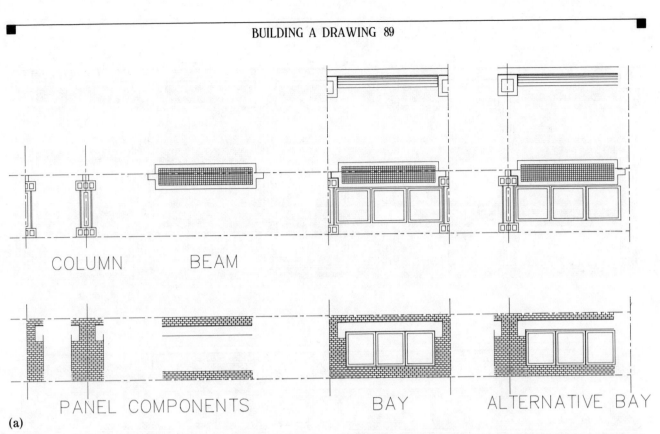

COLUMN   BEAM

PANEL COMPONENTS   BAY   ALTERNATIVE BAY

(a)

FIGURE 5-15   The building facade elements (a, left) can be combined into blocks representing structural column-bays. Note that the two building systems have different relationships to the column centerlines and floor levels. The column-and-beam block is assembled into a facade (b); by substituting the brick-and-lintel block the facade is transformed (c). In d, the blocks are rearranged into an alternate configuration.

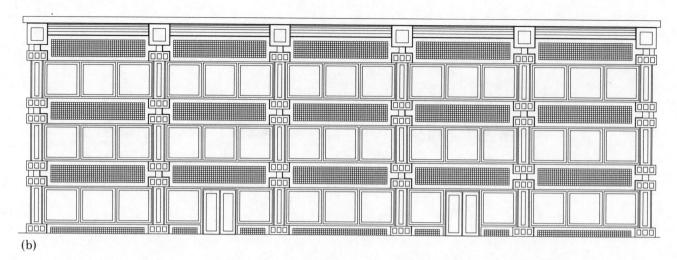

(b)

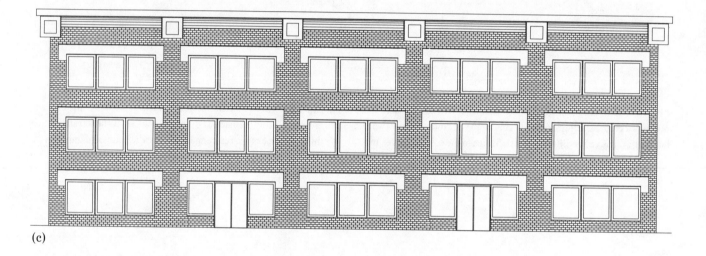

(c)

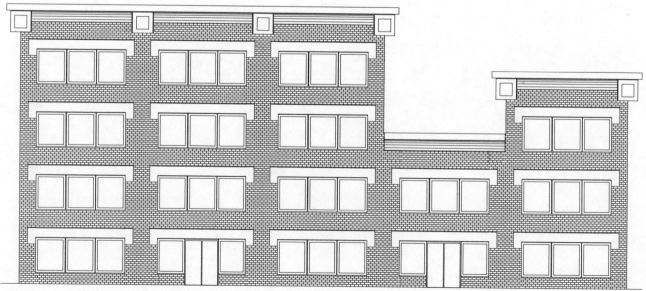

(d)

(Figure 5-16). Otherwise, if you drew full walls around each room they would overlap when you placed them next to each other. Again, the wall centerlines would be the reference. You might only work in this manner on a schematic plan, since you may want to treat walls as integral forms when you are drafting.

REPLACING BLOCKS

The ability to modify groups of previously inserted blocks is one of the most useful CAD tools. Whenever you wish to change all the insertions of a block within a drawing, you can easily replace them with a new

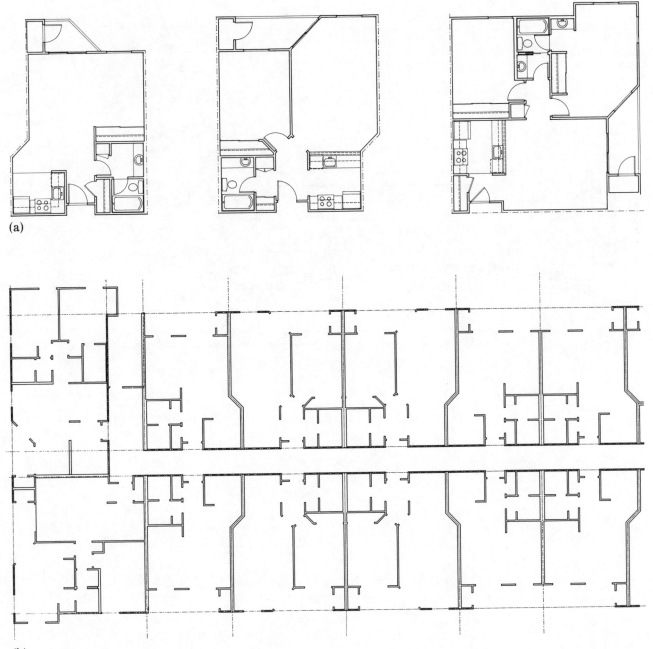

(a)

(b)

Figure 5-16   Three of five units (a) used in an apartment building shown with walls only (b) and with fixtures, doors, and counters (c). Arch. 1 Architects.

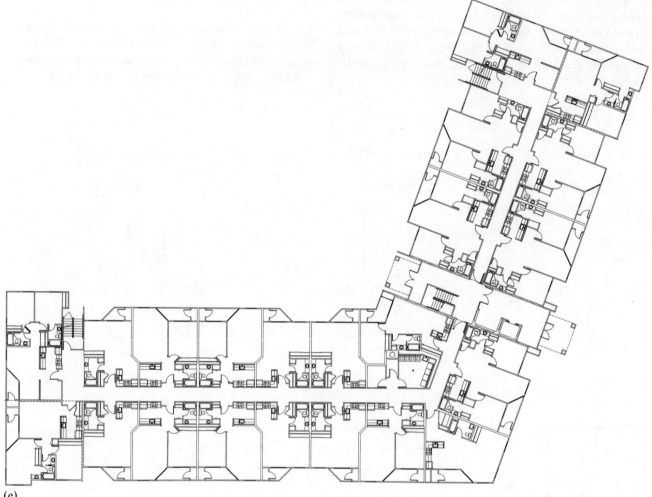

(c)

version. Any block, assuming it has not been unblocked, is a candidate: symbols, nested blocks, rooms, buildings. You can use this capability to either articulate a block or to substitute an entirely new one.

In Chapter 1, we described computer-aided drawing as a cyclical process: this is largely due to the ability to replace blocks. Most architects begin a project on a general level, then become more specific as the project progresses. Details are designed and refined as their context takes shape. As an elevation develops, a rectangular outline can be transformed into a window with mullions, casings, and shutters. By articulating blocks as you work, you can develop detail as you need it, without having to redraw the rest of your drawing.

Articulation

Think of block articulation as a link between a sketchpad and a finished drawing. A block, after all, is a drawing inserted into another drawing, so you can always go back and change the original. Work on a previously inserted block by hand, adding detail to it, perhaps working on tracing paper using a plot as a base. When you like it, draw it on the computer and replace its predecessor. You can replace an outline in a schematic plan with a fully developed room (Figure 5-16, b and c), or you can develop a repetitive detail in an almost complete working drawing.

You can, of course, modify a block directly on the computer, without "leaving" the larger drawing. First, explode a copy of the block, then modify it, in place if you like, then redefine it to replace the original. All the copies will be changed, as well.

Substitution

You can also replace blocks with wholly new blocks. They can be switched by changing the name of a new drawing to the name of a previously inserted block, then, substituting it into the drawing file. For example, a certain window symbol could be changed to another, or even to a door symbol. One 5′ × 7′ bathroom type could be substituted for another. You can dramatically transform a drawing by substituting a very different block, such as a brick elevation in place of a curtain wall. (The brick panels in Figure 5-15c were substituted for the column and beam in 5-15b.)

Articulation and substitution can be used to carry out "what if?" design studies. Since you can save your original drawing, you can safely try any new idea that comes to mind by replacing drawing parts. If you have several different blocks for which you have developed alternative versions, you can experiment with different combinations. "Interchangeable parts" can be used to conduct the kind of studies we carried out by switching layers in Figure 5-8. Like these alternatives, you can experiment with different materials, or you can change dimenions by replacing a block with a scaled version (Figure 5-17). You can also move all insertions of a block by replacing it with an identical block with a new insertion point. This could be used, say, to raise all the windows in a facade by 6″. Similarly, replacement is sometimes a convenient way to change the layer on which a block is drawn.

COMBINING BLOCKS

We have mentioned, in passing, nested blocks and families of blocks. These terms refer to ways of adding blocks together to produced complex, combined forms, which are single blocks in themselves. By combining blocks, you can manipulate large numbers of forms at once, but you still have the ability to revise one of the constituent blocks at any time.

Nests and Ghosts

"Nesting" brings to mind an image of forms within forms, or many forms within a single large form. A prefabricated window-wall unit, with several windows, is a good example (Figure 5-18). But a nested block might also consist of a cluster of furniture symbols with no visible connection, or a group of freestanding buildings that you wish to repeat in a certain configuration. If you unblock nested blocks like these, you get a cluster of smaller blocks, each intact. If you redefine a constituent block in a nested block, it will be replaced in each occurrence of the larger block.

Sometimes you will wish to add one detail to a number of different blocks. Ordinarily, you would have to redefine each block, adding the new element. Instead, you can use a nested *ghost block* to avoid redefining each block. A ghost block is a simple or invisible block that is carried around within a larger block. When you are ready, you can define it as a fully developed form, and it appears in each original block. You might, say, place a block that is a simple circle or a single point within several different blocks that make up a wall elevation. When you decide what kind of light fixture you want to mount on the wall, replace the point with a fully drawn light. If you have nested a ghost block into different kinds of larger blocks, you won't have to articulate and replace each of the larger blocks, only the single ghost block.

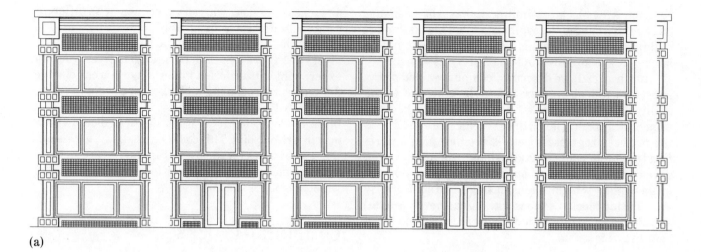

(a)

(b)

FIGURE 5-17   When the original block (Figure 5-15) is redefined as a
narrower bay, there are gaps between the new, smaller bays (a). The
spaces can be closed by moving the bays together (b).

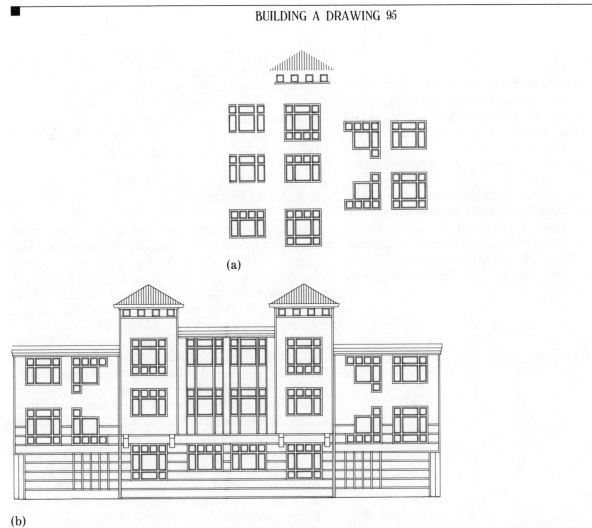

(a)

(b)

(c)

FIGURE 5-18   Nested blocks: a single square window is stretched into
rectangular windows and large squares, then combined (nested) into
several window assembly blocks (a). These, in turn, are nested into
partial-building blocks (b), which are combined to form the full building,
(c). David Baker and Associates.

Trees

Another kind of combination is *tree structured*. When two objects have a common form but different details, you can start with a common "parent" and make two new blocks. The "children" *contain* the parent, but are separate blocks themselves. That way, when you want to modify both in the same way, you simply change the parent.

For example, you might decide that all the windows on a building facade will have the same casing, but you will use both double-hung and casement units (Figure 5-19). Start with a block for the casing, then make a copy. Draw a double-hung detail into one and a casement into the other and define them as new blocks.

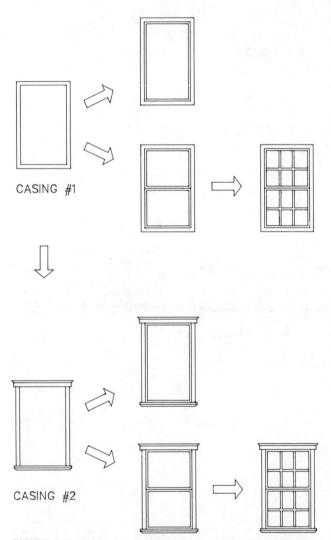

CASING #1

CASING #2

FIGURE 5-19   Tree-structured blocks: casing number 1 is developed into casement and double-hung window units; mullions are then added to the double-hung. By changing the casing to number 2, the "offspring" windows are automatically changed.

If you want to go back and change the casing for all your windows, simply modify the original parent. If you want to add mullions to *some* of the double-hungs, make a new block based on the first double-hung, add mullions, and make it into a new block. Since this "third generation" contains the plain double-hung, you can modify both by changing the original.

NAMING BLOCKS

A library is difficult to use without a catalog, and your library of blocks is no exception. Whenever possible, keep a visible record of the blocks you are using by plotting or printing them and keeping them in a notebook, on the wall, or, best of all, keyed into your tablet menus. Different blocks can look very similar. When you want to retrieve a block or edit your library, you don't want to have to scrutinize every block. Most programs allow you to name your blocks, so that you can save and recall them by a unique tag. Others require that you assign numbers to blocks, often grouped into libraries according to type (sometimes called *templates*). In this situation, a well-indexed notebook is particularly important.

Blocks should be given names that are easy to remember and as clear as possible. In addition to *what* you are referring to, you may want to know *how big* it is or *in what direction* it is oriented. If your blocks are nested or combined in series, you may want to identify them according to their place in the hierarchy. You might get three pieces of information into a block name, like "Door36LH," but beware, too much can be confusing. This is especially important if more than one person is working with your drawing library.

BLOCKS AND LAYERS

There are several very different strategies for coordinating blocks and layers. Although they may at times seem complex, they can give you tremendous control over your drawing. Our explanation here is oriented toward AutoCAD; if you are working with a different program, you will nevertheless find some useful strategies that can be applied to other systems.

A block can be made up of elements that are located on a single drawing layer or on many different layers. This fact has important implications regarding the ways you can display and plot your drawings: a multilayered block can be viewed with selected layers turned off, in various combinations. For example, a standard bathroom (Figure 5-20) might include layers for walls, plumbing, surfaces, dimensions, symbols, and notes, but, when you plot a presentation drawing, you may want to hide the dimensions, symbols, and notes.

You can also create a single-layer block using different colors, in order to plot it with different linetypes. A door symbol, for example, might be drawn on a single layer with different colors for the door and the swing arc, so that the latter might be plotted with a dashed linetype. This is not as hazardous as drawing with several colors on a layer might otherwise be, since you can handle the block as a single object; nevertheless, you will still have to display the entire block or no block.

Switching Layers

If you like, blocks can be drawn so that they may be placed on any layer, usually the current layer, at the time of insertion. A *reassignable* layer (layer 0 in AutoCAD), from which a block may be inserted to a new layer, is designated by some programs for this purpose. For example, you might draw plan symbols on this layer, and, when you place them in your drawing, you can put them on a layer for notes or symbols for the particular plan (first floor, second floor) you are working on. The bathroom fixture symbols in Figure 5-20 were originally drawn on a reassignable layer, then inserted on the plumbing layer. Your "library" drawings and symbols may all be kept on this reassignable layer, so that they will be available for new drawings with new layer names or numbers. When these blocks are inserted onto a new layer, they will also take on the color and linetype of the new layer.

Other blocks may be drawn and inserted on a specific (not reassignable) layer. By drawing a block on a specific layer as you work, you will assure that it is displayed and plotted with that layer. A block representing a paving pattern, for example, might only be for use on a site plan and can be drawn on the appropriate site plan layer.

Insertion Layers

When a drawing includes a number of levels, such as a multistory building plan, block insertions become a little bit more complicated. If you have blocks that are drawn on non-reassignable layers, like our bathroom block, you will want to be sure that you can display or hide each inserted bathroom along with the floor level on which it resides. Fortunately, you can control blocks according to the layer *on which they are inserted.*

A block that is drawn on layers "a" and "b" can be inserted on layer "c." For example, the bathroom block can be placed on the layer "2Floor-Walls." It can then be turned on and off, in its entirety, along with this layer, while its component layers (such as walls or plumbing) can still be turned on and off individually. This double-definition gives you an extraordinary amount of control over your drawing.

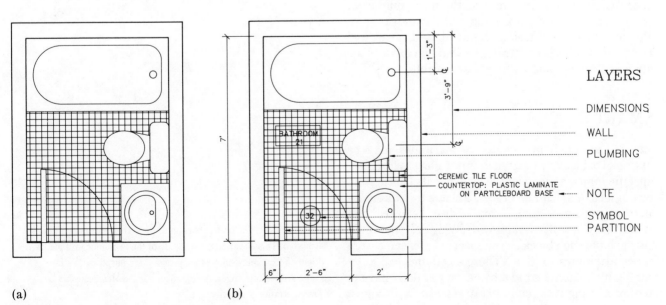

(a)   (b)

FIGURE 5-20   A bathroom block with layers noted.

Master Layers

The layers on which the block was originally drawn are called *master layers*. Typically, a set of master layers for a multilevel plan might correspond to the layers for a simple, single-level plan.

A single-layer block, such as a door symbol, can be inserted onto an appropriate layer, such as "2Fl-Wall": the choice of an insertion layer is usually obvious. When inserting a block that is drawn on several layers, on the other hand, you must make a more difficult choice as to the appropriate insertion layer. It may be a layer with which the block is closely associated ("2Fl-Wall," in the case of the bathroom) or a specific insertion layer that you have set aside entirely for blocks (Figure 5-21).

Sometimes, when you are drawing a very repetitious multilevel drawing (such as several parallel elevations), you might choose to do extensive work on a set of master layers, then place multilayered blocks on a single insertion layer for each wall surface (Figure 5-22, *a–b*). In the example, seven parallel walls (three are shown) are each assigned a single layer, and the entire building is assembled from blocks that were drawn on master layers like "Brick," "Concrete" and "Glass" (Figure 5-24 and Table 5-2). When individual details are required, layers like "Wall-2-Glass" are added.

Tactics for coordinating blocks and layers should be planned to save you from redrawing repetitious elements, while providing maximum flexibility for display and plotting. The more complex your requirements are, the more detailed your layering should be, and block structure must respond accordingly. Try to "keep it simple" by minimizing the total number of layers, using master layers for multilevel drawings. Be sure, however, in planning symbol libraries and master/insertion layer strategies that you follow your standard conventions as closely as possible.

SMART BLOCKS

As we explained in Chapter 3, attributes may be assigned to blocks, so that each time a block is inserted, specific information can be attached to it. This textual or numeric data can be processed later by a database management program. If you wish to keep track of items that you will insert into a drawing or if you would like to label each block as you insert it, you can assign *name* attributes to them. These attributes can automatically be attached to a block, so you don't have to bother naming it as you insert it; you can also assign a

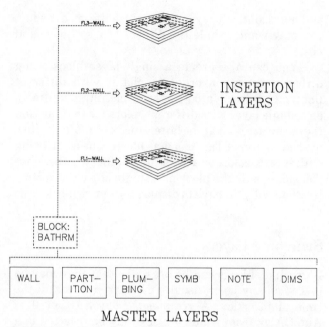

MASTER LAYERS

FIGURE 5-21   The bathroom block is drawn on the master layers, then inserted onto a convenient layer, such as the wall layer, for each floor of a multilevel building.

FIGURE 5-22   Three (out of seven) parallel walls of a transit station. The columns and arch forms are identical, but their arrangement varies in each wall, making the design an ideal candidate for block-assembly. Wallace, Floyd Associates, Architects/Planners, for the Massachusetts Bay Transportation Authority.

FIGURE 5-23   The central portion of the transit station with bricks displayed. This elevation is composite of the two outer wall planes (Figure 5-22 *a* and *b*) plotted for presentation purposes. Wallace, Floyd Associates, Architects/Planners, for the Massachusetts Bay Transportation Authority.

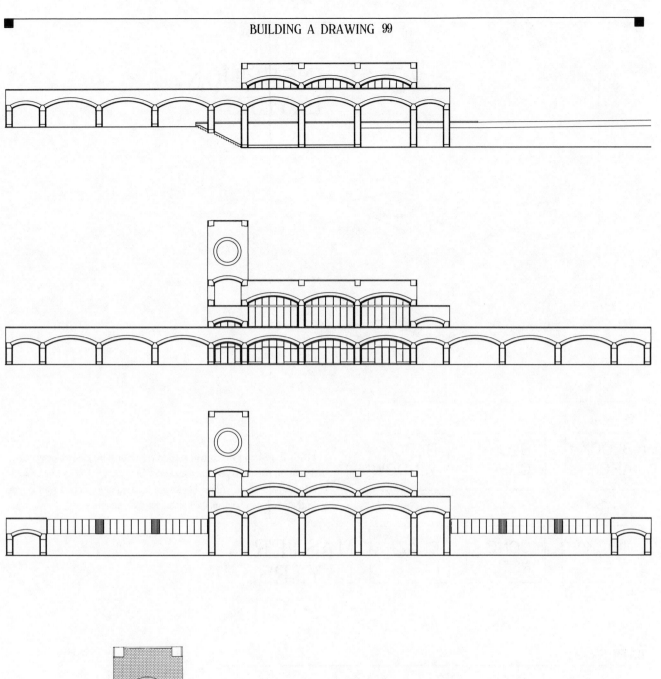

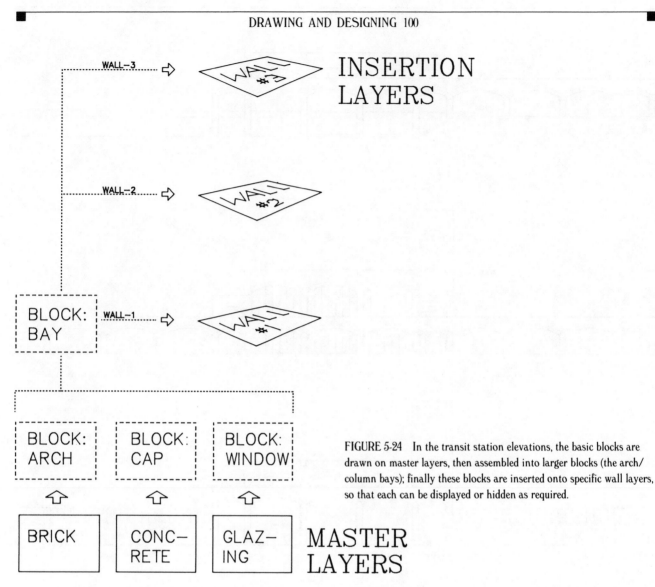

FIGURE 5-24 In the transit station elevations, the basic blocks are drawn on master layers, then assembled into larger blocks (the arch/ column bays); finally these blocks are inserted onto specific wall layers, so that each can be displayed or hidden as required.

MASTER LAYERS

TABLE 5-2

Layer name	State	Color	Linetype	
0	On	7 (white)	CONTINUOUS	LAYOUT
CENTERLINE	Frozen	21	CENTER	LAYERS
BRICK	On	6 (magenta)	CONTINUOUS	
CONCRETE	On	7 (white)	CONTINUOUS	
GLAZING	On	4 (cyan)	CONTINUOUS	MASTER
CANOPY	On	4 (cyan)	CONTINUOUS	LAYERS
HATCH	On	1 (red)	CONTINUOUS	
GRAPHICS-OUTLINE	On	3 (green)	CONTINUOUS	
GRAPHICS-DETAIL	Frozen	3 (green)	CONTINUOUS	
SOUTH-1	On	7 (white)	CONTINUOUS	
SOUTH-1-HIDDEN	On	7 (white)	CONTINUOUS	
SOUTH-2	Frozen	7 (white)	CONTINUOUS	INSERTION
SOUTH-3	Frozen	7 (white)	CONTINUOUS	LAYERS
NORTH-1	Frozen	7 (white)	CONTINUOUS	
NORTH-2	Frozen	7 (white)	CONTINUOUS	
NORTH-1-HIDDEN	Frozen	7 (white)	CONTINUOUS	

value or name to each individual insertion of a block. These *tags* can either be displayed or hidden, whichever you prefer.

By placing descriptive tag on, say, all the windows you are using, you can quickly tell what kind of window each window block represents. This is particularly useful when different blocks look alike, such as plan views of windows that are different heights. It can also be helpful to see the actual block names when you are working with different blocks that have similar or hard-to-remember names. You may also want to know, without manually counting, how many of each block you have used. Some programs will count for you; if not, a database program will do so.

Handles

A few CAD systems allow you to use these attributes as *handles* for manipulating blocks within a drawing. For example, you might use two types of partitions, "a" and "b," in the same drawing using the same graphic symbol, but identifying them with different attributes for "partition type." If you decided to erase partitions of type "a," you could pick them as a group and delete them. This is yet another way to group drawing elements, in this case blocks.

AUTOMATED DRAWING AND DESIGN

Any CAD program that combines a sequence of drawing tasks can be called **automated**: even a user-written macro for laying out a stair qualifies. However, automated architectural drawing tools can be extremely sophisticated. For example, there are readily available programs that can transform schematic outlines into dimensioned, three-dimensional models, *automatically*. These kinds of tools can save you tremendous amounts of time, but it is important to remember that they are only combining operations that you could do, one step at a time, by yourself. It's also important to realize that they have serious limitations: a program can generally carry out a task *one way*, when there are often other ways that are as valid or more valid. Thus, it is crucial to understand exactly what an automated drawing program does—and what it doesn't do.

FROM SKETCH TO FINISH

The most common (and perhaps the most useful) automated architectural drawing tools are those that turn lines into walls (double lines, in plan, or rectangular shapes in three dimensions) and those that clean up intersections where walls meet. These capabilities are so elementary that they are considered "standard equipment" for architectural computer-aided drawing.

There is a wide range of other automated drawing tools available—too many to explain in detail. Generally, they include:

- Door and window insertion tools. In plan, these can size a window or door symbol to your request, then "open up" a wall, place the symbol, and case the opened wall. These are also considered standard for architectural programs.

- Linear detail drawings, such as the insulated wall shown in Figure 3-1. These can also be used for section and elevation drawings; they often include hatching patterns.

- Layout and insertion of repetitive elements, such as the stair-construction routine cited in Chapter 3. Virtually any repetitious layout that requires custom-sizing or custom spacing of standard elements can be automated.

- Fully automatic dimensioning. Based on your criteria for locating dimensions arrows and numbers (such as inside or outside of walls), these utilities can dimension a drawing without requiring your help; typically they can pick out distances between wall intersections, windows and doors, and column centerlines.

- Schematic design programs. These enable you to sketch space outlines, based on area requirements and dimensional limitations (such as maximum spans), and assemble spaces in various combinations (Figure 5-25, *a* and *b*). When the adjacencies, sizes, and shapes of the spaces are correct, the software will transform a single-line diagram into a double-line floor plan, with wall intersections drawn correctly (Figure 5-25 *c* and *d*).

- Parametric drawing, which we will look at in more detail.

PARAMETERS: DRAWING BY NUMBERS

Parametric drawing automates the process of moving and scaling drawing elements. It can be used to conduct "what-if" design studies; it can transform working drawings when dimensions must be changed, and it can be used to customize standard details and symbols. Parametric drawing is not available with all

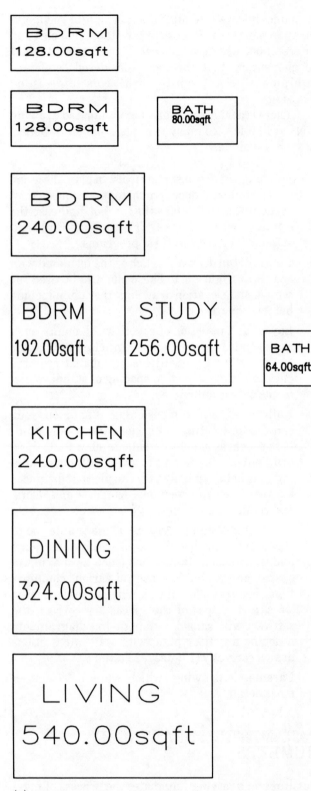

FIGURE 5-25   A house plan, developed from space planning to schematic design. First, spaces are blocked according to required dimensions *(a)*. (This example used AutoCAD AEC software, which calculates areas automatically.) Space shapes can be "pushed and pulled" as required. After the shapes are assembled into an acceptable diagrammatic plan *(b)*, the software automatically translates the diagram into a double-line wall plan *(c)* with different dimensions for exterior and interior walls, and wall intersections joined properly. The designer can then add windows, doors, and closets *(d)*.

(a)

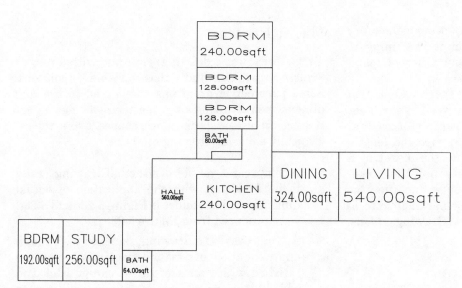

(b)

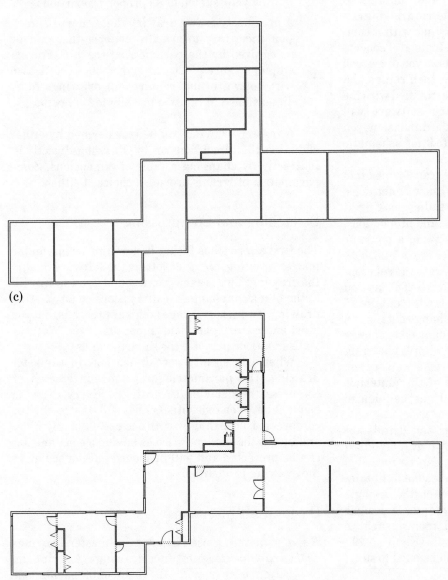

(c)

(d)

CAD programs (it is available as a supplementary "add-on" program for some), but it is gaining in popularity and appearing in many different manifestations.

Parameters are dimensional specifications that are applied to a drawing, but they work in a manner opposite to normal dimensions. Instead of *describing* the length of an object, they *prescribe* the length, instructing the computer to draw the object at a specific length. In other words, you supply the dimension, numerically, and the computer modifies the drawing accordingly. You can use parametric techniques on any type of architectural drawings: plans, elevations, sections, and details.

Sketching

Although "drawing by numbers" and "automated drawing" sound mechanistic, parametric drawing can be used to relax the process of drawing with a computer, without sacrificing precision. Instead of concentrating on dimensional requirements as you draw, you can use parameters to sketch freely, then return and dimension the drawing when you are satisfied with the basic configuration. The parametric software will automatically redraw your work to the dimensions you have specified. Thus, it is an ideal tool for schematic design and for sketching details.

A fully drawn design can also be transformed into one or more variations by substituting new dimensions. You can conduct "what-if" design studies, looking at various combinations of sizes, shapes, and proportions. You might "push and pull" room sizes of a house or examine different column spacings (Figure 5-26, *c-d*). You can compress a drawing to illustrate the relationships between isolated parts (Figure 5-26*b*), as you might do manually by drawing details with "cut lines."

Parameters can also be used to change details in a working drawing. For example, if you need to change wall widths in a plan, you can do so by simply changing the dimension for each wall. Likewise, a wall section can be modified if the dimensions of the materials (such as insulation, roofing, or trusses) must be changed (Figure 5-27).

Libraries of standard drawings and details are good candidates for parametric drawing. A standard detail, such as a window elevation, can be modified each time it is used (Figure 5-28): instead of maintaining a vast catalog of window elevations on disk, a single master will suffice. Standardized, adaptable designs can also be drawn for individual rooms (such as bathrooms or fire stairs), housing units (Figure 5-29), or whole buildings. Each can be dimensioned to suit a specific situation when it is used.

Master Drawings

To use parametric drawing, you start with a *master drawing* that, essentially, has variable dimensions. Some parametric programs enable you to use *any* dimensioned drawing as a master drawing; others require the use of special lines, shapes, and symbols. Typically a master drawing might be:

- A compressed version of an actual drawing, ready to be filled out with the application of actual dimensions. The studies in Figure 5-26*c* and 5-26*d* were produced from Figure 5-26*b*.

- A "first pass" at a drawing, sketched with rough approximations of sizes and spacing. After you are satisfied with your sketch, you can go back and add dimensions which the software will use to redraw your sketch to its proper proportions.

- A previously drawn drawing that you will dimension according to specific criteria that can be recognized by the parametric program. For example, Figures 5-26 through 5-30 were drawn with software that requires all drawings to be dimensioned in relation to a single *base* point.

A master drawing can be transformed by either changing the dimensions on the drawing directly or indirectly by changing a table of dimensions. Some parametric programs provide a choice of either.

Stretching and Compressing

The first approach is filling in new dimensions on the master drawing, and then letting the software modify the drawing. This is as easy as it sounds; you simply fill in the blanks or change the dimensions on an existing drawing. The disadvantage to this approach is that you must enter *every* pertinent dimension, even if all the walls in a floor plan are the same thickness.

When you specify new dimensions in a master drawing, the parametric program can stretch or compress the drawing accordingly. Every drawing element between two witness lines will be stretched or compressed accordingly, with one exception. Symbols and blocks that are specified as having a constant size can be protected and will be moved but not scaled as the drawing is modified.

Customized Insertions

A second method is used for adapting master drawings *as they are inserted* into other drawings. A script can be written (either with the help of a parametric

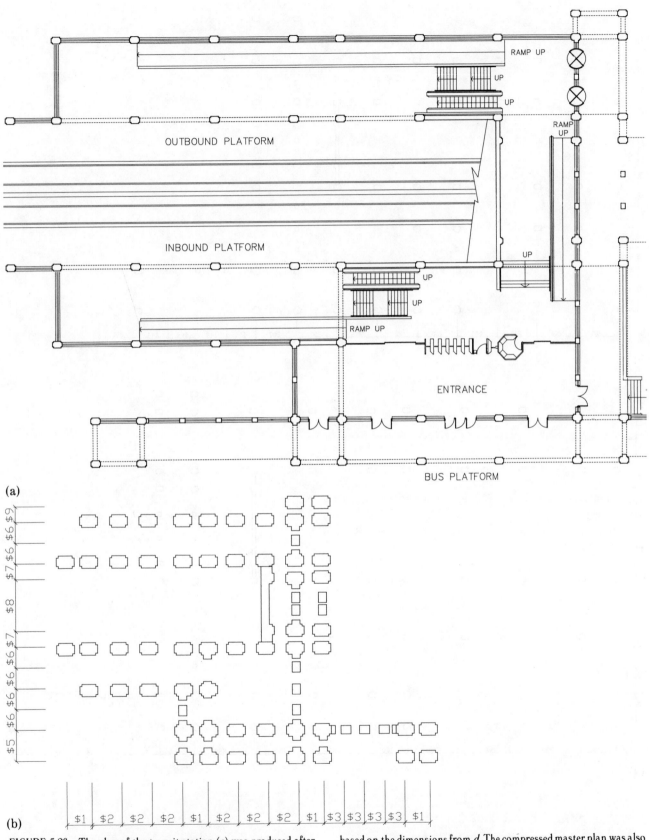

(a)

(b)

FIGURE 5-26   The plan of the transit station (a) was produced after
many trials of different column spacings. Figures c and d are column
plans that were automatically developed by assigning dimensions
(shown here in inches) to the master drawing (b). The actual plan a is
based on the dimensions from d. The compressed master plan was also
very useful in studying the relationships between adjacent columns.
Wallace, Floyd Associates, Architects/Planners, for the Massachusetts
Bay Transportation Authority.

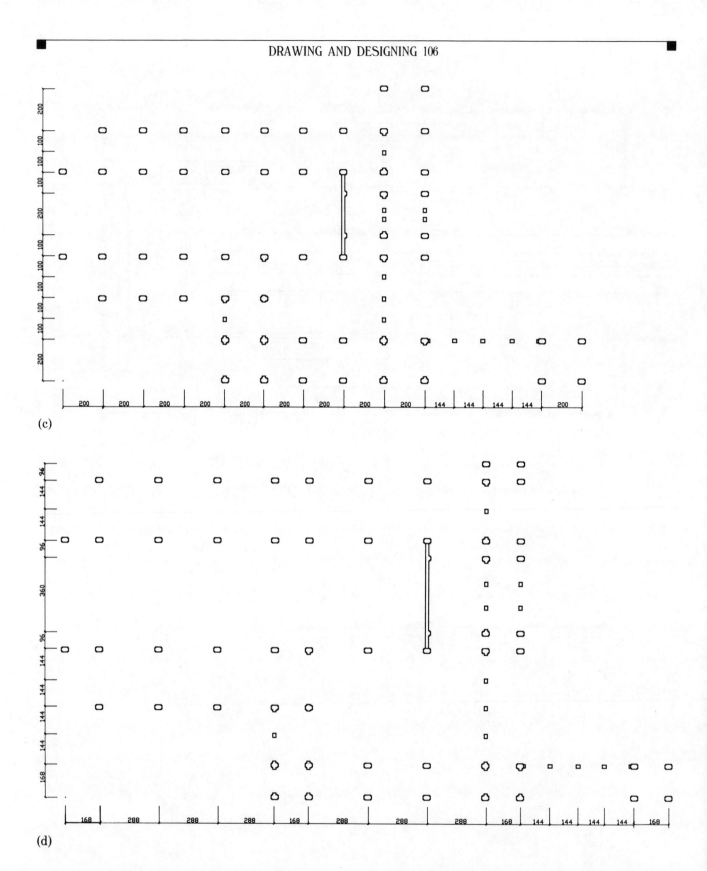

(c)

(d)

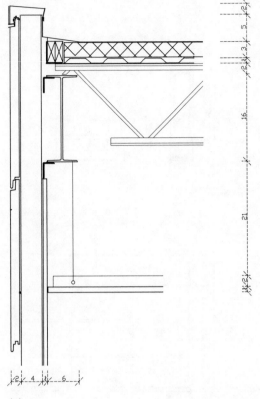

(a)

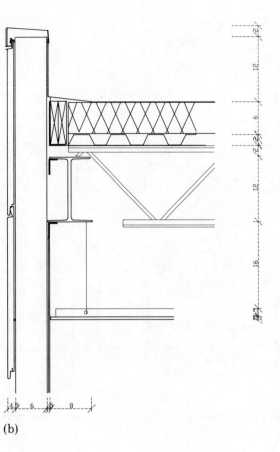

(b)

FIGURE 5-27   These wall sections were drawn parametrically by substituting new dimensions in the original drawing. Note that the bar joist was "protected"; its size was unaffected by altering the dimensions. Buday Wells, Architects.

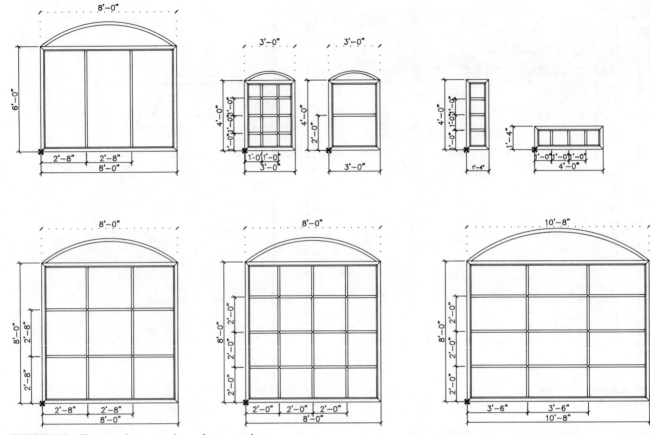

FIGURE 5-28   These windows were drawn from a single master
drawing, using a user-written question-and-answer sequence to specify
the number of mullions and the inclusion or omission of the arch.
The program (Synthesis) automatically dimensions each window.
Transformer CAD.

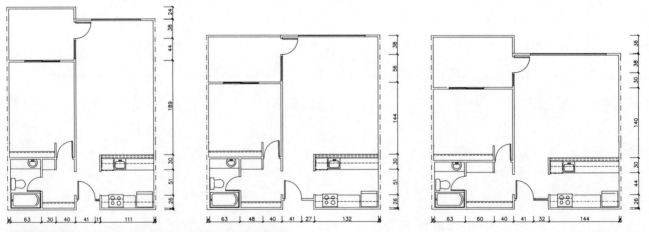

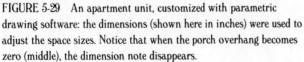

FIGURE 5-29   An apartment unit, customized with parametric
drawing software: the dimensions (shown here in inches) were used to
adjust the space sizes. Notice that when the porch overhang becomes
zero (middle), the dimension note disappears.

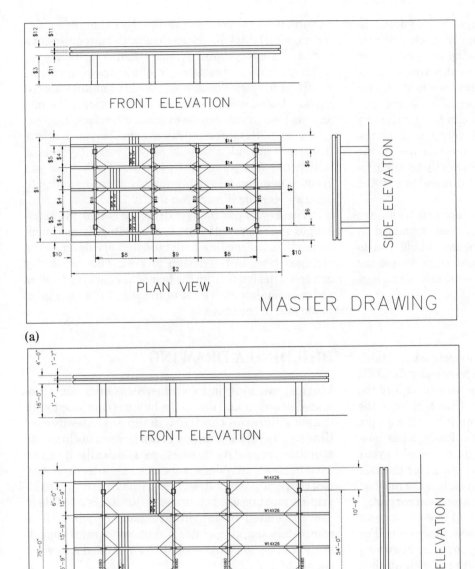

(a)

(b)

FIGURE 5-30   This framing drawing for a steel canopy structure was set
up with a master drawing and a script that included formulas for
calculating most of the dimensions. The parametric program (Synthesis)
assists in setting up the script and formulas. The user need only specify
total length, width and height; all other dimensions (which are represented
by a "$" in the master drawing), were calculated by the software and
the dimensioned drawing was drawn automatically. Beam sizes were
specified by the user and noted automatically; however, parametric
software can also be used to do engineering calculations, as well.
(See Chapter 7.) Haddco Industries, Inc.

program or with a user programming language, directly) that will prompt you to supply specific dimensions each time you insert a drawing or symbol. For example, a parametric program for drawing window symbols in elevation (as in Figure 5-28) might request the perimeter dimensions, number of mullions, and casing type. The master drawing can be modified by relatively simple formulas that are placed in the script: in the window example, the spacing of the mullions can be calculated automatically by the program, by dividing the perimeter dimensions by the number of panes of glass.

Many architectural programs use this technique routinely for insertion of symbols from standard libraries. The most desirable versions enable you to adapt the drawing libraries themselves, as well as the prompts, and help you to develop new master drawings and insertion scripts.

Parameter Files

Some parametric programs enable you to set up a table of variables and formulas called a *parameter file*. This table can be set up to prompt the user to supply the necessary dimensions. Parameter files eliminate the need for you to do any programming in setting up a master drawing for adaptation. Typically, a parameter file would list the variable name (as cited in your master drawing dimensioning), a prompt for the user to enter a value, and any formulas (such as the mullion formula) that are needed to place an element correctly.

A parameter file could be set up to customize an entire structure with only a few new dimensions. For example, a steel canopy structure could be drawn by asking the user for the length, width and height: then all the other dimensions are calculated according to the formulas in the table (Figure 5-30). Using a reference table in this manner, all the wall thicknesses for a building plan may be specified by answering a few prompts, or even a single prompt as to "building system: a, b, or c."

Parameter files are more laborious to set up than a simple master drawing with variable dimensions. However, once a table is set up for a specific building system, it can be used many times, and new values can be substituted to create new files. By changing values for, say, wall thicknesses, each new file can represent a new building system. By maintaining a library of different building systems, a single drawing can be modified to reflect dozens of possible combinations of materials and construction methods. Quantity counts and cost estimates can be extracted for each alternative, as well. Parametric drawing enables you to create libraries that link a wide variety of assembly details with wall, floor, and roof graphics. Each time you create a new construction assembly, it can be added to a parameter file library "on the fly."

The key to parametric drawing is that the sizes, shapes and construction types of building elements can be modified according to details that are designed or changed later in the design process. This capability can free a designer from the fear of having to redraw or redimension an entire set of drawings if a change is made late in the project.

BUILDING A DRAWING

Whether working in two dimensions or three, automated drawing and design techniques combined with drawing libraries can free a designer to spend more time on other design issues. It can be used to eliminate mundane, repetitive tasks, or, paradoxically, it can be used to create mundane, repetitive architecture. Any tool that can produce drawings without careful consideration must be used cautiously. Since it is possible to use automated design in situations in which it is completely inappropriate, it requires careful consideration to decide what should be automated and what should not.

Layering, blocking, and design automation are the tools that make computer-aided design flexible and efficient. If you work out strategies for using these together effectively, drawing may become the least laborious part of creating a design. Your techniques for using layers, libraries, and automation will have a significant effect on your design work, so consider carefully the implications of your tools. No matter how advanced the tools become, you will still, essentially, be assembling a building as you build a drawing.

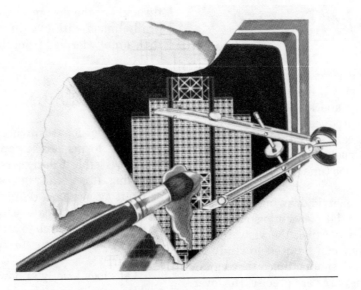

BEYOND THE
SECOND
DIMENSION

CHAPTER 6

Two-dimensional drawing is a kind of code for representing physical forms. Plans, sections and elevations are flattened versions of reality that compress large amounts of information into a clear, useful form. But like any code, you have to learn to use it.

Many nonarchitects are unable to readily understand architectural drawings, leading to difficulties in communicating with clients and the general public. Among architects, even the most experienced designers must look at two or more drawings to visualize three dimensions and must

mentally "decode" symbols for objects like walls and doors.

No "flat" drawing can convey the physical reality of a proposed building, so designers resort to other means of visualizing their work. The first is, simply, imagination: when you read a plan or section, you are translating the code into a mental picture of three-dimensional forms and spaces. To an experienced designer, the process seems effortless, but it is only as effective as the designer's imagination.

THE PURSUIT OF REALISM

Perspective drawing is a second means of looking at designs three dimensionally. Quick sketches often can be used to try out ideas; elaborately constructed perspective renderings can produce very accurate views. Unfortunately, sketches can be wildly inaccurate and misleading, while constructed perspectives are tremendously laborious and too time consuming to use as a serious design tool.

Isometric and axonometric drawings are useful techniques for projecting flat views into space. Since parallel lines are drawn parallel, the views do not appear realistic, but they can be used to study the relationships of forms and spaces. Since they can be measured accurately, they are very precise. However, it may require several views of a structure to fully portray it, and iso/axonometrics are also labor-intensive drawing techniques.

Physical models are often the most realistic way to represent designs. Occasionally architects will build full-scale mock-ups of parts of a building, but most models are built to scale. Rough "working models" are useful during the design process; highly detailed models can be used to portray finished designs. Yet physical models also require large amounts of time to build.

The work that goes into three-dimensional drawings and models is often difficult to justify because much of it is repetition of work that has already been drawn in two dimensions and must be transferred to the new medium. When design studies are carried out in perspective, axonometric, or model form, they must then be transferred back to a two-dimensional form. Thus, many architects consider three-dimensional work redundant as well as expensive and try to minimize it, despite its usefulness as a design and presentation tool.

Can a CAD system build a physical model? Not really, but "CAD/CAM" can help to build models. By hooking a microcomputer (and software, of course) up to the proper tools, such as a laser cutting-tool, you can automatically cut out model pieces that have been extracted from your drawings. Then you can manually assemble the pieces. Although this is an elaborate manufacturing process, it may be justified in situations where complex, highly detailed physical models are required. While the cost of this hardware and software is falling, it will remain relatively expensive because physical models are static, difficult-to-change media that are best suited to displaying finished designs. Electronic models, on the other hand, can be used

throughout the design process, and they can be integrally linked with two-dimensional drawings, rather than simply derived from them.

SPATIAL DESIGN

Three-dimensional drawing and modeling software, in its many forms, makes spatial representations far more accessible to designers than any form of physical modeling. It generally operates on the same hardware as drafting systems, requiring only small additional (software) investments. Unlike manual perspective drawing, it allows you to create multiple views of your work without having to redraw it, over and over (Figure 6-1).

Let's look briefly at how you might use an "ideal" architectural computer-aided design system.

Models

You could start a project with organizational sketches, in plan, then draw volumetric massing studies, in three dimensions, develop the plan further, and then work on some specific sections and elevations. You would transform your floor plan and massing studies into a **model** with walls, floors, and roofs, and you would move these elements around until you were satisfied. You would simultaneously be locating door and window openings, and refining the shapes and surfaces of the various forms. As you worked, you would be able to view the model, in perspective, from *any* viewpoint, inside or out. When you are ready to document the project for construction, you would *extract* two-dimensional representations of plans, sections and elevations, then dimension and annotate them. Any changes that you make during this last phase would be reflected in the original electronic model. Finally, the model is available for presentation purposes and might even be used as a reference on the construction site.

This process is called **integrated three-dimensional modeling.** "Integrated" means that the two- and three- dimensional functions are connected, so that you can go back and forth between them without losing information. *Modeling* is a process that creates a *spatial* database that you can "cut" through in any plane and create a new view. In effect, this process allows you to produce an entire project, start to finish, in a form that you can view two or three dimensionally from any point at any time.

As we said, this is an "ideal" system. Many "integrated three-dimensional drawing" programs are not

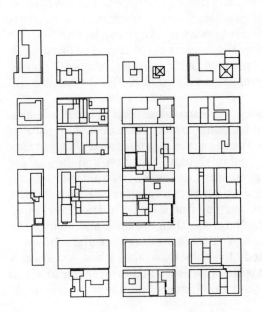

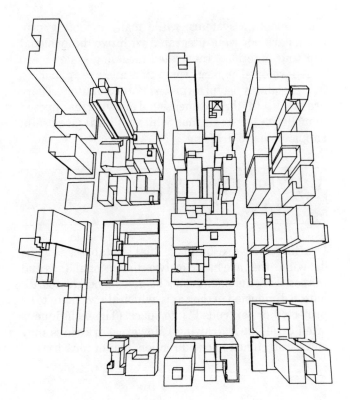

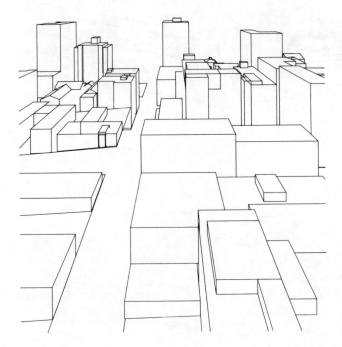

FIGURE 6-1   An urban model (Seattle's Capital Hill) viewed in plan, then in perspective from three different viewpoints. An unlimited number of different views may be extracted from a model. Courtesy of MegaCADD, model by NBBJ Group, Seattle.

true modeling systems, while many modeling programs are not well integrated with two-dimensional drafting functions. Integrated modeling systems are well developed on large computers and are appearing in increasingly useful forms on microcomputers. There are also useful three-dimensional drawing (as opposed to modeling) systems that, while not ideal, are useful supplements to drafting.

EXPANDING YOUR DRAWINGS

Drafting software builds a "flat" database, that is, drawings that are based on two-dimensional lines and shapes. These elements may be given a height coordinate, a dimension in the z axis, which allows them to be projected or "extruded" into space. (The technique is often called $2\frac{1}{2}$-D drawing.) However, drawings may only be stretched in one direction, that of the z axis.

DRAWING IN SPACE

You may actually draw in a three-dimensional mode with most projective systems. When you draw a line it will appear as a plane; a rectangle as a box, and a circle as a cylinder. However, you will always be drawing on a single plane or a set of parallel, "stacked" planes, because you cannot draw directly on the vertical planes.

Typically, you can choose a bottom or *base* elevation for an element, so that you can specify both its position and size in space. As you draw a plan, you may specify a "default" base elevation and height for everything you draw, and, when you want to draw, say, a half-height wall, you can specify a new z coordinate. In practice, you may find it easier to draw everything at the default values, then, go back and change the special cases. You can also assign specific z values to symbols and other blocks, so that when you insert a window, it will be positioned at its proper height. If you want to look at a multistory building in space, simply

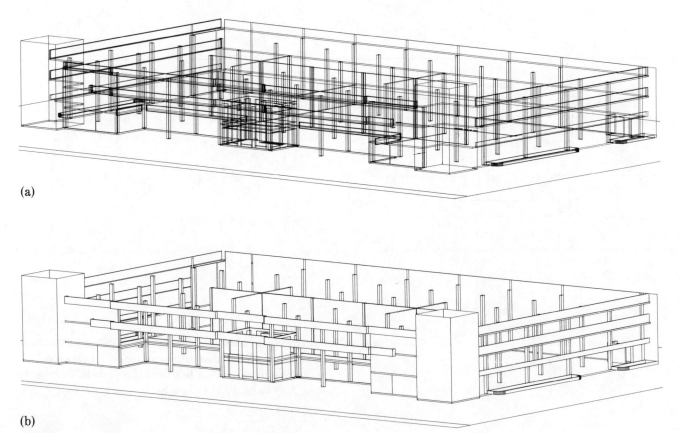

(a)

(b)

FIGURE 6-2   A projected "$2\frac{1}{2}$-D" view of a parking garage, as a wireframe *(a)* with hidden lines removed *(b)*. This is a parallel-line view, rather than a perspective: parallel lines are displayed thus. Arch.1 Architects.

locate the base elevation of each set of plan layers at the correct height: they will be shown as stacked floors and walls. The perimeter walls in Figure 6-2 were constructed in this manner.

Even though projective drawings are limited to parallel planes, you are not restricted to drawing plans. Facades, for example, can be viewed after you have located windows and doors on walls, even though you cannot turn these into two-dimensional elevation drawings. However, two-dimensional elevation views can be turned into three-dimensional views by using the height (z) dimension to give a wall depth. Several elevations may be "stacked" and viewed as parallel walls in space.

Since $2\frac{1}{2}$-D drawing is "extruded" some programs are limited to forms with flat (i.e., parallel to the ground) tops, and most allow curves only on the horizontal planes. One solution to this problem is a technique for "freezing" a view and adding the necessary lines. This is essentially a rendering method, since the additions will not be reflected in the drawing database.

USES AND LIMITS

Drawing complex three-dimensional drawings with projective software can be time-consuming, since you are often limited to drawing in plan, using numerical coordinates, rather than using planes or shapes in space. The more sophisticated programs provide shortcuts, but significant limitations are inherent to the tool.

Projected three-dimensional drawings are used most effectively for schematic design studies and for evaluation and presentation of well-developed work.

When schematic design work can be conducted using simple forms, projective drawings provide a quick, easy way to look at the spatial implications of your decisions. As you draw a plan, it's a simple matter to draw each wall at its correct height, and to insert doors and windows. You can toggle between three-dimensional views and the plan view to see the results of your work, change wall heights and move openings as you wish. Simple studies of roof forms and overhead definitions can also be carried out. You can conduct "what if" experiments, plotting variations for purposes of comparison.

Effort and Value

When you want to develop a design beyond this schematic level, however, it is often too much trouble to continue locating every form and symbol accurately in

three dimensions. Even if you do, the value of seeing every last detail three dimensionally is questionable. But most important, if you go to the effort of accurately projecting a facade from a plan drawing, you still must draw two-dimensional elevation drawings from scratch: you can't transfer them.

Instead, it's often more practical to take a well-developed two-dimensional plan and assign height coordinates to the more important elements, such as walls, other openings, and objects. By leaving everything else "on the floor," you can simplify the projection, making it easier to read. If you choose, you can display the remaining plan elements, including notes and symbols, on the floor within the projection for reference.

When you are drafting in two dimensions, it's not realistic to consider the three-dimensional implications of every single line. Try, instead, to go back and adjust the details when you want to look at a three-dimensional view. It's usually easier to change the heights of groups of elements than to set them accurately one at a time.

This process is greatly simplified by three strategies. First, try to reuse any of the elements you drew during schematic design, if they are still appropriate, since they already have the appropriate height values. Second, try to make sure that your library drawings have appropriate z coordinates before you start. You might even consider making custom versions of a block for various situations, such as windows of the same width but different heights. Walls too, can be drawn at a common "default" height, and if there are numerous wall heights, you can go back and change them later. Third, you can use your layer organization to make it easy to assign heights, if many or all of the elements on a particular layer, such as walls, can be given the same values.

The resulting projected plans can be used for design reference, by viewing spaces in a building or whole buildings in context or for presentation. They can be plotted and rendered or displayed on the screen.

The ultimate usefulness of projective three-dimensional drawings is as a supplement to your design and presentation methods. They can add to your understanding of a building or help you to convince a client. They do not, however, provide the multiple-drawing capabilities of three-dimensional modeling.

ELECTRONIC MODELS

Three-dimensional modeling software, as we said, creates a *spatial* database, in which every object is defined as a line, shape or plane in space. The modeling process is inherently different from drawing, and it is especially well suited to architectural design. (Figure 6-3, *a* and *b* illustrate the difference between a projected dome and a modeled dome.) It is similar to drafting only in that the final result may be, if you choose, a plan or elevation on paper; it is similar to projection only in that both methods may produce wire-frame images.

An electronic model can be viewed and worked on from any point, in any plane. Although you can work from a single, two-dimensional view by assigning *z* coordinates as you draw in plan or elevation, it is helpful to look at several "flat" views at once, such as a plan and two elevations, and, preferably, a three-dimensional view as well. Therefore, modeling programs that display several views on "split screen" or on two monitors are easiest to work with. When you add

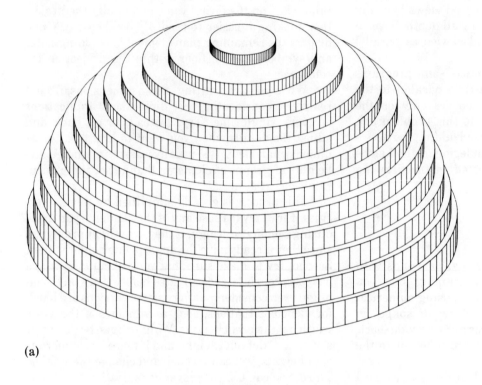

(a)

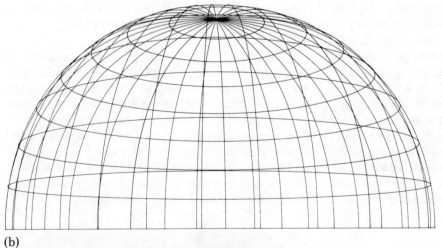

(b)

FIGURE 6-3   A projected dome *(a)* built with stepped cylinders and a modeled dome *(b)* without hidden lines removed. The model includes curves in vertical planes.

an object to one view, it simultaneously appears in all the other views; likewise, changes are recorded and displayed in all views. In essence, you are viewing the model through different windows (Figure 6-4).

If you wish to draw a facade on an exterior building wall, you simply build up the wall, with windows and doors at their proper thickness. When you make a section-cut through the wall and the floors that intersect it, you will get an accurate section. In this manner, the model can be used to generate a virtually unlimited number of individual drawings (Figure 6-5 a–c).

Three-dimensional modeling does much more for an architect than simply create new drawings. When you draw in two dimensions you are using symbols for walls, doors, and other elements; as we noted earlier, when you read a two-dimensional drawing, you are "decoding" a representation of a *part* of an object. Modeling, instead, lets you deal with whole objects. Even when you are drawing "in plan," you can see your work in its spatial context. The potential result is a truly three-dimensional design process; the mental gymnastics required for linking drawings in different planes are no longer necessary.

VARIETIES OF MODELS

There are three basic types of modeling software, based on lines, surfaces, and shapes. (Some programs use more than one of these approaches.) Each method has its own unique characteristics, but they all enable you to construct forms in space that can be translated into two-dimensional drawings.

Lines are the basic element in two-dimensional drawing, but few modeling programs are based on them. Although it is possible to create models by drawing lines in space, it is difficult to translate these into anything more than wire-frame models. In order to create opaque planes or objects, groups of lines must be linked into "closed" objects. Drawing individual lines is a useful supplement to drawing planes and objects directly, but by itself, it tends to be cumbersome.

Drawing surfaces in space is similar to projective drawing, since each vertical plane can be defined by a line with three-dimensional coordinates. It is different, however, in that you may draw in horizontal, vertical, or oblique planes, defined by any three (or more) points in space. Each plane can be "cut" anywhere, allowing

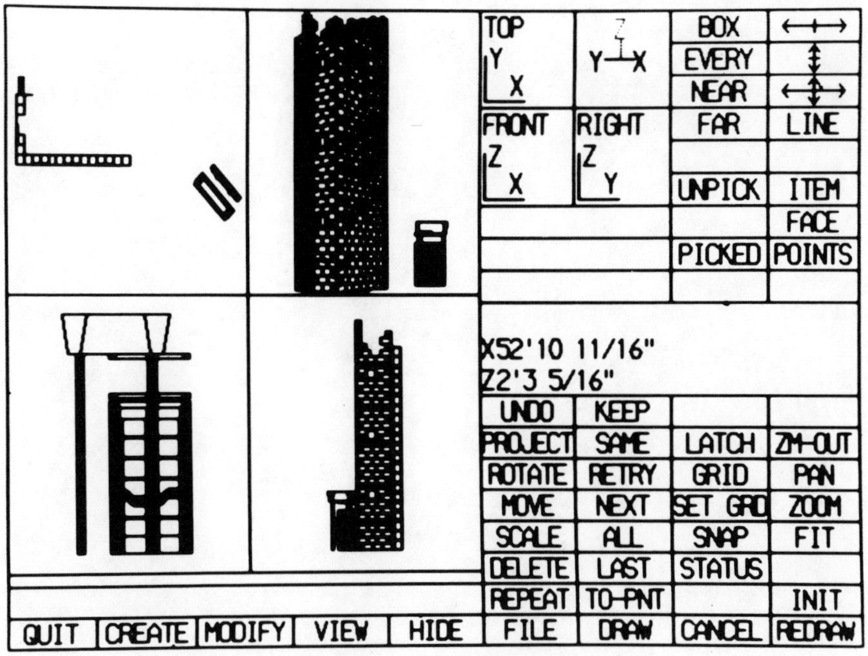

FIGURE 6-4 The views on the left side of the screen are plan and perspective (top) and two elevations (bottom). Note that the views are zoomed independently, allowing the isolation of the entry at lower left. A single view may also be chosen for full-screen work. Courtesy of MegaCADD.

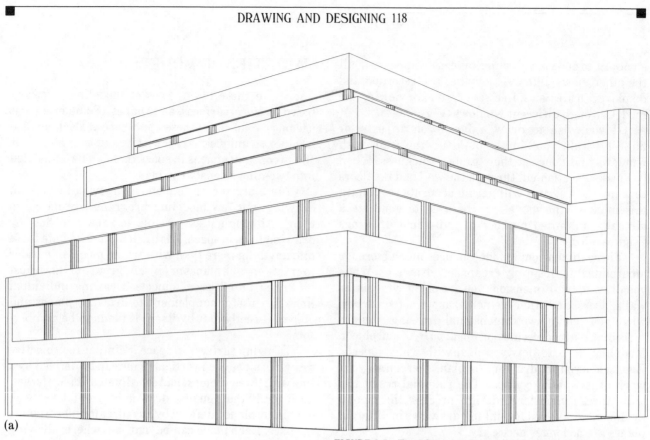

(a)

FIGURE 6-5 The 3-D model of this office building *(a)* was used to produce the elevation *(b)*, which was then developed with a drafting program *(c)*. Arch.1 Architects.

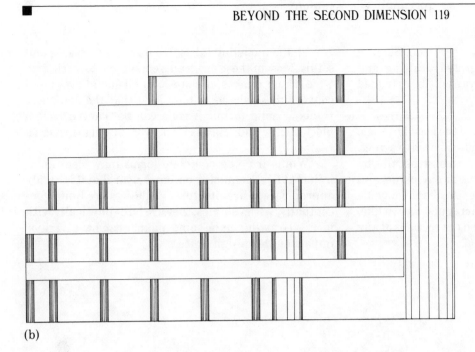

(b)

(c)

you to create cross sections (Figure 6-6, *a–b*). Surface modeling is well suited to integrated drafting and modeling, because drafted lines can easily be extruded into planes.

Modeling software that is based on *shapes* is, paradoxically, the most intuitive and the least familiar. These systems are the epitome of object-based drawing. Objects are defined as a closed forms, generally by drawing shapes in two dimensions, in any plane, and then stretching them into space. A shape may be regular, with parallel sides, or as irregular as you like. You may rotate objects in space and cut sections at any location.

Shape modeling takes two forms, wireframe and solids. Most of these programs enable you to work with wire-frame images of shapes, but some allow you to convert these shapes into objects that the computer treats as solid forms. A solid can be "carved" like a block of clay and "cut" as if you were slicing through a real wall.

While drawing complete forms may seem unfamiliar at first, it quickly becomes clear that it is highly appropriate to architecture. Buildings are built, conceptually, with volumes; they are built physically with forms. Drawing in the same manner can have a major impact on the design process.

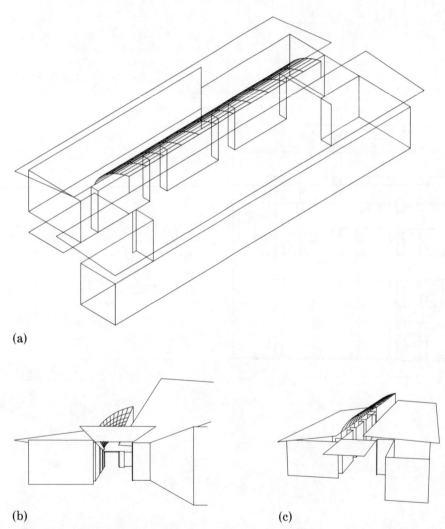

(a)

(b)　　　　　　　　　　(c)

FIGURE 6-6　Three views of a model constructed with planes. This is a schematic view; architectural plane-modeling software can also create double-planes for walls, floors, and roofs. (In *a*, the hidden lines have not been removed.)

VOLUMES AND FORMS

Whether you are using software that utilizes lines, surfaces, shapes, or all three, you can approach modeling a building in one of two ways: using either volumes or forms.

Most designs start with a diagrammatic organizational scheme, which is then usually developed into a plan. Instead of moving from diagrams into a simple plan design, a modeler may immediately begin thinking in terms of the *volumetric* implications of early design decisions. Interior spaces can be thought of as the three-dimensional volumes that they really are, rather than flat outlines. Schematic designs can be based on spatial relationships; even diagrams can be sketched three dimensionally.

The exterior shape of a building can also be designed as the plan evolves. Conversely, site and contextual forces may influence the massing of the building, which in turn affects the internal spaces. This sort of "push and pull" is usually done in two-dimensional plans, perhaps using sketches or physical models to study massing. Volumetric modeling lets you "sketch" with spaces, assembling and modifying them, and extracting plans, sections, and elevations as required.

The second approach to modeling is through designing *forms*, or solid objects, as opposed to simple volumes. By drawing floors, walls, and a roof, a design can be *built* in a realistic manner. Buildings may be assembled one object (or group of objects) at a time, just as a building is built. As in two-dimensional drawing, you may create (or purchase) libraries of forms, inserting them into your model as objects that can be scaled, revised and replaced (Figure 6-7).

Such a *form* model can be constructed directly over the base of an earlier volumetric model. Walls, for example, can be applied to the face of a building mass; repetitive elements, such as windows, may be repeated as if they are prefabricated pieces. When a volumetric base-model has been covered and infilled with walls, columns, doors, and windows, it can simply be removed, leaving an enclosed, detailed building (Figure 6-8 *a–b*).

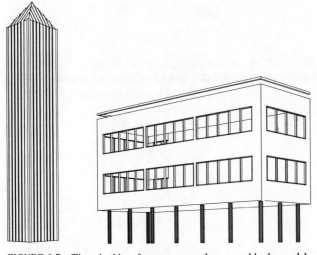
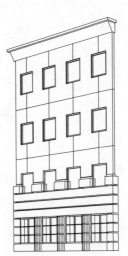

FIGURE 6-7   These building forms were used to assemble the model in Figure 1-10. David Baker Associates.

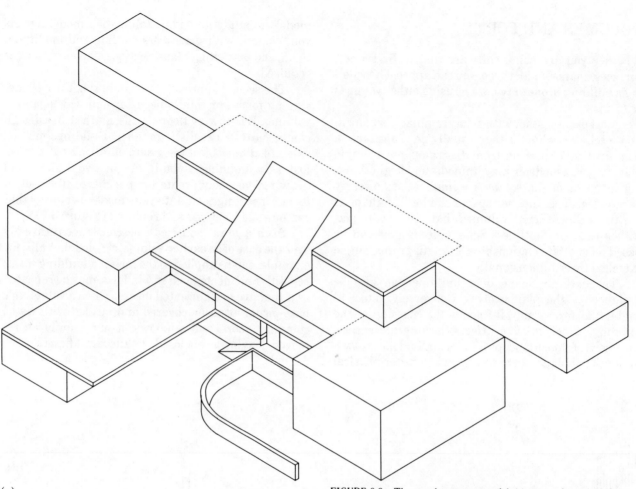

(a)

FIGURE 6-8   The simple massing model *(a)* was used as a base for a
fully-detailed building model, shown here as a cutaway isometric *(b)*
and a perspective view *(c)*. The massing model was erased as the walls,
floors, and roofs were drawn.

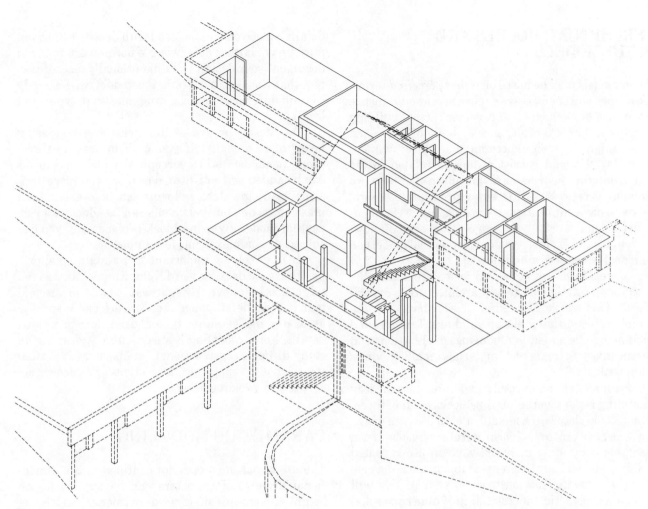

(b)

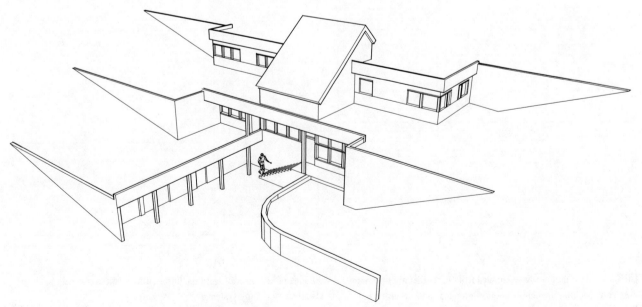

(c)

PERCEPTUAL MODELS AND BUILT MODELS

Form models may be based on either *perceived* forms, the shapes and surfaces we experience, or *built* forms, assembled of elements that represent actual building materials. For example, a wall built of perceived forms might be a single rectangular object, while a "built" wall would consist of objects related to the actual units of construction (Figure 6-9 *a–d*). These two techniques represent different approaches to design; they also have implications regarding the development of details and working drawings. They are not, however, mutually exclusive, since a perceptual model can be transformed into a built model.

Models based on perceived forms are, naturally, good for simulation of the way architecture is experienced. They serve as a kind of shorthand for the complex objects that make up buildings. Textures and shading can be added to renderings of elevations and perspectives to represent materials, making views more realistic.

Built models, on the other hand, simulate the way a building is put together. Using blocks made of three-dimensional shapes, the metaphor of "building a drawing" can be taken to an almost-literal conclusion. If you assemble a building of parts, you can use repeated building elements in different combinations to develop a consistent, efficient construction system. You will also gain a realistic understanding of dimensions and

details, since you will be faced with decisions that you might have missed otherwise. When you are ready to document your design two dimensionally, each drawing that you extract from the model will already contain information regarding material types and locations.

As a design progresses, it reaches ever-increasing levels of complexity. If you wish to develop three-dimensional details in a perceptual model, built forms can be added and substituted as more and more decisions are made. Just as forms can be overlaid on a massing model, built elements can be added to a perceptual model. By using block replacement, you can substitute complex forms for simple ones.

It is, of course, important to maintain an appropriate level of detail as you develop a model. Just as you might choose to develop key areas of a two-dimensional plan in great detail, you may choose to focus on specific areas of a model, either typical conditions or unique details. Form modeling is a particularly good way to study difficult constructional details, since it is often impossible to represent intersections and corners accurately in two dimensions.

PARAMETRIC MODELING

The use of parameters is not confined to two-dimensional drawing. Parameters can be applied to the height dimensions of three-dimensional models, as

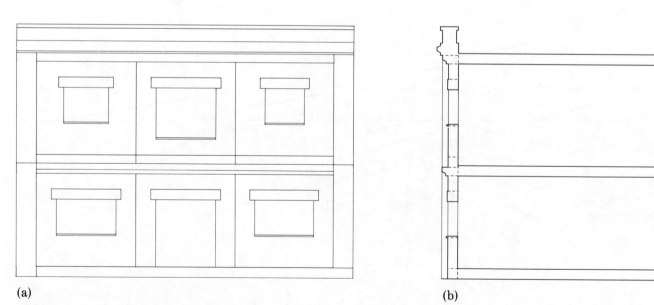

(a)

(b)

FIGURE 6-9   This model was assembled from parts that approximate building construction: the details are not intended to be accurate, but the idea of adding wall sections, lintels, and cornices can help to visualize a building system.

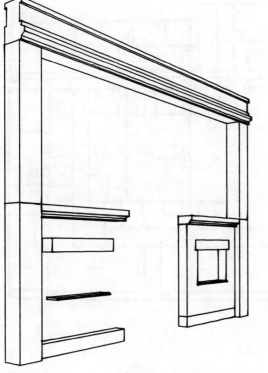

(c)

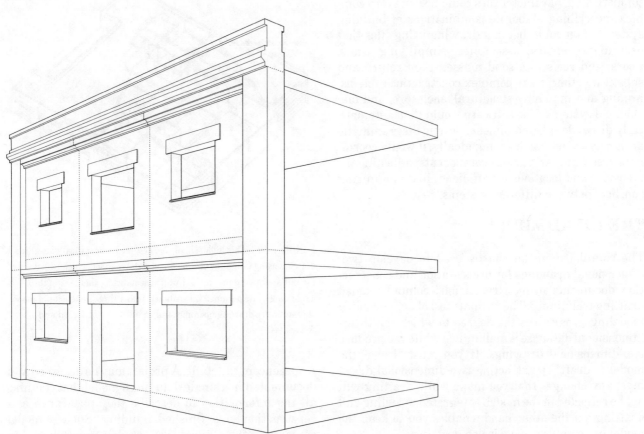

(d)

well. Working with realistic architectural forms in three dimensions can be very labor intensive; it's almost like actual building. Parametric modeling is one of the solutions to this problem.

Parametric modeling software enables you to specify parameter files that represent three-dimensional construction assemblies, such as wall types, wall–floor intersections, window and door openings, and roof slopes and overhangs. You can begin a project by drawing a schematic, single-line outline plan, then let the program transform it into a full three-dimensional model, differentiating interior and exterior walls, drawing roofs with the pitch and overhang you have previously specified (Figure 6-10).

In order to make customized assemblies, such as new wall types or roof overhang details, new (or modified) parameter files must be designed. Once a new file is developed, it can be incorporated throughout the project, then the model can be adapted to suit specific conditions. Since the construction system for a whole project can be changed by modifying a single parameter file, this semiautomatic process can actually *encourage* custom detailing.

As parametric modeling software becomes more sophisticated, parameter files could become very complex, describing elaborate combinations of building systems. You could begin a drawing using files that describe schematic assemblies, simplifying walls, floors, and roofs into solid masses, then return and substitute other, more complex construction systems, mixing and matching structural, enclosure, and mechanical systems. The software would then automatically draw, detail, and dimension your diagrammatic design as a working drawing; ideally, it would coordinate assemblies of various components, adjusting dimensions and locations for efficiency and minimizing conflicts between different systems.

THE IDEAL MODEL

The completed model can be used to develop two-dimensional drawings for presentation and construction documents using "traditional" computer-aided drafting techniques. The ultimate test of an integrated modeling program is the degree to which the three-dimensional database is maintained while you produce two-dimensional drawings. If you must "leave" the model to draft, by extracting two-dimensional drawings, any changes that you make while drafting will not be reflected in the model. Integrated modeling and drafting, on the other hand, enables you to keep the model up to date as you develop drawings.

Thus, our "ideal," truly integrated design process encourages a straight path, using a single medium,

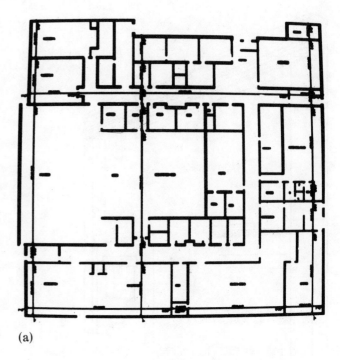

(a)

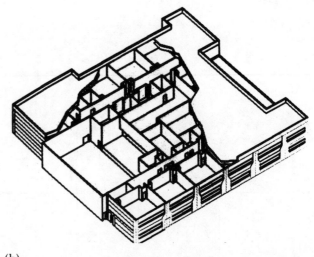

(b)

FIGURE 6-10   This high school was designed schematically as a line drawing using Computervision's Personal Architect, which transformed the initial drawing into a solid-wall schematic *(a)*, then, using the Technology File parametric capability, into a three-dimensional model, automatically drawing openings and roof details *(b)*. Heard and Associates.

from concept to details. A project may be designed and documented in a single data file, a model that contains all the information to describe the appearance and construction of a finished building. Such a model contains, in three dimensions, models of each building component, such as walls, doors, and windows, with all relevant information attached to them. When you wish to use a plan, section or elevation, it can be extracted. When you want to plot dimensions and symbols for a particular view, it can provide them. Likewise, sizes, quantities and engineering data may be listed. In a way, it is like the master builder's model that served as the primary reference on the medieval construction site.

Although truly integrated architectural CAD programs are beginning to appear, it may be a few years until they reach the ease of use that has become common to simpler drafting and modeling software. Nevertheless, it seems clear that this is the ultimate destination of CAD in architecture.

SEEING AND COMMUNICATING IN THREE DIMENSIONS

As we have seen, computer-aided design in three dimensions is far more than a tool for producing impressive perspective drawings. There are a number of different ways of presenting three-dimensional images, and they are not only useful for impressing a client: they are immensely valuable in helping you understand your own work.

Imagination has always been as important to a designer in evaluating a design as in creating it. Architects have always relied on "the mind's eye" to visualize future constructions, supplemented by simplified, often inaccurate sketches, or through laborious individual renderings. As a result, many a designer is surprised by unforeseen results when a building is completed, because it is impossible to imagine or draw all of the countless situations that occur in any building.

Initially, most designers treat three-dimensional drawings and models as a substitute for making physical models or renderings. It doesn't take long to begin to see the differences: these tools enable you to use techniques that have no real precedent in manual practice, for both design and presentation.

VIEWING MODELS AND PROJECTIONS

Several tools are available for viewing and enhancing projected drawings. The most basic viewing method displays a parallel-line image of objects in space (Figure 6-2). You may choose a viewpoint around, over, or under the objects, but lines are always shown parallel, as if you were rotating and tilting an isometric. Although this technique is lacking in realism,

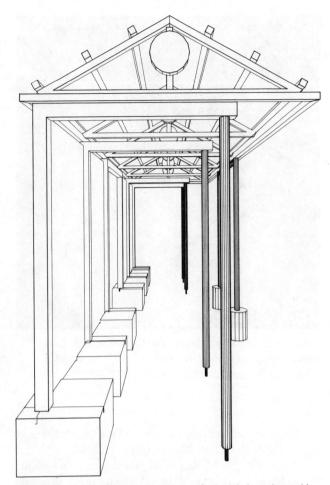

FIGURE 6-11 A "one point" perspective of a bus shelter, obtained by selecting a viewpoint and target on a line perpendicular to the front wall-plane. David Baker Associates.

it may be used to display all lines at their actual dimension, so that you can take measurements off of a 3-D plot. This can be the best way to document a complex object or an intersection of two objects.

To make a view more realistic, projections can also be displayed with vanishing points. Again, you can choose your viewpoint, but the result is a multiple vanishing point perspective of the wire-frame projection. A rectangular building, for example, will be represented as a three-point perspective. On occasions when a simple one-point perspective is useful, such as a section/perspective, a viewpoint can be chosen oriented perpendicular to a plane (Figure 6-11).

Since the overlapping lines of a wireframe can be visually confusing, you will probably choose to work on all but the most simple drawings in two dimensions, then view them three-dimensionally from time to time. **Hidden line removal** is used to automatically erase

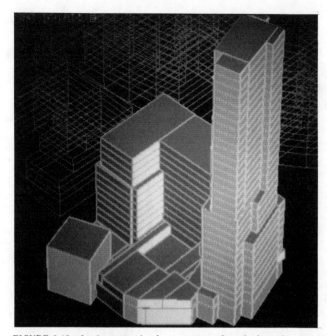

FIGURE 6-12 In this example of automatic surface shading, the wirefame image has been redrawn over the surfaces to add detail. Polshek and Partners.

lines that are *behind* other objects. (The illustrations in this chapter have had hidden lines removed, with the exception of Figure 6-2*b*.) After you choose a viewpoint, the software can calculate which surfaces obscure others, treating each as opaque. The process of removing hidden lines is generally used to created images for viewing, storing, or plotting. Once you have created a hidden line image, you generally cannot continue to draw on it. In addition, hidden line removal on complex drawings can be time consuming, since the program must conduct a large number of calculations. Although most hidden line utilities will miss a few lines or remove a few extras, it is still vastly preferable to erasing lines by hand. It is an especially important tool for turning wire-frame images into renderings, since complex wireframes can be incomprehensibly cluttered.

Automatic **surface shading** is offered by most surface modeling and solid modeling programs, and by a few projective systems. Any surface, as defined by an extruded line or curve, may be painted with a solid tone, giving forms the appearance of being solid objects. Unlike rudimentary "paint" programs, the tone is part of the database and will appear automatically when viewed from any angle. Some advanced software will create "translucent" tones that show lines behind a surface; another feature allows you to choose one or more light sources and automatically create

shadow and tone studies. These are useful for both design studies and video-based presentations (Figure 6-12).

RENDERINGS AND PRESENTATIONS

The simplest way of using a three-dimensional projection or model is by plotting and hand-rendering wireframe views, which helps to "soften" and interpret a design. Studies of different materials, colors, and lighting can be carried out this way; renderings for presentation can be laid out by the computer, then shaded to add emphasis or change details.

Surfaces and Colors

However, hand-rendering is a laborious process, even on top of a computer-generated wire-frame image. As we explained, some three-dimensional programs enable you to shade surfaces automatically, in some cases allowing shadow studies with user-specified light sources. The latter technique produces variations in tone that can look very realistic, particularly when more than one light source can be specified.

Bit-mapped "painting" or rendering programs can be used to capture a three-dimensional image as it is displayed on the screen: the CAD vector graphics are frozen into a pixel-based image. You can no longer use all your CAD editing tools on this image, but you can render it by drawing lines on top of the image and shading areas with textures or colors. Painting an image is a quick, convenient way to make wireframe drawings look more realistic (Figure 6-13).

FIGURE 6-13 This interior image was extracted from a 3-D model and "painted" using a rendering program.

Although computer-toned drawings sometimes look somewhat cartoonish, they can be very helpful in evaluating surfaces. By substituting different colors and textures, you can view tens or even hundreds of alternative combinations. Using tools like these, an architect can study and present more combinations of material, color, and light than has ever been possible.

Many architects are conservative—or downright nervous—when it comes to choosing colors. Choices are often made by holding paint chips and carpet samples and imagining them in a finished building. With three-dimensional software and hardware that can display hundreds or thousands of colors, the guesswork is eliminated. Choices can be based on accurate simulations of colors as they will actually be seen in context, not on mental visualizations.

Points of View

Perspective renderers and photographers know that the choice of viewpoint is crucial to the impact an image has on the viewer. Besides choosing the subject matter carefully, the viewing angle determines which objects block other objects and which forms are juxtaposed with others. Small changes in angle can have a major effect on the composition of a view. Height too, is important: the view from four feet off the ground can be very different from that at six feet (or eight feet or twenty feet). Renderers often discover this too late; the computer lets you experiment by moving the viewpoint around before you save or plot an image (Figure 6-14 b and c).

Once you have chosen a viewing angle and height, you must still determine the distance for your view. Perspective-generating software is like a sensitive camera zoom lens. A close view is like a "wide-angle" lens, giving an impression of extreme separation between objects in the foreground and those in the background. A close view tends to feel "spatial." Distant views, on the other hand, render objects as if they were very "flat," as if viewed through a telephoto lens. You can use these differences to your advantage by choosing spatial or flattened views as they are appropriate to your project (Figure 6-14, a and b).

Architects are often seduced by their own renderings. If you choose the most flattering viewpoints to show your client, be sure you look at the less flattering viewpoints in private. Computer-generated perspectives give you an opportunity to see what everyone else will see when a building is built: you can make sure that there are no unpleasant surprises.

Stereo viewing is another useful trick that can be done with little more than a pair of hand-held slide viewers. If you create two three-dimensional views from viewpoints that are only a few inches apart, like a pair of eyes, and make a slide of each, you can look at each through a separate viewer and recreate an old stereoscope. The result is a sense that the model jumps right off the paper; it looks like a true physical model or even like the real thing. You can also create stereo views by plotting two views and focusing one eye on each image (Figure 6-15) or plotting the views in two colors, then placing similarly colored cellophane over the opposite eye, like watching a 3-D movie.

In addition to impressing clients, this technique can be used effectively for studying building massing in context, for evaluating enclosed spaces, and for examining curved or multiplanar facades. Stereo viewing is an excellent replacement (or supplement to) elevation shadow studies, the traditional technique for simulating multiple planes.

Computer displays have been developed that enable a viewer to see 3-D images if equipped with special glasses and the proper software. Another interesting viewing technique that is under development is holographic projection. Using laser projections, solid-appearing objects (based on computer models) can be viewed in space from any angle, without special glasses. When holography finds its way into computer-aided design, it will be an intriguing way to view electronic models as if they were physical models; perhaps someday holograms will replace flat screens as everyday CAD displays.

Moving Around and Through

Beyond renderings and photographs of individual views, you can create sequential views around and through buildings, combining them into actual animation. The ability to generate unlimited views means an architect can visually "walk" through or around a building, looking not just at the individual spaces, but at the *sequence* of spaces. It can help an interior designer place furniture, evaluating alternatives with a realistic view of the architectural design. It can enable an urban designer to walk down a simplified street, as in the urban model in Figure 6-1, and evaluate a large project from many different viewpoints (Figure 6-16 and 6-17). Predrawn 3-D models and drawings of major cities are already appearing, and CD-ROM promises to make these widely available.

A spatial model allows you to see as many sides of a form, a building, or a city as you want; to see, theoretically, every viewpoint that future users will see. With this ability, there is no real reason for architectural "surprises" to happen: designs can be inspected in advance regarding scale, sight lines,

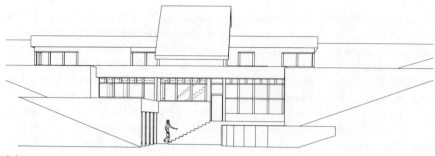

(a)

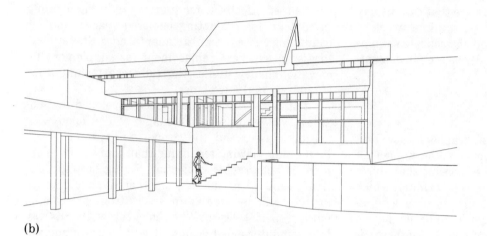

(b)

(c)

FIGURE 6-14 The first two views *(a* and *b)* are from exactly the same
angle with the same target, but from different distances. The first is
flattened, since it is taken from a distant viewpoint; the second is more
spatial, since the viewpoint was close to the model. The third view *(c)*
is from the same distance as the second, but the angle and elevation
have been changed.

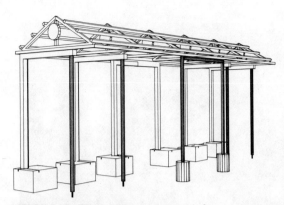
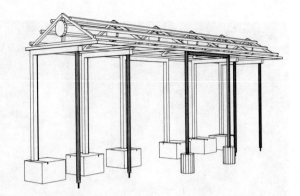

FIGURE 6-15   These two views were made from viewpoints a few inches apart, like two eyes. Lacking slide viewers or color plots, you can still see a three-dimensional image by focusing your left eye on the left image and your right eye on the other—no easy trick. Try it, but be patient; it takes some practice. Move the page toward and away from your eyes. Try putting a sheet of paper between your eyes. David Baker Associates.

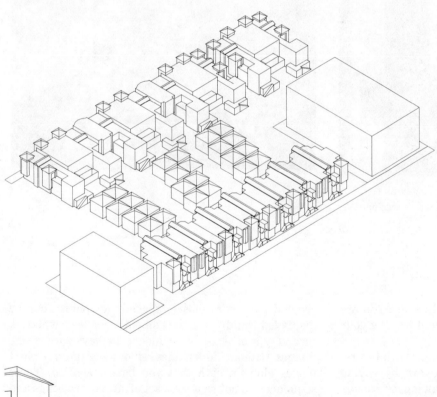

FIGURE 6-16   Two wireframe views of an urban housing project. David Baker Associates.

FIGURE 6-17   Four views of a large urban building in context,
produced using 2-D/3-D software with automatic surface shading.
Courtesy of Sigma Design.

alignments, and general aesthetics. In short, you are
virtually able to build a project without leaving your
desk.

"Walk arounds" and "walk throughs" can be created on even the simplest 3-D software by saving
sequential views of a projected drawing or model.
These can be rapidly displayed in sequence to produce
"one step at a time" walks. (A sequence might also be
photographed on-screen or be plotted and photographed, then displayed on a slide projector or video
recorder.) Although not true animation, step-by-step
sequences are far more effective than viewing individual images.

Programs that run on very fast computers can
display *real-time* sequences that flash by like real
animation. Stored images, which have been previously

created from very closely spaced viewpoints, can be
displayed rapidly to create smooth, realistic walks. A
second type of real-time sequence displays wire-frame
images, without hidden lines removed, as the viewpoint
moves along a path that you have specified. These
sequences do not require a set of stored drawings and
can be viewed spontaneously at any time. They are
limited, though, to fairly simple drawings that can be
viewed without hidden lines removed.

Sequences need not be realistic to be useful.
"Flyovers" are a good way to view buildings in context;
you can also create special effects by removing walls
and roofs, or walking *through* walls to illustrate neighboring spaces. Use your imagination: remember what
you wished you could look at if you could have gotten
inside a scale model (Figure 6-18 *a–d*).

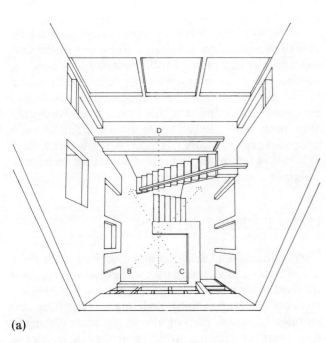

(a)

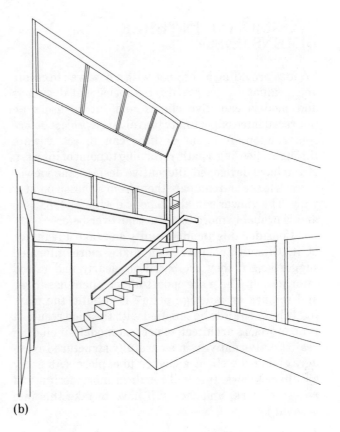

(b)

(c)

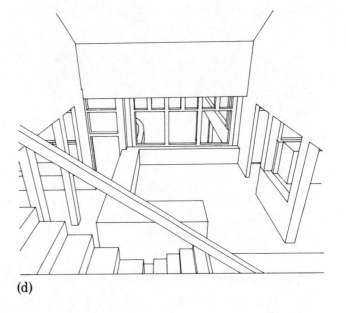

(d)

FIGURE 6-18 Four views of a house interior. In the first (a), with the roof lifted off, arrows indicate the viewpoints and targets for the others.

INTERACTING IN THREE DIMENSIONS

Besides providing a designer with a new way to create and evaluate a design, three-dimensional drawings and models can give clients and future users an unprecedented opportunity to evaluate a project before construction. A client or user can direct a walk through, choosing a path, returning to point of interest. If you have developed alternative designs, the viewer can ask to see and compare them from a chosen point of view. The viewer can also *suggest* design alternatives and is probably more likely to than ever before.

Consider this an opportunity and take advantage of it. Clients and users can make more informed suggestions if they are based on clearly understood information. The more opportunity a client has to see and remark on a design before it is built, the more likely he or she is to be satisfied with the final result. It is up to you, as architect, to present models, including realistic alternatives, in a carefully structured manner, giving the client a chance to explore. (As every architect knows, this will result in more design and redesign work, and fees will have to take this into account.)

Architectural drawings have always been a barrier to numerous nonarchitects. For every client that can easily read a plan, or fully understand a building section there are many who can follow with only a vague understanding. Three-dimensional images and sequences can eliminate this barrier so thoroughly that we should expect clients to *demand* a full tour of a proposed project before it is built. Why shouldn't they? While it is important that clients trust an architect's judgment, seeing is believing.

GREAT EXPECTATIONS

Three-dimensional drawing and modeling is the field of computer-aided design that will grow (and change) the most in the next few years. Expect to see increasing levels of integration until modeling and drafting are seamlessly joined. Expect also to see some elaborate new ways of viewing architecture, such as stereo animation or even holographic model projections. By that time, we should be able to develop three-dimensional design strategies to push the tools to their limits.

COMPUTERS AND THE DESIGN PROFESSION

PART 3

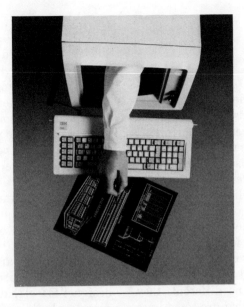

NEW TOOLS, NEW DESIGN STRATEGIES

CHAPTER 7

It's understandable that most of us try very hard to get computers to do what we're accustomed to doing by hand. Isn't that what they're for?

Remember McLuhan's words:

> A new medium is never an addition to an old one, nor does it leave the old one in peace.[1]

Computers serve as an extension of our hands, but they are an entirely different medium than the pencil, pen, or typewriter. Inevitably, we are adopting new working methods with our new tools.

As our methods of designing, drawing, and building change, our roles are changing, too. By looking ahead, perhaps we can avoid some of the pitfalls that await us and take advantage of some of the opportunities. In this chapter we will examine some of the technologies that are available, and others that we can expect to see in the near future, and try to understand their impact on architecture. We might ask: As new tools allow us to work in new ways, can we improve the way we design and build? Are there ways of practicing architecture that we haven't even thought of?

ARCHITECTURAL STRATEGIES

Architectural design is based on a designer's ability to visualize and record design solutions. Tools and media are an important part of this process. If inadequate, they can get in the way; if exceptionally good, they can help to unleash creative powers. In some cases, design tools can actually influence design. For example, a design that is conceived using modeling clay is likely to take a different form than one that is developed strictly on paper. Likewise, a clay model may inspire different forms than a stick model. The former might be considered more appropriate for exploring masonry building systems, the latter, wood or steel. Various computer-aided design tools are no different: they affect the design process in ways that are sometimes subtle, sometimes conspicuous.

Since we have already looked closely at the tools, let's take a brief look at some common approaches to architectural design and examine the effects that computer-aided drafting and modeling may have on them. If you consider how CAD affects your personal design approach, you should be better able to devise strategies that support your work.

PLAN AND FUNCTION

Since the early days of the modern movement, *functional* architecture has been described in many ways. Initially it was used to call for buildings that were machinelike in their support of activity and their simplicity of detail. Later, the term was applied to minimalistic buildings of all kinds. More generally, we can refer to a functional design method as one that uses organizational principles and space requirements as primary design criteria.

A design method that relies heavily on the organization and development of plans can make excellent use of two-dimensional drawing software for design. Since areas can be calculated easily, and rooms, walls, doors, and windows can be moved at will, it is particularly easy to assemble blocks of space, "pushing and pulling" pieces until they fit. You can make the transition from diagram to developed plan without drawing and redrawing each piece.

[1]Marshall McLuhan, *Understanding Media: The Extensions of Man*, New American Library, 1964, p. 158.

Completing the Plan

Functional, plan-derived design best serves as a base for studies of elevations, sections, materials, and details. While working in plan alone, designers often will design a two-dimensional building, then develop sections and elevations as an afterthought, neglecting three-dimensional relationships and visual issues. The two-dimensional nature of drafting software can encourage a designer to work *exclusively* in two dimensions. This is particularly problematic with software or customized front-end packages that are specifically oriented toward drawing plans. When software is exclusively plan oriented, it is considerably more difficult to start working on, say, a section on the computer. Software that is strictly two dimensional can inspire a false sense of completeness that can lead a designer to feel that a well-developed plan represents a complete building. This is one of the major dangers in using two-dimensional drafting software for design: it sometimes takes even more mental effort to address the third dimension than does manual drawing. There can also be a tendency to focus on the computer as a sole tool: in this case, it is important to accompany plan development with sketches, on paper, of nonplan design issues.

A two-dimensional, functionalist design strategy can benefit from any drafting or modeling software that allows three-dimensional views to be created from plans. By frequently checking 3-D views, you can use level changes, multistory spaces and variations in ceiling height *as a plan is developed*, rather than after the fact. As we explained in Chapter 6, massing and elevations can be developed simultaneously. The ability to work in two dimensions and three dimensions at the same time may bring new life to the notion that "form follows function."

FORM AND SPACE

There are many approaches toward architectural form-making, and almost as many kinds of three-dimensional CAD software. When you are trying to figure out how to choose or best use a 3-D program, it may be helpful to give some thought to how you perceive and design buildings. A good "fit" between your software and your design method is particularly important when you work in three dimensions.

Exterior Form

Exterior-oriented, *geometric* or *sculptural* approaches to design tend to treat buildings as freestanding objects or assemblies of simple forms. They may produce smooth, tight-skinned buildings or more complex aggregations that respond to site influences and functional considerations.

Three-dimensional modeling is particularly appropriate to this kind of design approach, since modeling is easiest using simple forms. Quick model "sketches" can be drawn with software that supports modeling with shapes. Unlike small physical models, electronic modeling can be used to add detail, develop nuances, conduct shadow studies, and explore interior-exterior relationships without relying on elaborate renderings or resorting to two-dimensional representations. Simultaneous development of interior spaces and exterior forms can be used to effectively knit together inside and outside.

Spaces

A more volume-oriented, spatial design method is characterized by a focus on enclosure and the *shape* of spaces and the use of planes to define layers of spaces. Both three-dimensional projection and modeling are well suited to spatial design methods. If you start with a plan view you can extrude it into the third dimension, stretching each wall to an appropriate height. If you are starting from scratch, many programs allow you to sketch walls (and partial walls and columns) in three dimensions. By switching between plan and various perspective views, you can continually evaluate the spatial implications of every design decision.

Constructional Design

A *constructional* approach to design, which makes use of design procedures that are appropriate to specific building systems, produces recognizably different forms in wood, masonry, steel, or concrete. This approach typically emphasizes the distinctions between different construction components: structural (primary) elements; nonbearing, enclosing (secondary) elements; and moveable, operable and replaceable (tertiary) elements. A clearly differentiated layering system supports this kind of hierarchical system by allowing you to define and maintain different families of forms. By placing structural and nonstructural elements in distinct sets of layers, you can better envision the building system as you design, then communicate it more clearly by plotting layers by building system.

Drawing libraries that are organized according to hierarchies of material types can be helpful, as well. Constructional architecture has often used realistic physical models as a design tool: sticks for wood and steel, sheet materials for concrete and masonry, and so on. Perhaps more than in any other approach, the working method influences the ultimate built form. Computer-modeling programs that use shapes are ideally suited to this kind of *additive* design method: Buildings can be assembled from libraries of columns, beams, wall elements, window units, floor and roof sections, and so on.

Not all modeling software is well suited to a construction-based design approach. A system that is heavily automated and assumes that you will be using certain materials or connections may be a handicap. For instance, if a program automatically translates volumes into uniformly thick walls, and you wish to design an articulated post-and-beam building, you may have problems. If you wish to use and express a wide range of materials, flexibility is important.

IMAGE AND PLACE

Ornamentation and Articulation

One of the many possible uses of drawing libraries is the stockpiling of standard details for surfaces, patterns, decorative elements, and articulated structural details. These details may be custom designed, they may be traced from sources such as historical references, or they may be purchased from materials suppliers or "image vendors."

In recent years, ornamentation has grown in popularity since the austere days of unreconstructed modernism, and CAD may encourage that trend. Since decoration must be grounded in buildable reality, we may find a trend towards standardized decorations that can be extracted from disk-based manufacturer's libraries. These libraries, which might eventually be used to automatically produce customized building parts via computer-aided manufacturing techniques, would be remarkably similar to the millwork catalogs used by Victorian-era carpenters. Integral ornamentation, decoration that grows out of the inherent qualities of a material and its function in a building, may likewise be facilitated by manufacturing techniques that link architectural computers with the production shop.

Contextual Design

Design that is sensitive to its neighbors in terms of siting, massing, scale, or detail can be called *contextual*. If a building is to respond to its surroundings, it helps to be able to see the design in context as you work. Although posting photographs of neighboring buildings or landscape is always helpful, you should always be able to see the implications of design decisions in context: in plan, elevation, section, and especially in three dimensions. Because of the difficulty inherent in redrawing adjacent buildings at many different scales, and because of the unwieldiness of site plans at large scales, it is often difficult to view a large-scale drawing in context.

Because of the computer's ability to "change scales" effortlessly, it is feasible to keep context drawings visible as you work. In addition to drawing adjacent buildings in plan, it is often helpful to see a building plan in its larger context: a neighborhood, town, or urban area. Elevations and sections of neighboring buildings and site conditions can also be combined with your own elevations and sections to view facades in context.

Since three-dimensional models can be used to view a design in context at any time, at any scale, and from any viewpoint, they are far superior to physical models. Massing models (shapes with little detail) are quick to draw and can be readily produced as any project is started. As predrawn city models become available, there will be little reason for any urban project to be designed "out of context." When contextual models are used *throughout the design process*, it becomes difficult to ignore the implications that design decisions have on a place. Sensitive design does not automatically result from the ability to see a project in place at any time, but it doesn't hurt.

STANDARDIZATION

As computer-aided design makes drafting and modeling faster and more efficient, there are greater and greater incentives to make extensive use of standard drawing libraries and repetitive forms and details. We have seen that there are numerous advantages beyond simply saving work, but there is considerable skepticism among some architects about CAD's applicability to "nonrepetitive" design.

Repetition can be used to create cost-efficient, visually consistent, and potentially attractive designs, or it can produce bargain-basement, boring, cookie-cutter architecture. These results are generally determined by budget and an architect's competence, not by tools. Although computers make the use of repetitive forms very easy, repetition was a means of achieving visual consistency and constructional efficiency long before computers arrived. Keep in mind, too, that repetitive elements can be used in many different ways. For example, the house in Figures 5-5 through 5-9 is a fairly unconventional design, determined by a specific site, program, and the client's desire to build

into a hillside. Nevertheless, the design uses standard wall thicknesses, windows, doors, fixtures, and so on, and the plans, sections, and elevations were all developed rapidly from an electronic model.

Standardization has long been increasing in the construction industry, and architects have learned to use standardized components because they are less expensive to both design and build. It is not uncommon for entire buildings to be built with factory-fabricated parts, such as precast concrete, steel trusses, factory-glazed windows, metal partitions systems, and ready-to-assemble HVAC systems. This kind of **building systems integration** was pioneered in the 1960s, and the degree of coordination between structural systems, exterior and interior systems, and mechanical systems has gradually been increasing since then.

Well-integrated building systems, that is, those which can be combined easily and without conflict, are ideally suited for computer-aided design, particularly three-dimensional modeling. When appropriately powerful hardware and software are developed and manufacturers introduce comprehensive drawing libraries of their products, we can expect to see semiautomated design systems that are geared toward specific design methods, and perhaps toward specific building systems.

TOWARD AN INTEGRATED DESIGN METHOD

The design and construction of buildings requires the knitting together of diverse materials and building systems. There are often very clear separations of processes and disciplines: consultants work independently on the same part of a building; drafters and specification writers often work with minimal communication. These habits have developed because they allow parallel, semi-independent work. Parallel work is necessary in complex projects, but it makes communication and scheduling tremendously important.

It is usually the architect's job to orchestrate these specialists, their work, and the building systems they create. This task of coordination can often be simplified by an increased level of integration in the design process: integration between people, between building systems, and between media. Computer graphics and data management provide a convenient means for standardizing and exchanging drawings and information, from schematic design through the completion of construction.

NEW KINDS OF DRAWINGS

Since drawings are no longer bound by the limitations of paper and pen, the word "drawing" can now refer to a *set* of meshed drawings that can be viewed and managed interchangeably. Electronic models, unlike their physical counterparts, are not limited by materials or scale. A "model" can now be an accurate representation of a building, complete with all the information necessary to produce working drawings.

Drawing Types

The drawing types that are produced in each phase of an architectural project are being changed by computer drawing methods. Not only are highly developed drawings possible at a relatively early stage, but drawing types that were difficult or impossible to produce without computer assistance can be used. We have mentioned some of these in previous chapters. The first three, listed here, are essentially extensions of overlay drafting techniques that were discussed in Chapter 5. The others are new forms of traditional three-dimensional drawing techniques.

Multidisciplinary drawings, consisting of discipline-specific layers drawn over a common base, can be plotted in different combinations, as required. They enable you to address specific trades and combinations of trades simultaneously, to prevent conflicts between different materials and building systems, and to illustrate and clarify construction sequences.

Multilevel plans, with two or more floors of a building overlaid, allow you to avoid redrawing repeated elements, and help to maintain continuity between floors.

Combined **section/elevations,** in which surface elements are overlaid on section cuts, lets you view exterior elevations, interior elevations, and wall sections in combination.

The ability to work in three dimensions *conveniently* brings both **perspective** and **iso/axonometric** drawings into the realm of everyday design, presentation, and documentation tools. Individual views are valuable, but series of sequential views, inside–outside views, and 360° rotations are ideal ways for an architect to convey physical and spatial information (Figure 7-1 and 7-2). These sequences need not be limited to paper output, but may be viewed in animation, as we have seen in Chapter 6.

Three-dimensional working drawings may not replace plans, sections, and elevations, but they may prove a valuable supplement. Difficult corner details and objects like cabinets are good candidates for dimensioned, 3-D drawings like axonometrics. Three-dimensional plans are useful for space planning and landscape drawings and could be used routinely for some kinds of working drawings (Figure 7-3). In the

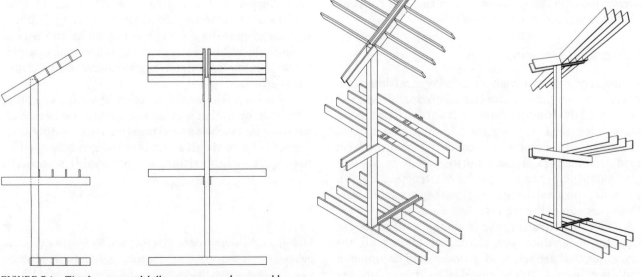

FIGURE 7-1 This framing model illustrates a complex assembly; each of the drawings that are extracted from the model could be dimensioned.

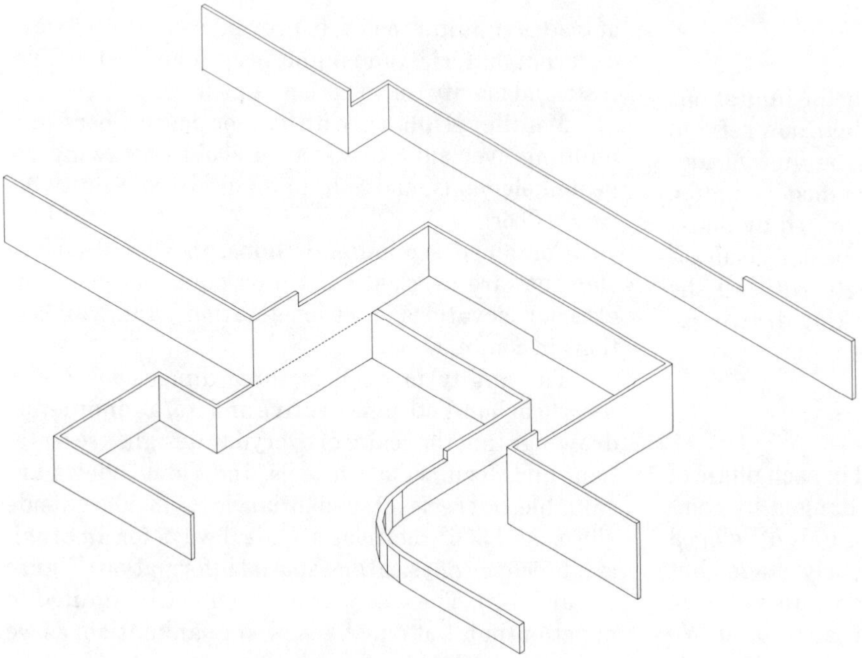

FIGURE 7-2   A view of a terraced foundation was extracted from the model in Figure 6-14. This and other extracted models can be useful in describing subsystems and their interrelationships in three dimensions.

past, anything that could be conveyed graphically *more clearly* than in text, has been drawn. If the computer will automatically produce height dimensions and can plot them in a readable way, why not use dimensioned axonometrics from time to time? If section and interior elevation information are being drawn into the same database, you can plot cutaway axonometrics, or section/perspectives.

Integrated Drawings

Ultimately, the synthesis of overlay drafting techniques, the computer's data-handling capabilities, and integrated drafting/modeling software will produce a truly integrated working method. Two-dimensional drawings will become a secondary documentation media, instead of a primary working medium. We will always use plans and sections for construction, but in a three-dimensional design process, they are inherently linked together (Figure 7-4).

Integrated drafting and modeling, as described in Chapter 6, enables you to extract almost all the drawings that are required to design and document a building from a single model. The design process becomes a matter of *building a model*, then choosing

the appropriate views to display and plot with corresponding notes, symbols and dimensions. Think of the process as three-dimensional overlay drafting: it's as if you had three sets of sheets, one horizontal and two vertical (at right angles), interlocking with each other (Figure 7-5). Of course, any work you do on one set will be reflected in the others. The efficiency of two-dimensional computer-aided drafting is multiplied: instead of parallel development of plans and sets of section–elevations, each evolving individually, a network of integrated drawings further reduces duplicated efforts.

Since a model would be too complex if *every* bit of project information was included, simplified drawing conventions (such as a solid mass for a wall, rather than a model of a studwall assembly) and symbols must be used, just as in drafting. Every simplified modeled

▶

FIGURE 7-3   This working drawing of a post office lobby was projected into three dimensions to illustrate the relationships between the plan and various elevations. Buday Wells, Architects; property of US Postal Service.

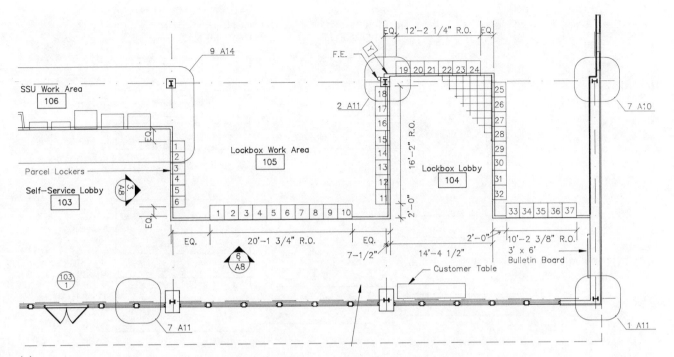

(a)

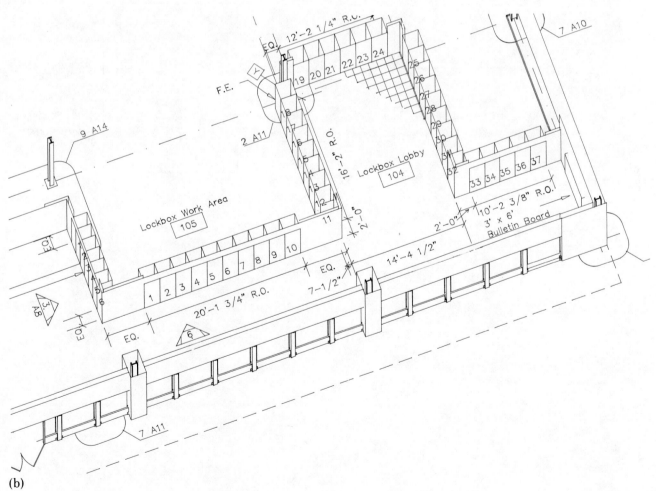

(b)

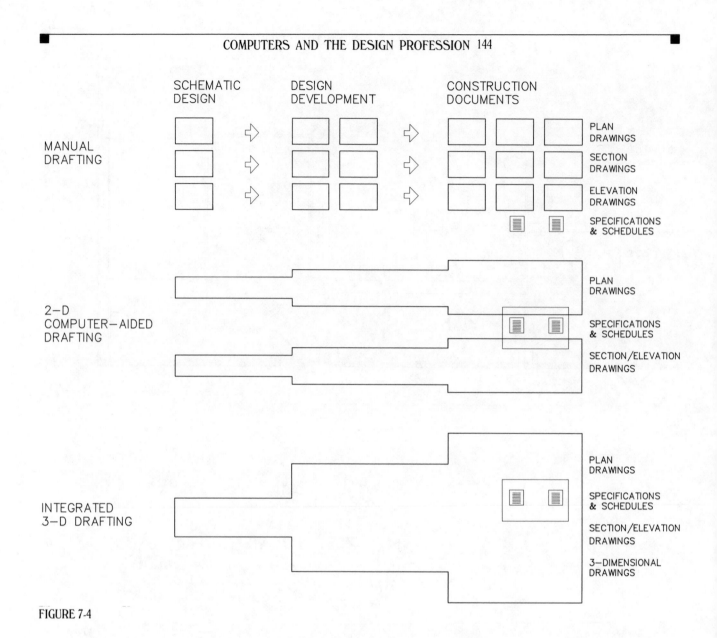

SCHEMATIC DESIGN

DESIGN DEVELOPMENT

CONSTRUCTION DOCUMENTS

MANUAL DRAFTING

PLAN DRAWINGS

SECTION DRAWINGS

ELEVATION DRAWINGS

SPECIFICATIONS & SCHEDULES

2-D COMPUTER-AIDED DRAFTING

PLAN DRAWINGS

SPECIFICATIONS & SCHEDULES

SECTION/ELEVATION DRAWINGS

INTEGRATED 3-D DRAFTING

PLAN DRAWINGS

SPECIFICATIONS & SCHEDULES

SECTION/ELEVATION DRAWINGS

3-DIMENSIONAL DRAWINGS

FIGURE 7-4

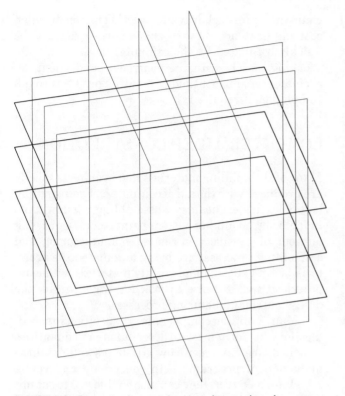

FIGURE 7-5   Planes (or drawing sheets) meshing in three dimensions.

element can be linked to a separate detailed model that describes its dimensions and materials in detail. When the detail is revised, the full model is updated.

You gain, above all, consistency and continuity. When an entire project is contained within a single data file or a set of linked files, there can be no changes that are omitted from other drawings. It's almost like actual building: you can't put two things in one place.

COMMUNICATION AND CONTROL

Drafting with multiple layers can help to break down some of the barriers to project coordination that are inherent in paper drawings. As a design evolves, the architect is faced with monitoring the simultaneous progress of different designers, drafters, and consultants, keeping their information up to date, and accommodating modifications that often occur at the last minute.

Communication

Communication among architects, consultants and builders often makes the difference between the suc-

cess and failure of a design project. If an architect and consultant use the same (or compatible) CAD software, information can be exchanged electronically with improved speed and accuracy.

Generally, drawings and information are exchanged in person at meetings, by mail or messenger, and projects are discussed by telephone. Even a large, "under one roof" architecture and engineering firm must exchange information with outside parties, while small firms sometimes send drawings out every day. The exchange of paper drawings is costly, inconvenient, and slow. It frequently means that various consultants receive different versions of a drawing set and that drawings have been changed between the time prints are sent and received.

Once a set of drawings is drawn with a computer, it becomes much easier to share than a set of paper drawings. Of course, prints and sepias may still be exchanged, but a whole project can be copied onto one or two disks and exchanged much more easily. Instead of sending drawings by messenger, they can be transmitted over the phone with a modem: a fairly large drawing can be sent in 10 to 30 minutes. (Computers can also be linked to telefax printers to produce "hard copy" at the other end of a phone line.) Once a consultant has an electronic copy of a drawing, he or she can make paper copies at any time.

When an architect and consultant have the same drawing, they can discuss it by phone, but to point and sketch they need to meet in person, unless they have a visual telephone link. Video phone connections rely on special phone circuits that are not yet widely available, but the increasing speed of modem links is making rapid transmission of electronic drawings feasible. Very fast phone links can enable you to exchange sketches or actually work on a drawing over phone lines, while talking.

Seeing Clearly

Layered drawings and models can help you to pick apart a project by discipline, seeing any one part in relation to any other part. If you can see many kinds of information at once or in chosen combinations, you may find it easier to keep a handle on a complex project. Layering can help you to be sure that the contributions of individuals or consultants mesh properly; it can also simplify the coordination between various disciplines. Revised layers can be distributed via disk or modem at any time and inserted into a consultant's base drawings. The simplicity of this updating process can help prevent the kind of conflicts that result from consultants working in isolation on outdated base drawings.

Quick Changes

As we have seen, database management capabilities, built into graphics software, provide the opportunity to link designs with materials lists and specifications. Since materials and construction methods can be specified, recorded, or changed *at any point* during design and documentation, it is easier to make material choices and specification writing part of the design process. After-the-fact schedule-writing and specification writing can be avoided, as can many of the errors that result from changing drawings without changing schedules or specifications.

The ability to quickly modify a design and automatically update documentation can encourage an increased spontaneity in design. Traditionally, major changes during the final stages of documentation are to be avoided, while changes during construction are often traumatic. Unfortunately, it is often during the working drawing stage that mistakes are discovered and new ideas arise, but it's "too late" to change anything, since manually redrawing one or more sheets is too expensive. If major changes can be made by moving groups of objects and notes or by substituting alternatives, design can safely continue until the final plots are made.

These capabilities can relieve some of the pressures of "fast track" design, in which design continues during construction. Quick drawing and rapid revisions are crucial to fast tracked projects, as are frequent, precise communications with consultants and, of course, the general contractor. Fast-tracking may be one of the first applications in which CAD routinely appears on the construction site. Nevertheless, fast tracking is still a costly, somewhat risky technique, and, while computer-aided design methods can speed the process, they do not reduce the expense or risk.

Design *revision* during construction can have advantages. Every architect knows the feeling of standing in an unfinished building, thinking "if I had only thought of that sooner . . ." and wishing a change was still possible. With the ability to replot drawings and update materials lists and engineering, changes can be made much more readily during construction. Change orders, amendments to the contract documents, are usually more clear if they include revised graphics; with computer aid these changes may then become part of the final record drawings. Change orders often involve, for example, changes or relocations of repetitive elements that are very difficult to change on paper drawings, but must be done quickly. Using CAD you can avoid the difficulty of major changes on finished drawing sheets. The construction cost implications of every change order can also be quickly estimated by the computer, as we shall see. Working closely with the contractor and client, an architect can thus continue to modify a project through completion, if required.

COMPUTER-AIDED CONSTRUCTION

Many of the building materials that architects specify are produced with the aid of computers. From drilling bolt holes in steel beams, to assembling window units in factories, to mixing custom paint colors, a growing number of construction-related manufacturing and assembling processes are being automated. As architects begin to design and specify materials with computers, it makes sense to look for ways to link the design and manufacturing processes.

Many building components are specified in schedules, long lists of items with descriptions and quantities attached. We have seen how attributes and database management programs help you create and revise schedules *on paper;* they can also enable you to submit lists, on disk or via modem, in a format specified by a building product's source or manufacturer. These lists can go directly into the supplier's computer and be used to order or even to custom manufacture the needed items. Not only is this process quicker than ordering verbally or on paper, but it is far less error-prone, since copying is eliminated. Since few large jobs are completed without a few ordering errors, which often require days or weeks of waiting for reorder, this can be a very useful tool.

Computer-aided manufacturing techniques often use CAD-produced drawings as guides for machine cutting, drilling, and assembly of components. These drawings are the electronic equivalent of shop drawings. With compatible CAD systems (or interchange capabilities), it is possible to develop shop drawings from architectural CAD drawings, then use them directly in production of, say, wood cabinets or steel framing members. Automated production techniques can also be applied to wood millwork, sheet metal fabrication, concrete-form design, and numerous other decorative or structural elements.

The first steps toward bringing computers to the construction site were taken in a similar manner by the prefabricated housing industry in the 1970s, when computers were used to produce detailed layouts of different panel and roof truss variations. Computer-aided manufacturing is now commonly used in truss construction for dimensioning, automatically engineering, and controlling the cutting and assembly. In some cases, local retailers and contractors have the software to design the trusses for factory assembly. In Japan, prefabricated-housing manufacturers are using CAD/ CAM for a wide range of component design and assembly tasks. Although these operations are done in a factory setting, it's easy to see how these techniques can be used on a construction site, as computers become less expensive, more durable, and more portable. In addition to viewing drawings on video displays and plotting details as needed, it is possible to use specialized printers and plotters to produce full-scale templates and layout tapes for wall construction.

Mechanical engineers often produce electronic models that are used directly, on a video screen, in the production process. Is it too farfetched to think that on-site electronic models will soon be an important part of the construction process? On a construction site, the traditional stack of drawings may be replaced with a computer model, ready to display dimensioned views on request. As software allows sophisticated cross-referencing between models and detail libraries, you will be able to point to a detail and automatically call the appropriate drawing to the screen. Builders will be able to pick areas of interest and display them in two- or three-dimensional views. Selected strings of

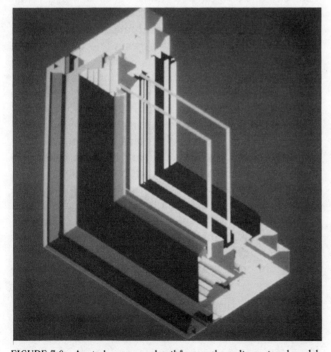

FIGURE 7-6   A window corner detail from a three-dimensional model with surfaces shaded (in color). CADS, Inc./Design Professionals, Inc.

dimensions can be displayed and printouts can be generated on-site each time a view is requested (Figure 7-6).

THE INFORMATION DELUGE

Every design firm has a library of manufacturer's catalogs, handbooks, design references and magazines. Keeping these resources current and readily accessible is a daunting task; some large firms hire librarians to keep references organized. Computers have increased the flow of information significantly, since writing and publishing has been speeded up considerably. Huge information databases, many of which contain information on building materials and systems, real estate and development, and the construction industry, can be tapped, for a fee, with a modem-equipped personal computer. However, one new form of data storage, compact laser-disk (CD-ROM, see Chapter 2), offers even better means of getting a large portion of this deluge under control.

CD-ROM has the unique advantage of being able to store encyclopedic quantities of information on a single inexpensive disk. This information can be cross-referenced so as to be quickly and simply accessible via a small computer. It can also be *extracted* and used directly in text or drawings. In short, it is an ideal medium for storing the immense amounts of information that make up an architectural reference library.

Manufacturer's catalogs, including the multivolume Sweet's, make up the bulk of any architectural library. As these become available on CD-ROM, they will take up less space and be easier to update, and they can also serve as a vast library for standard details. Traditionally, these catalogs have supplied representative tracing details; now they can contain full sets of details for all their products in a form that can be inserted directly into CAD drawings. Electronic catalogs can be used much more readily as mix-and-match source books, much like the old pattern books used by 19th century house designers.

As the various other elements of the architectural library become available in electronic format, we may find that they too are more useful. Cost-estimation manuals, which must also be updated periodically, are far easier to use on disk, since retyping tables is unnecessary. Building codes, including electrical, plumbing, and handicapped, may be easier to manage if they are carefully cross-referenced on a single disk, enabling you to extract all the codes pertinent to a specific building type. A reference book such as *Architectural Graphic Standards* could become an interactive tool, providing generic graphic details that could be inserted and modified in your work. Such a reference could also supply ready-to-use numeric spreadsheets to calculate dimensions, spans and insulation requirements, rather than listing passive tables. Finally, we may soon find libraries of architectural books and complete editions of periodicals available on CD-ROM, with full-color illustrations of a myriad of architectural projects, ready to be called on for reference at any time. Compact disks make libraries of three-dimensional models as feasible as libraries of drawings, so don't be surprised to see three-dimensional architecture magazines, with buildings you can "walk through," in the near future.

EXTENDING YOUR REACH

Architects are expected to be familiar with many specialized fields. For this reason, we work in teams, make use of libraries of reference material, and consult with experts in fields like engineering and construction. Although this arrangement is often satisfactory, it sometimes disrupts the continuity of the design process: consultants aren't always there when you need them. Sometimes we must design small projects with minimal input from consultants, while at other times the design of a large project will require specialized information simply to converse with and coordinate consultants. When problems arise that can be solved without a consultant or when a consultant is not available, you may want to make use of specialized, discipline-specific programs. You may also find tools that enable you to extend your in-house capabilities and provide services that were previously beyond your reach.

When new skills or new tools are introduced into a profession, they tend to be adopted by individuals who quickly become "specialists." This often occurs within a design firm upon the introduction of computer-aided design, and it can happen with other tools, such as the ones outlined in this section. However, increased specialization persists only if a tool is so difficult to learn or use that it requires a significant extra effort. In some cases, new software will continue to require users to be specially trained but may help bring specialized skills into the design process. The trend, however, is toward generalized, easy-to-use software that can be used without great extra effort.

We will look, here, at some examples of specialized software that can extend your abilities to visualize and solve design-related problems; in the next section we will examine software that goes one step further, toward actual decision making.

INTEGRATED ENGINEERING

Traditionally, architects estimate structural and mechanical requirements by rules of thumb or rough calculation, then refine these estimates with the help of a professional engineer. For example, an experienced designer can usually estimate structural sizes very accurately. Since engineers are often not trained to understand the architectural implications of their decisions, it is important that architects be closely involved in the design and specification process. Architecturally-oriented engineering software can provide a way for an architect to try out designs that require engineering expertise or to evaluate consultant's work independently.

Number Crunching

Nongraphic engineering software has greatly reduced the amount of "number crunching" that an engineer must do, allowing more time for the study of alternatives and reducing the likelihood of math errors. Some architectural firms have adopted these programs for in-house engineering, enabling them to make very accurate "first passes" at calculations, which an engineer can use as a base for more detailed work. When designers can conduct "what-if" studies as they design, they have an opportunity to evaluate the practicality of their ideas. This process is especially effective when architect and engineer are using the same software and can exchange information via computer.

Architects are usually familiar enough with the principles behind structures, HVAC, lighting, and other disciplines that they can use engineering-calculation software that requires only basic information (such as areas, uses, and occupancy levels). Engineering software for architects must be easy to use, but it must not give the impression that it is replacing the function of engineers. It should simplify the calculation of straightforward problems and provide the ability to approximate solutions to difficult problems, while making clear the need to consult with specialists for all but the simplest situations.

Graphic Engineering

Another kind of engineering program brings engineering directly into the design process. *Graphic-based* engineering programs work with computer-aided design software: for example, as you draw structural elements you can specify materials and loading conditions and the computer will calculate the size of a beam or column for you, based on the dimensions you have drawn. An integrated HVAC engineering program can perform heat-loss/gain calculations based on your drawing or model, totalling surface area, volume, window area, and insulation values, based on climatic information (from a climate database) and the orientation of the building.

Graphic-based engineering was first developed

FIGURE 7-7   These two illustrations, photographed directly from a full-color screen image, were created using Lumen lighting-engineering software. The program allows a designer to position natural and artificial light sources and specify their direction and intensity, permitting "what-if" studies of different lighting configurations. Points of view may be selected in three-dimensional space. Lighting Technologies, Boulder, Colorado.

for large computers, but programs are appearing that work with microcomputer CAD systems. As it becomes widely available and easy to use, this tool will become an invaluable part of the design process. When you can conveniently check structural sizes as you work with a high degree of accuracy, you can avoid many of the clearance problems and detailing conflicts that often appear late in a project. Even more important, you can try out different structural systems and immediately see the resulting sizes, or you can try out shading systems and see the heat-gain figures. You can look at a variety of alternatives, even new, unfamiliar ones, with confidence that your results will be realistic and accurate. Of course, your assumptions must be correct, so you must be familiar with an engineering discipline or work closely with an engineer, or both.

Computer programs have been developed for most aspects of architectural technology, including solar energy applications, lighting (Figure 7-7), acoustics, plumbing, site engineering, heating, cooling, and most aspects of structural engineering. More and more of these programs feature graphic interfaces, opening areas that have traditionally been strictly numeric to the visual world of the architect.

Architects will continue to rely on engineers for the expertise to suggest solutions to difficult problems and to validate all calculations. However, integrated engineering may ultimately improve the quality of building engineering by bringing it directly into the design process and giving designers greater use of skills that they have long considered too cumbersome to fully develop.

COST CONTROL

Electronic **spreadsheets** are computer programs that enable you to set up tables that include invisible, embedded formulas that will automatically calculate and recalculate rows and columns of numbers. Traditionally, manual (paper) spreadsheets, assembled by combining lists of materials with unit costs from reference guides, have been used for estimating construction costs. Because this process is so labor intensive and error-prone, electronic spreadsheets for cost estimating were one of the first computer tools to be adopted by the construction industry.

Although a project's cost is rarely determined before it is bid by contractors, a designer is responsible for keeping it as close to budget as possible as the design progresses. Generally, this is accomplished through estimates based on rough costs per square foot, although a project will sometimes be submitted to a professional estimator or contractor for a preliminary estimate. The traditional tools for producing estimates are detailed cost-data reference books, which are updated yearly, and a pencil and paper. Now that the pencil and paper are essentially obsolete, the cost-estimating books are being produced in electronic database format. The information from these databases may be transferred into a spreadsheet program and used to quickly estimate the cost of a proposed project. From the earliest schematic design to the completion of working drawings, these tools enable you to keep a running estimate of project cost. Initially, costs may still be calculated from tables that link floor area or building volume with data regarding building type and construction system; later, you can use CAD attributes to list precise materials and quantities and calculate costs with excellent accuracy.

Computerized cost estimation is so easy that any architect can use it while working on a project. A typical estimating spreadsheet will have a row for each material or assembly and columns for quantities, labor, and material costs (per unit or square foot), adjustment factors like local multipliers or inflation indexes, and totals. Once you have set up the basic spreadsheet format (or you can use purchased front-end programs for your spreadsheet) and you have chosen lists of materials, all you need to do is enter quantities, roughly at first and precisely later. Programs are available that will automatically enter material quantities, based on the attributes you specify as you draw. Using this kind of *integrated cost estimating*, you can keep track of the cost implications of design decisions as you make them; you can conveniently conduct what-if studies of alternative construction types and space sizes as you consider them.

PROGRAMMING AND SPACE PLANNING

The creation and analysis of a building program (using the word in the architectural sense, meaning the requirements for a proposed project) can be a very complex task. It must include space sizes and adjacencies, functional requirements, site considerations, budget allocation, and a range of other criteria. One of the more difficult parts of digesting a program is understanding the adjacency requirements of a large number of spaces. In a building program with many different kinds of spaces, it can be very difficult to represent these relationships either graphically or verbally. It is often even more difficult to *use* an analysis, once it has been carried out, in design and space planning.

Affinities

One tool for grappling with adjacency analysis is the *affinity matrix*. By listing the proposed rooms or areas along two perpendicular axes, a grid is created on which a rating is applied to the desirability of locating two spaces next to each other. Although this technique has been around for years, it is not especially popular because once an analysis is conducted, it is still difficult to refer to the matrix in a convenient manner.

Software for producing computer-assisted matrices is available to make the task of analyzing adjacencies less difficult. It assists by providing a predesigned format that can be linked to the area requirements and organizational hierarchies of program itself. After you assign numbers that represent the desirability of all possible adjacencies, the software will display desirability factors in color tones or hatch patterns, rather than numbers (Figure 7-8a).

In order to make the matrix more useful, it can be used with a schematic-design graphics program. The matrix adjacency values can be linked to two-dimensional shapes that represent the relative sizes of each area. After you specify a tentative building perimeter, organized according to a proposed circulation scheme, the program will arrange the spaces according to the most desirable proximities and the constraints of available space. They may be displayed with their adjacency color codes or with a different coding, such as department or use type.

A space-planning program may be used to assign spaces in a multistory building (*stacking*), or to lay out preliminary floor plans (*blocking*) (Figure 7-8 *b* and *c*). After a schematic organization is developed, it may be transferred into a drafting or modeling program for further development. This is an example of software that automates the design process according to *design rules*. We will look at this and other examples of *rule systems* more closely later in this chapter.

Space Planning

"Space planning" is often an important part of the design of an office or institutional building. An architect, interior designer or facility planner must plan the organization of offices, equipment, workstations and their required electrical and mechanical support, based on the architectural design and the user's needs. Sometimes this is part of the design process; in which case an architect can use symbols with attributes to keep track of areas and equipment quantities throughout the design (Figure 7-9). Often space planning is an after-the-fact undertaking by an outside consultant. In this situation, design work by a consultant can be greatly simplified by the use of computer-based architectural and mechanical drawings. Information can be assembled quickly by the consultant, and much redrawing can be avoided. (In many cases the architect may be compensated for the material supplied to outside consultants.)

Work cubicles on moveable partition systems are an excellent example. Manufacturers of these systems often provide drawing library catalogs of their products in formats for several different CAD systems. Typically, these can be used in numerous configurations, which you can experiment with as a building design takes shape (Figure 7-10). These graphics can be used to test space sizes and clearances, then to help locate mechanical and electrical systems. They can be used for cost estimating, and finally, for actually ordering partitions.

PLANNING AND URBAN DESIGN

Computer-aided mapping, a highly specialized form of computer graphics, is often used with database management techniques for analyzing and solving planning and urban design problems. When a multitude of factors, such as census data, demographics, property ownership and turnover, and traffic movement, must be simultaneously considered in a complex planning problem, computers can be used to sort them into reports and into visually coded maps. This information may then be used in developing design criteria and in making planning and design decisions.

One of the problems with computerized planning has been that planners, armed with mainframe computers and huge databases, have had a near monopoly on the information that is the foundation for planning decisions. Urban designers and planning consultants have had to rely on sometimes sparsely published information or on the willingness of planning bureaucracies to prepare reports on request. Planning departments have been able to use their control of information to buttress planning decisions, which often go unchallenged. Constituencies that are not adequately represented by planners have often been forced to rely on undocumented, subjective arguments in proposing alternatives.

The large databases that are maintained by federal, state, and local agencies are becoming available in small-computer formats that can be used with common database management software. Simultaneously, maps of cities are appearing in formats that can be used by low-end CAD systems. This availability enables architects, urban designers and planning consultants to work more effectively. There is also the

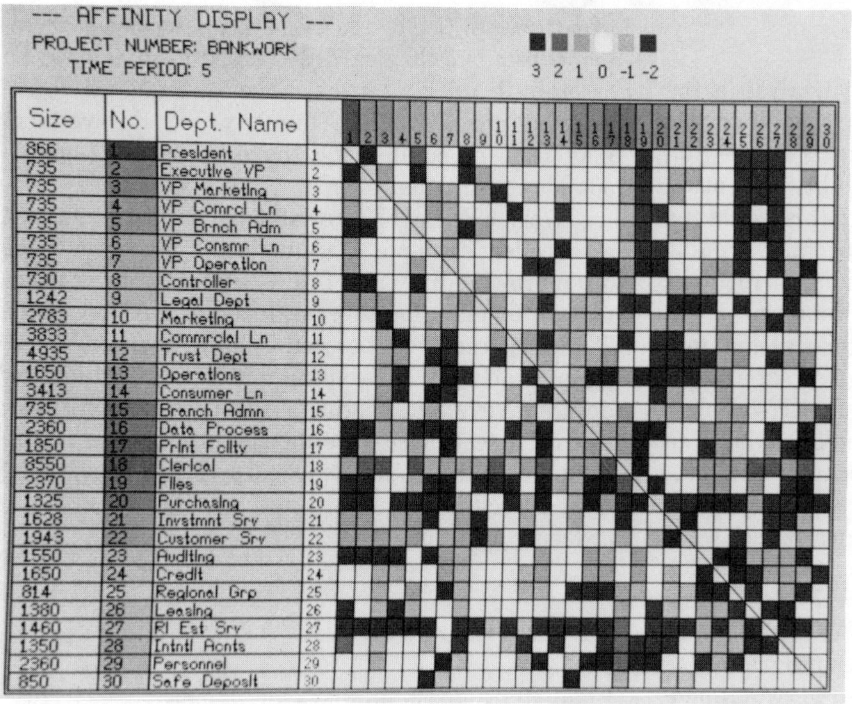

--- AFFINITY DISPLAY ---
PROJECT NUMBER: BANKWORK
TIME PERIOD: 5

3 2 1 0 -1 -2

Size	No.	Dept. Name	
866	1	President	1
735	2	Executive VP	2
735	3	VP Marketing	3
735	4	VP Comrcl Ln	4
735	5	VP Brnch Adm	5
735	6	VP Consmr Ln	6
735	7	VP Operation	7
730	8	Controller	8
1242	9	Legal Dept	9
2783	10	Marketing	10
3833	11	Commrclal Ln	11
4935	12	Trust Dept	12
1650	13	Operations	13
3413	14	Consumer Ln	14
735	15	Branch Admn	15
2360	16	Data Process	16
1850	17	Print Fclty	17
8550	18	Clerical	18
2370	19	Files	19
1325	20	Purchasing	20
1628	21	Invstmnt Srv	21
1943	22	Customer Srv	22
1550	23	Auditing	23
1650	24	Credit	24
814	25	Regional Grp	25
1380	26	Leasing	26
1460	27	Rl Est Srv	27
1350	28	Intntl Acnts	28
2360	29	Personnel	29
850	30	Safe Deposit	30

(a)

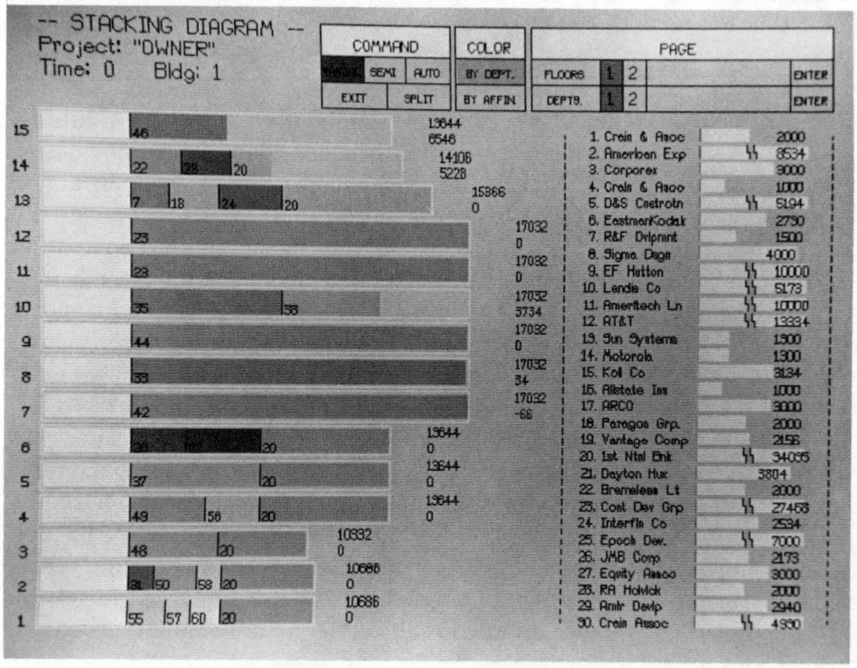

-- STACKING DIAGRAM --
Project: "OWNER"
Time: 0   Bldg: 1

COMMAND		COLOR		PAGE		
SEMI	AUTO	BY DEPT.	FLOORS	1	2	ENTER
EXIT	SPLIT	BY AFFIN	DEPTS.	1	2	ENTER

Floor		Values
15	46	13644 / 6546
14	22 28 20	14106 / 5228
13	7 18 24 20	15366 / 0
12	23	17032 / 0
11	23	17032 / 0
10	35 38	17032 / 3734
9	44	17032 / 0
8	33	17032 / 34
7	42	17032 / -66
6	36 20	13644 / 0
5	37 20	13644 / 0
4	49 56 20	13644 / 0
3	48 20	10332 / 0
2	31 50 58 20	10686 / 0
1	55 57 60 20	10686 / 0

No.	Name		Value
1	Crain & Assoc		2000
2	American Exp	⅍	8534
3	Corporex		9000
4	Crain & Assoc		1000
5	D&S Cnstrctn	⅍	5194
6	EastmanKodak		2750
7	R&F Drlprnt		1500
8	Sigma Data		4000
9	EF Hutton	⅍	10000
10	Landis Co		5173
11	Ameritech Ln	⅍	10000
12	AT&T	⅍	13334
13	Sun Systems		1300
14	Motorola		1300
15	Kal Co		3134
16	Allstate Ins		1000
17	ARCO		9000
18	Paragon Grp.		2000
19	Vantage Comp		2456
20	1st Ntnl Bnk	⅍	34035
21	Dayton Hux		3804
22	Bramlees Lt		3000
23	Cont Dev Grp	⅍	27458
24	Interfin Co		2534
25	Epoch Dev.	⅍	7000
26	JMB Comp		2173
27	Equity Assoc		3000
28	RA Holvick		2000
29	Amr Devlp		2940
30	Crain Assoc	⅍	4330

(b)

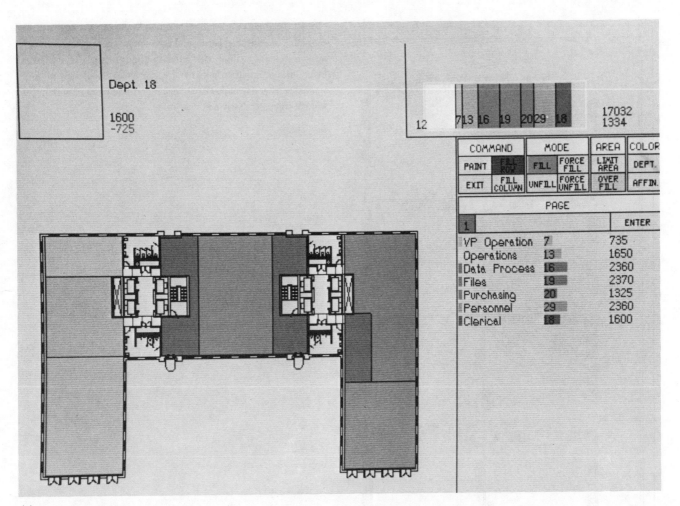

(c)

FIGURE 7-8   These three photos from a color display illustrate a computer-assisted schematic design and space planning program. In (a), an affinity matrix is used to chart desirable proximities, using color coding to signify degrees of preference. In the following illustration (b), the various spaces are allocated ("stacked") to different levels of a multistoried building, according to affinities. Finally, the computer can "block" space within each floor according to area requirements and desirable proximities (c). The designer can intervene at various stages or allow the computer to conduct a number of studies using different criteria. Sigma Design; images created with Space Planning/Facilities Management Software.

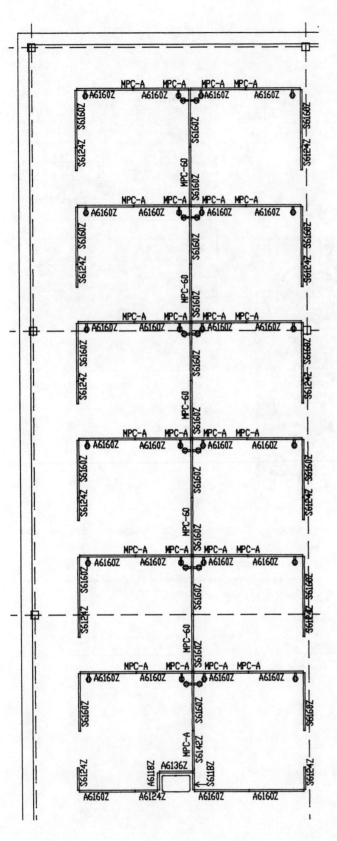

FIGURE 7-9 This workstation/partition layout utilizes attributes to keep track of individual panels and accessories. The attributes can be easily counted to facilitate cost estimating and ordering of components. In an office plan that includes hundreds or thousands of these workstations, it is nearly impossible to count partition types accurately without computer assistance.

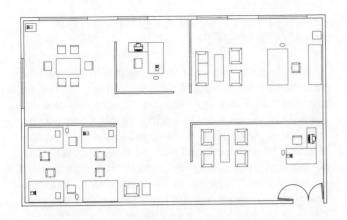

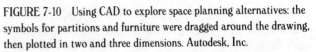

FIGURE 7-10 Using CAD to explore space planning alternatives: the symbols for partitions and furniture were dragged around the drawing, then plotted in two and three dimensions. Autodesk, Inc.

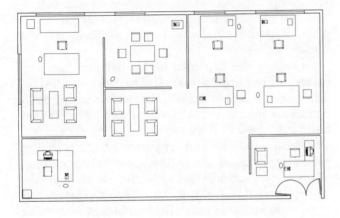

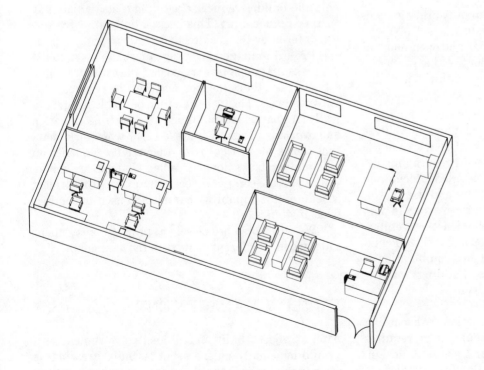

potential for simplifying land use analysis, resource, and utility mapping, as well as planning of services such as transportation, schools, recreation facilities, and libraries. Mapping software, which links databases with geographic or political maps, is increasing in sophistication, and discipline-specific programs are becoming available for many specific analysis and design tasks.

Mapping

Here are some examples of planning problems that might be handled with the assistance of computerized mapping.

- A transportation designer wishes to ensure that all residents live within a 10-minute walk of a mass transit stop. He or she can conduct a "what-if" study of various routes, with the computer illustrating walking distances from proposed stops.

- Prior to beginning a large construction project, an architect's consultant needs to know the sizes and condition of subsurface utilities serving the site. This information might be kept routinely on the consultant's computer, rather than buried in a city hall file or, worse, scattered among several utility companies. A map could quickly be produced that illustrated routes, sizes, elevations, and age of utility lines.

- Before designing a new community athletic facility, an architect might produce a set of maps illustrating the locations, types, and open-hours of other nearby facilities, in order to reduce unnecessary duplication of facilities within short distances.

- Census data, already available in electronic form, can be used with mapping graphics to analyze population distribution. A school district can use this to project future enrollment, geographically. It can combine this data with detailed information on the conditions of its facilities and use the information in conjunction with census data to plan maintenance and new construction. An architectural consultant could develop a prioritized capital improvement plan, based on a combination of neighborhood requirements, building maintenance requirements, and budget.

While large amounts of information are becoming widely available in electronic form, it often requires specialized skills to analyze it and use it in design. Nevertheless, this increased availability promises to enable designers to provide more thorough planning analysis at a lower cost.

CONSTRUCTION PLANNING AND MANAGEMENT

Although construction management falls outside the architect's role in all but designer–builder firms, an architect must always consider the construction sequences in which a project will be built. Construction scheduling will often have a major impact on the selection of materials and details, since a smooth flow of work is enormously important in keeping costs under control. It is often very helpful to examine construction sequences during the working drawing phase, in order to develop an efficient building system. The earlier construction planning begins, the better, and computerized project management can help a designer (or construction consultant) to start planning when it would otherwise be too difficult or time consuming.

In situations in which highly detailed cost estimates are required, a carefully considered schedule can be used to estimate both labor and financing costs by calculating the overall construction time. When a builder is chosen before contract documents are finished or in a design-build arrangement, this planning can be very detailed. If a builder is selected via bidding, a "suggested" construction sequence may nevertheless be very useful in pointing out efficient construction methods, which may result in lower bids. A competent plan, which the builder may take over and use, may help the builder reduce scheduling costs, which may further reduce bids. (This is essentially an extra service offered by the architect.)

Project management programs enable you to list the tasks that must be carried out, the estimated time for each task, the sequences, and the interrelationships between tasks. The tasks can then be displayed graphically as a bar chart that illustrates the time, duration and overlap of each, (Figure 7-11) or a network chart that shows the *critical path*, the activity sequence on which other tasks depend. When changes are made, you can let the computer recalculate the entire project schedule; this capability can also be used to conduct what-if studies.

We will look more closely at project management software in a different context in the next chapter.

FACILITY MANAGEMENT

After a project is built, an architect's involvement with a building usually ends. A set of "as built" drawings is often turned over to the client as a reference for space planning, interior design, maintenance and repairs, or future renovation. When modifications are made to the

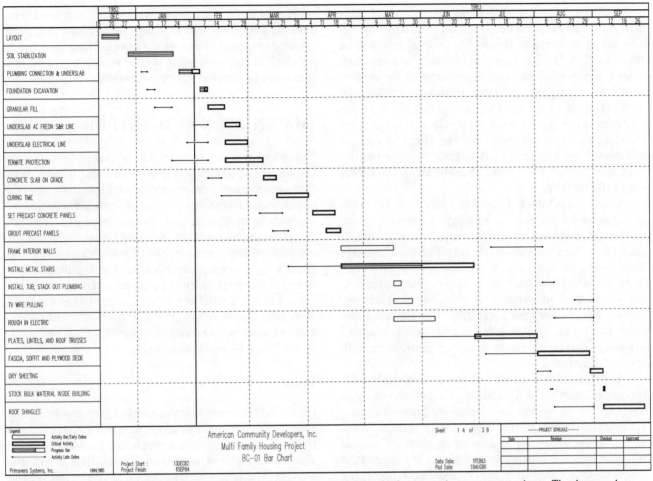

FIGURE 7-11 A bar chart (or Gantt chart) illustrates the timing and overlap of various activities in a construction project. This chart also highlights the critical path, the sequence of activities that must be completed before succeeding activities can begin. The chart can be quickly revised as time estimates are altered or as the project progresses. Primavera Systems, Inc.

building, these drawings are used as a base for the creation of new drawings.

All the activities that are required to operate a building are often lumped together under the title **Facility Management.** Specialization in facility management has become a profession in itself, particularly for large buildings and complexes. However, since managing a building is largely a matter of implementing the functions that a building is designed to support, some architects have begun to add facility management to the services they offer.

Management of a building or complex includes an extension of architectural services like space planning and interior design, but also goes far beyond architecture. It includes everything from inventory control to energy and communication systems to maintenance and renovation. Most important of all, facility management includes fitting organizations and operations

to a building, and vice versa. Although these services are a major departure from traditional architectural services, there are some persuasive reasons why architects might choose to continue their involvement with a building after the initial construction is finished. Some of these reasons involve CAD.

The best time to begin managing a facility is before it is built. To begin with, architectural drawings and materials lists often form the base on which facility management is built, and electronic drawings and databases are far more useful tools to the facility manager than are paper drawings and lists. An accurate set of as-built drawings can be used for years for management purposes, and lists of partitions, fixtures and mechanical equipment can be maintained and updated, *if they are created in a form that will continue to be usable.* Essentially, the architect must provide drawing and data files in a manner that can realistically be used for a set of tasks that are radically different than construction. Although the addition of a new set of concerns to the design process is not to be taken on lightly, it is a service that can be added to a design contract or handled separately. A set of electronic drawings and a database can be supplied as a part of the fee, or the architect can retain these, under contract to use them for future services. It is far more efficient and less expensive for the client to pay for additional work by an architect than to pay a facility manager to start from zero, assembling all the necessary information.

Once an architect offers this additional service, it becomes more feasible to maintain a continuing involvement, either as an actual manager or as a consultant. Many large commercial and office buildings are undergoing almost constant changes, and often no one is in a better position to manage reorganization, modification, and renovation than the original designer. Remember that CAD drawings contain more than meet the eye, and familiarity with a set of drawings can be almost as useful as familiarity with the building itself.

Specialized computer software is available for facility management. In addition to systems that help operate HVAC, electrical, lighting, plumbing, and communications systems, there are programs available to plan, prioritize and estimate costs for capital improvements. Although these systems are beyond the scope of this book, they are increasingly becoming relevant to the practice of architecture. It may be that this kind of planning and control will lead architects into a cradle-to-grave involvement with the buildings they design.

EXPERT ASSISTANCE

Can a computer program create architecture? Can computer-aided design software design without human aid? The mere thought of this conjures up images of runaway computers forcing their will upon the public. Although the reality is not so dramatic, the notion of automated design is disturbing to the architectural profession. It is important to remember that computers don't do *anything* on their own: they must always be told what to do and how to do it. The issues we are facing concern *who* decides which tasks will be automated and *who* provides the instructions to the computer.

Are architects interested in handing over any of their creative work to machines? Even if not, are there reasons why clients might begin to opt for computer-generated designs? Before we answer these questions, let's look at how we design, then at what kinds of design tasks can be carried out by a computer.

IMAGINATION AND METHOD

There are two common schools of thought regarding the nature of design. One, the more traditional, says that architecture is an intuitive art form that depends on the inspiration and talent of the individual designer. According to this school, design requires creative imagination as well as judgment that is based on experience and intuition. The other, which has gained popularity in recent decades, is that architecture is based on rational, learned methods that may be articulated and analyzed. Both views are true to some extent, since even the most "natural" designers have consistent ways of working, and since a design that has no "inspiration" may be especially boring.

Lists

If you wanted to explain to a nondesigner how to design a building, you could list a sequence of steps to follow. If the list was complete enough, the person might be able to design a reasonably sound building. We might wonder, though, who has designed the building: the person who wrote the list or the person who used it. Many basic design assumptions will be built into the list, but unless the list was extraordinarily specific, the building would reflect the personal experience and cultural values of the person using the instructions. Even with a very precise list, two different people would probably produce somewhat different results.

A specific design sequence like this is an example of a rigid design method. Design methods of many kinds have been described and taught at various times. Some are analytical, based on understanding and making use of existing or historical architecture. Others are procedural, advocating a series of steps to be followed. Still others are based on the use of specific requirements or rules. Some of these methods, such as Alexander's concept of *pattern languages*, are attempts to systemize the ways we tend to work subconsciously (or wish we worked). Others, such as a building code, are attempts to proscribe the results of our work, in order to guarantee a certain kind of product.

When a portion of the design process is reduced to a step-by-step sequence or a set of interrelated principles, it can potentially be simulated in a computer program. However, as we all know, designers do not work in a strictly linear fashion and depend upon being able to use ideas from a historical example one minute and from a structural principle the next. A successful design method recognizes this and depends upon it; even a mundane method like a building code usually allows a designer free reign on many issues. If a design method is to be successfully automated, it must either be capable of using a tremendous web of factors, or it must depend on a human to do so.

Making Decisions

Since computers are good at comparing things and making choices based on these comparisons, they can be programmed to carry out sequences of steps that are based on predetermined decisions. You can tell a computer that if certain conditions exist, then certain actions should be taken. This kind of "if-then" ability can allow a computer to simulate decision making, even though it must initially be told what decisions to make under each set of circumstances. The computer can be told that groups of factors are similar and that various combinations will produce similar results; it also can be told to remember the decisions that you have made in the past, and when similar circumstances arise, it can take the same action "by itself." The computer begins to appear that it is "thinking" and "learning," even though it is only acting according to the instructions and information it has been given by a human.

Just as the architect's list of steps for the nondesigner would carry the architect's knowledge and values, so do programs for automating design. Since the "decision-making" abilities of the software are based on a human's expertise, such programs are called **knowledge-based systems** or **expert systems.**

Almost any architect will be quick to point out that architecture is too complex to squeeze into an expert system. There are too many areas of expertise, linked in ways that are impossible to fully articulate, to capture in a computer program. Most computer programs use a *tree-structured* decision-making process that progresses from one "if-then" decision to the next. A map of all the possible decision paths forms a branching, treelike diagram. As Alexander pointed out in his essay "A City Is Not A Tree,"[2] real-world relationships can not be simplified into linear hierarchies. Instead, they are more like a lattice with

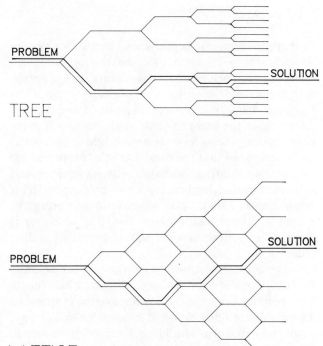

FIGURE 7-12 Decision making: the tree represents sequential, linear logic; the lattice allows decisions to jump from one path to another.

branches that intersect and cross (Figure 7-12). Likewise, architectural design decisions intertwine in countless ways that a machine cannot be programmed to duplicate.

In the foreseeable future, no computer will be able to take a client, a building program, a site, and a budget and combine them into a design that considers the full range of organizational, contextual, constructional, social, and aesthetic possibilities, *as well as a human designer can.* However, expert systems can be written that will address *part* of the design process, for better or worse.

Since architecture is so complex, it is difficult, perhaps impossible for an individual architect to become an expert in every area of the field. Working with consultants is often adequate, but consultants are not always as responsive, knowledgeable, or imaginative as we might like. Here, then is a possible role for packaged expert systems in architecture, as a supplement to the personal knowledge of an architect and his or her consultants.

We can look at several examples of supplementary expert systems, and then we will examine the notion of expert systems for design.

---

[2]Christopher Alexander, "A City Is Not a Tree," *Design*, February, 1966.

RULE SYSTEMS

Perhaps the simplest kind of knowledge-based system allows you to create sets of *rules* that the computer will use to either check your work or modify it. A program that checks your spelling is a rule system, since the computer has a list of correct spellings and a set of instructions for comparing it with what you type. Likewise, a *design rule system* might check your drawings to see that your walls are the proper thickness (differentiating, perhaps, between interior and exterior, bearing, nonbearing, and plumbing walls); it might check to see that the windows in your elevation were the proper height above the floor levels, or it might check your design with the appropriate building code.

Going a step further, the rule system can actually modify your work for you, according to whatever instructions it has been given. Perhaps you have specified a particular window type and location for each type of room you will use in a building. Once you have named the rooms in your plan, the program would add the appropriate windows without further prompting. This kind of technique is a useful supplement to the parametric drawing techniques we discussed in Chapter 5.

Parts of Problems

In theory, any problem that can be reduced to a finite number of variables can be automated by writing rules that cover various sets of conditions. Design problems, or *parts* of design problems, can sometimes be reduced to a manageable number of variables. Once this is accomplished, each design issue can be addressed and resolved according to a script of rules.

For example, bathrooms in commercial and institutional buildings are usually designed using standard fixtures, partitions, and wall surfaces, and using standard dimensions and layouts. The variables in a given situation might include the number of fixtures, available space, the entry location, and the plumbing-wall location. Each time a designer solves this problem, he or she will usually go through the same steps; in fact, bathroom design and detailing is not a particularly creative job. A computer program can be written to carry out these steps, assembling the graphics from a drawing library and creating material schedules and specifications.

Similar programs have been written for numerous concise design problems, such as exit stairs, elevators, moveable partitions, and the detailing of assemblies such as curtain walls and integrated ceiling systems.

Engineering problems, including structural, HVAC, acoustics, and lighting are particularly conducive to systematic rule-based solutions.

Many of these examples are repetitive tasks that often amount to "busywork" in a design or engineering firm. Large amounts of a designer's time can be spent designing similar details, over and over, which may not be the best use of a professional's abilities. Although drawing bathrooms is often used as a training ritual for novice designers and drafters, it can be argued that near-mindless work is a waste of time and that more creative work is better training. It can also be argued that it is important for any designer to learn the simple rules that go into designing a bathroom, otherwise, we may forget how to design them, or, more likely, simply assume that the computer is always right. Needless to say, it isn't: it often requires a human's "common sense" to understand the *context* of a particular problem.

Computer-generated drawings must, of course, be checked carefully, even though programs can be written that will flag most errors and uncertainties. It requires an understanding of design criteria to check designs, so it is important to retain this experience. Perhaps the most useful rule-based systems are those that can suggest alternatives and facilitate "what-if?" experimentation, since these leave the final choices to a designer.

More complex problems can be attempted by expert systems, but the programs must, of course, become correspondingly more complex. These programs are written not only to reduce repetitive work but also to provide a tool to solve problems that are difficult to do intuitively. Some engineering problems, such as complex statically indeterminate structures, can *only* be solved with computer assistance. Subjective problems like programming, building design, and building systems design can also be automated. Should they be?

CAN A COMPUTER DESIGN?

The compilation and analysis of a building program is an example of a process that can be undertaken by an expert system. Once a designer (or client) has placed values on the various adjacency relationships, the software can combine this information with the size of the spaces, then suggest alternative layouts. Of course, the more information that can be considered, the better. For example, the size and shape of the site should be considered, as should likely access points. The software might be able to choose among a list of organizational schemes (such as linear or centralized), or the designer might specify which is more appropriate.

There is nothing mysterious about the process: The program has been designed to locate spaces according to "if-then" logic. If the site is long and narrow, for example, and the rooms are small and must open to common circulation, then a double-loaded corridor might be suggested, with primary access at one end and service at the other. The software could be used to automatically generate dozens of possible organizations for one building program. Since it can consider a multitude of variables quickly, it may see relationships that a human designer would miss, or it might be able to suggest alternative organizations that a particular designer might not think of. However, the opposite is also possible: The software might well miss good options, if its programmer failed to consider enough different routines for solving a particular problem.

Here is one of the problems with expert systems: Experts are rarely infallible, and the results of a less-than-perfect expert system are worrisome. If the program is used to simply suggest alternatives, then it can be useful and relatively harmless. If, on the other hand, it is seen as the sole source of alternatives, then the insight of a human designer will be omitted from the process, perhaps at the expense of "the best" solution. As everyone knows, computers have no "common sense" and can miss a solution that seems obvious to a properly trained person.

If a human designer is completely withdrawn from the design process, the expert system becomes the sole judge of what is best. We all know horror stories about computers making ridiculous decisions that were not caught by people until too late, but could computer-aided design go this far? "Expert" systems might best be treated like entry-level designers, who may be given projects to work through but would rarely be expected to produce a finished design, unassisted.

Building Types

Expert systems have been written that automate the design process for specific building types. Buildings that require extremely specialized knowledge to design, such as hospitals or factories, can be condensed into elaborate sets of rules that must be managed by particularly sophisticated expert systems. In theory, a well-crafted expert system could enable a competent designer who has little experience with a specific building type to undertake a project that he or she might not have otherwise attempted. Such an expert system would be similar to a good design reference,

except that it would be an *interactive* design tool that would be capable of making suggestions and evaluating a designer's work.

Architecture in a Can

When expert systems are applied to simpler problems, the result may have different implications for architects. Imagine a house-design expert system: the software could request detailed program, site, and budget information from the client by asking the same questions an architect asks, regarding issues like space requirements, proximities, material preferences, and even about subjective matters like "image." The program would then organize the space, develop the massing and specify a building system and appropriate detailing. The process would be similar to that of the "expert" architect (or architects) after whom it was modeled. In theory, the result would be a building that the expert would have designed.

One early architectural expert system (produced at MIT, in 1972) was an attempt to write a program that could create Frank Lloyd Wright-esque Usonian houses. Given the program and site plan of one of Wright's clients, the software produced plans and a perspective that were remarkably similar to Wright's actual design.

If we assume that a house-design program works as intended, the next question becomes: who needs an architect? Perhaps the client may not need to hire an architect if he or she can buy a software package that does the same job. But remember that the client is essentially hiring an architect *in absentia*. If a market for "canned" design systems develops, it may become possible for any architect to mass-market design services by "recording" his or her design method. Although this seems somewhat bizarre, we may find CAD software publishers producing mass-marketed architectural expert systems for use by nonarchitects. Programs like this might be particularly attractive to housing developers or franchised businesses. A popular design program could produce the most widely built "style" in history.

The legal and professional implications of this scenario are hard to imagine, but several things are apparent. Many people who cannot afford custom design service at present may gain access to almost-custom automated service, and the architects who contribute to the software will be taking the place of those architects who design, say, developer tract housing. It also seems likely that designers will lose work if custom-design programs are good enough. Why hire an architect when you can buy one? However, architects may be able to use these systems to expand their base for custom services on many kinds of "low end" architectural projects, including commercial, retail, and industrial buildings. If an architect can use a computer to do the most time-consuming, expensive parts of the design process, providing personal service and quality assurance throughout, perhaps new markets may be opened up.

Finally, expert systems are being developed by architectural firms, initially for their own use, and later for sale to other firms. By using a purchased expert system for tasks like code analysis or bathroom design, a small firm can take on larger projects or make greater profits on small ones. This may also be true for more elaborate expert systems, but this brings us back to the question: who is the designer, the software author or the software user? Will the firms that use expert systems become design "subsidiaries" of the author firms? This may prove true in the case of rigid, proscriptive software; nevertheless, easy-to use, flexible expert systems may enable small firms to make better use of limited budgets and small staffs.

THE ELECTRONIC WORKPLACE

CHAPTER 8

There are no right and wrong ways to use a computer-aided design system, any more than there are right and wrong ways to design buildings or organize design offices. No two firms function identically, so there's no reason to think that one CAD strategy will work for everyone. Some ways may be more conducive to design work, others to production, and others may simply feel more comfortable. "Comfort" may seem like an intangible notion, but it is tremendously important in matching people and tools: CAD should fit your working style so that

you are hardly aware of its presence. If the tool doesn't fit, you may have to change either your style or your CAD setup; over time, they should evolve to fit each other.

Computer-aided design affects many of the most fundamental practices of a design firm. In addition to changes in design and drawing techniques, it imposes new roles and new routines on drafters, designers, managers, and support staff, in large firms and small practices alike. Some of these changes may significantly simplify day-to-day operations, while others may seem like bothersome concessions to automation.

Don't expect CAD to automatically organize your office: you have to do that. If your organization is a mess, using a computer will only automate your mess. Instead, do some thinking about how you work, what you do effectively, and what you do poorly. Whatever you do well, make sure that the CAD system will support it, not change it. Adapt the system as much as you can before you change what you are doing well. Try to use the transition period as an opportunity to improve problem areas. If you need to work on, say, drafting standards or project management, you can focus on these aspects of computer use. Use the tools to work on the problem, but don't expect tools to solve problems by themselves.

PLANNING: A LONG TERM VIEW

Design work inevitably requires a focus on the project at hand: it is often difficult to make plans beyond current work and marketing targets. For many firms, the most important planning concerns personnel—how many employees to maintain and how to keep them busy. Since architecture has been a labor-intensive profession, with relatively small equipment investments, this is to be expected.

Computers are among the most expensive investments some firms will ever make, so they require careful long-term planning. Not only can the initial costs of computer-aided design systems be high, but there are the continuing expenses of upgrading hardware and software, adding new workstations, and training people. Long-term planning is required for financing these investments, and strategies must be carefully developed for upgrading and expanding. Since architectural firms depend on an often-unpredictable flow of projects, planning ahead can be difficult. Add to this the ever-changing technology of computer hardware and CAD software, and you have a daunting planning task.

By setting up goals for the purchase of equipment and the training of personnel, then adapting these goals according to actual events, a relatively steady plan can be maintained. Develop a formula for timing new purchases, based on the amount of work to be done, the number of people and the rate of training, the amount of cash on hand, cash expected, and acceptable levels of debt. As each new project starts, the plan can be checked against the project's requirements ("do we have enough workstations?"), possible conflicts with other projects ("how do the schedules compare?"), and cash flow ("can we buy that new workstation now?"). In short, the process is similar to the traditional personnel hiring process, except that the long-term goals and financing commitments take on an increased importance.

FOUR STAGES

The introduction of CAD into a new setting seems to follow a four-stage process in large and small workplaces alike. Although the amount of time spent in each stage varies, the sequence seems almost inevitable.

First, when CAD arrives, a few people concentrate on learning to use the system and getting it "up to speed." Often these are the people who initiated the move to CAD or helped choose the system; sometimes they are people who have previous training, either in another workplace or in school. They are not necessarily people in management positions and are frequently at or near the entry level. Whatever their level of experience, the early users are either experienced with computers or are interested in exploring a new way of working and generally have a great deal of enthusiasm.

Meanwhile, the rest of the firm is usually interested in the system, but somewhat uncertain or nervous about it. There is often apprehension about the changes CAD will bring. In a larger firm, management will want to see results, but may not wish to get directly involved.

Second, there is a learning period, in which the general level of enthusiasm grows, but with occasional disillusionment. Since experience is low, there is much hit-or-miss usage as people discover what tasks the software is most appropriate for, and learning occurs largely by trial and error, with tips and cautions passed along verbally. There are often unforeseen expenditures, as training and purchases proceed on an ad-hoc basis. Projects, and pieces of projects, are often assigned to CAD randomly or according to personnel and equipment availability, with frequent changes in plans.

Third, there is a period of retrenchment as management feels a need to control expenses and scheduling conflicts. New controls are developed: more planning goes into deciding which project can best use CAD, criteria for setting up project teams are modified to emphasize computer skills, and project managers and project architects begin to become more familiar with the system. With experience, careful budgetary controls based on long-range plans are instituted, with procedures for modification over time.

Finally, the computer system becomes an accepted tool that requires little extra planning. Training is complete at all levels; teams know when to use CAD and when not to; scheduling is routine, with procedures for handling conflicts and charrettes. When budgets equal expenditures, management can virtually forget about the system, until a new level of technology comes along that may begin the process all over, but with the benefit of several years of experience with computer-aided design. CAD systems, like any other asset, must eventually be replaced, so the four stage process may become a cycle.

Every firm wants to arrive at the last stage as quickly as possible. The process can be speeded somewhat with the assistance of experienced people and the institution of a thorough training regimen, but nothing can substitute for actual project experience and careful evaluation of the results, followed by planning that uses the insights and talents of all involved.

STARTING ON THE RIGHT FOOT

As you introduce CAD into a design practice, it's crucial that you know from the start exactly what your goals are, even if they change as your experience grows. If your primary concern is automating drafting, then focus on this; if you have secondary goals,

then set up a timetable for reaching them. CAD can be used for many purposes, but you don't have to master them all at once.

An incremental approach might start with the aspect in which you most need to increase productivity, such as drafting plans, then gradually move to elevations and sections, then details, then begin full use of attributes, and finally a move into schematic design and three dimensions. Alternatively, you might choose to begin with an aspect you find the most interesting, say three-dimensional modeling, then begin producing presentation drawings, and finally move into two-dimensional drafting. The choice is up to you, but be sure you have good reasons, and try to plot a course in advance.

In a design firm, scheduling is based on the flow of projects as much as it is based on the calendar, and a CAD implementation program should recognize this. Try to choose projects that are appropriate to the aspects on which you will focus, but also be sure that you start with projects that are limited in size and not overly ambitious in schedule. There is no need to start with a project that will be designed and drawn completely on CAD; it may, in fact, be months or even years before you reach that point.

Even more crucial than *what* you will begin with is *who* you will begin with. We will examine, below, the various roles that people play in using a CAD system, but the most important factor is that people be interested in using the system. You can't force someone to use CAD, so the most effective way to introduce it into a firm is by letting the people who are most enthusiastic try it first, hopefully sparking interest in others. In addition, it is important that, from the start, CAD use not be limited to entry-level drafters. Everyone on a project team should be familiar with the CAD system; it is especially important that a project architect or project manager know its capabilities and limits, and these are best learned through direct experience.

Start Slowly

Perhaps the most important rule in starting out with computer-aided design is to *start slowly*. It can be very tempting to plunge into a big job with a new system, expecting an efficiency increase that will compensate for initial learning-time. This reasoning is particularly seductive if the job is being used to "pay for" the system. Whatever the circumstances, *don't start with too much riding on the job*.

In a large firm, it's usually a good idea to have someone around who has some experience with CAD to shepherd people through the learning process, to set up the system, and to help establish office conventions. In a smaller firm, this may not be feasible and is not necessarily as important. A small office is better suited to learning by trial and error, and information is shared more easily.

Training

When all CAD software was terribly difficult to learn, it was standard practice to train "CAD operators" outside the office, sometimes in far-away training centers. It could take anywhere from weeks to months of training to achieve proficiency, and when these people returned they were inevitably pigeonholed as specialists who were too valuable to do anything else. As CAD has become easier to use, the time required for outside training has been reduced to days (or eliminated), and training programs have appeared in most cities. Since CAD is now taught in most architecture schools and drafting programs, new employees often need no further training. They can often help introduce new techniques to co-workers.

It is not unreasonable to learn to use computer-aided design and drafting on the job, in the office, especially if there are experienced people around. All that is required is employee time, computer time, and a willingness on the part of the firm's management to support the learning process. The latter is particularly crucial, since pressure from one's boss to "produce" can make learning more difficult. Set aside time specifically for training people, and allocate a budget for covering training time. Since the firm will benefit from improved CAD skills, everyone, from an entry-level drafter to a project architect, should be fully paid for learning time.

"On-the-job training," for an individual or an entire firm, can be handled through a series of tasks. A novice should start with a short period of simple drawing operations to become familiar with the software and the manuals. This may begin with simple line-drawing, continue with a taste of each important feature, and end with drawing something that is of personal interest. This point can be reached in a day or two with easy-to-use software and an experienced co-worker or instructor available. After this, a student can begin working on useful work like developing drawing libraries or pieces of projects, *without time pressure*. It's a good idea to keep a list of noncrucial projects for training purposes. Finally, it is helpful if a beginner can spend some time on a project that has few time pressures before moving on to normal work. While this may not always be possible, it is highly desirable. The more time you have to explore the capabilities of the system, the more you will be able to take advantage of it. This applies to experienced people as well: try to reserve some time now and then to experiment. Allocate time (and a training budget) for this.

There are two drawbacks to on-the-job training. First, it takes longer than attending a training program, which is geared toward fast instruction. Second, it requires the use of valuable computer time. If the office is busy, it may be impossible to assign a workstation to training. Inevitably, workstations that are purchased for training purposes are taken over for jobs when things are busy, so you may be forced to choose between a flexible training schedule and sending people to a training site outside the office.

Outside Assistance

A compromise alternative is the use of a **service bureau**, especially when you are starting out with CAD. A service bureau is a drafting service that will produce drawings for you. Usually, drawings should stay "in-house" through production, but a service bureau that uses the same software as your firm can often provide suggestions, training, and general hand-holding as you get started. If you get into a pinch, they may be able to take over a drawing and finish it quickly. Even after you no longer need drawing assistance, they can continue to provide training services.

COSTS AND BENEFITS

Let's look more closely at some of the less obvious factors that need to be considered in evaluating a computer-aided design system.

The initial costs of starting up a CAD system, with many trial-and-error expenses and high training budgets added to hardware and software expenditures, are not typical of the long-term experience. However, there will be a continuing need to train people, explore new working strategies, and choose and implement new software. Some of these will be offset by the growing familiarity with CAD in the design profession: soon all training will be a matter of upgrading skills, not starting from scratch.

It is particularly difficult, perhaps impossible, to measure the value of improved design quality. Factors such as accuracy, drawing clarity, and increased thoroughness are intangibles, yet they are among the most important reasons to use computers. They must be evaluated subjectively, but they *must* be evaluated in order to know how effectively your CAD system is being utilized and how it can be improved.

Don't draw conclusions too soon. It takes a long time to reach a point at which the system functions at a high level of productivity. If at first you are producing no more work than you produced manually, don't panic. Keep an eye on productivity, but don't forget to consider improvements in quality, and, as you develop drawing libraries and office conventions, consider the work that may be saved on subsequent projects. Remember that the greatest gains in productivity are to be found in modifying and developing a drawing, not in the initial drawing stages.

It is common to find the same amount of time being spent on computer-aided design as manual design, only with a higher percentage being spent on design than on drawing. Is this a problem or a benefit? This question is intrinsic to the philosophy of a firm; in fact, it is intrinsic to the future of the architecture profession.

Efficiency

As design and drawing can be done more efficiently, there is a tendency for architects to lower their fees in order to obtain work. This may have a serious impact on the type and quality of work that results. A competitive frenzy to outbid other architects (and nonarchitects) for work may drive fees down to the point at which there is little choice but to rubber-stamp repetitive designs and details across the landscape. If fees drop to the level of the minimum labor costs required to produce a building that will stand up, the profession could be transformed into an electronic assembly line.

On the other hand, if architectural fees remain fairly steady, then productivity increases will encourage more thorough design and production. Most architects know that design work tends to expand to fill the available time (and then some). There are great benefits to spending more time on design, and clients must be made to understand this. Fortunately, it is not difficult, as we will see later in this chapter.

The methods for billing for computer use vary from office to office. Some attach an hourly fee to computer time, while others raise their overhead factor in billing clients, either for all work or, in some cases, for work done by computer users. As computer use becomes more widespread, it is becoming more convenient to include computer costs as general overhead. There are, however, two exceptions: first, although you can't usually bill clients for training time, you should set up a formula for billing a fair percentage of training time spent on project work. It is often acceptable to split a labor rate between two budgets, one for training and the other for project work, if the criteria is clear and records are kept carefully. Second, when a client requests extra services based on the capabilities of the computer, such as plots of multiple three-dimensional views, these expenses are generally billed separately under the terms of the architectural contract.

Most design work is done with pressing deadlines, and computers will not alter this fact. Yet it's good to remember an axiom from a well-known architect, and apply it when you can: "Architecture should not be done in a hurry."

PEOPLE: COORDINATION AND CONFLICT

No one kind of office organization is most appropriate for using computer-aided design: Virtually any setup can accommodate new tools if they are chosen and implemented wisely. Design firms are organized in many different ways, but there are roles that are common to most firms, large and small. Likewise, there are roles that must be filled to effectively use a computer-aided design system.

OFFICE GEOGRAPHY

Design firms tend to be organized either vertically, in which a team works on a project from start to finish, or horizontally, meaning a staff of specialists passes a project from department to department. In theory, CAD can be used equally well within either structure, especially if everyone has access to a CAD workstation. In practice, this is not always so.

Horizontally organized firms generally have a distinct drafting or working drawing department, and this is usually the first group to use a CAD system. Unfortunately, it is also often the last. In a firm with a drafting department, working drawings are often considered distinct from the design process, and designers may avoid the production of working drawings completely. Thus, the potential for using CAD as a design tool tends to be neglected: when designers use it, they tend to ask the drafting (or graphics) department to produce a set of presentation drawings. Thus, much effort is duplicated, and designers fail to learn to use a valuable tool.

There are three reasons for this situation.

- There is often an attitude in large firms that drawing is for drafters, only.

- CAD systems were once too difficult for designers to learn without becoming full-time drafters.

- CAD systems have been physically isolated in a drafting department, often isolated from the design department.

The first two factors are changing quickly. Designers are quick to see that CAD, modeling in particular, are useful design tools, and software has become far simpler to learn. There is still, however, a tendency to segregate computers into isolated areas, removing them from the design process. This not only makes it difficult for a designer to work on the system, it makes it inconvenient to even talk with the person who is drawing. If separate departments are maintained, it is crucial that designers have easy access to computers for design purposes. Furthermore, it is equally important that design and drafting departments use similar software and drawing conventions. There is tremendous labor saving potential in being able to swap disks back and forth between departments, but there is also potential for confusion and time-wasting if they are exchanged in dissimilar formats, such as different layer schemes.

These are problems that vertically organized offices should not have to face—yet often they do. Small firms that have worked in teams for years have been known to create a "CAD Department" because they assume that computer-aided drafting is a specialized skill and that computer-aided *design* is not worth the effort. The introduction of specialization into a team-oriented design process can cause havoc at worst and will slow down the design process, at best. Cooperative design requires a familiarity with the project on the part of all members of the team. Assigning a CAD specialist who is not familiar with a project to draw a designer's work requires extra explanation and introduces new opportunities for error. There is, again, a tendency to isolate drafting computers from the main-

stream of the office design work, which discourages others from learning to use the CAD tools (Figure 8-1).

If there is a single set of rules for office geography, it should be: *keep people near their tools, and don't isolate people from each other.* Ultimately, everyone in a design firm should have direct access to a computer. At that point, the matter becomes an issue of office design, which architects should be well equipped to handle.

ROLES AND HIERARCHIES

In the early days of computer-aided drafting, when tremendous investments were required to train people, the role of "CAD Operator" was created. The specialists that filled this role often had little architectural training, and those who did rarely had the opportunity to use it. Although the job had a certain kind of prestige, it was also considered a dead-end. Could a CAD operator ever hope to become a project architect?

Fortunately, the role of CAD operator is no longer necessary, since learning to use CAD is no longer a career in itself. Nevertheless, the role persists. There was a time when it was easier to teach architecture to a computer operator than it was to teach computers to an architect; now it is unnecessary to train nonarchitects to work with architects. The persistence of the role of CAD operator has an even more negative impact. The idea that using a computer can lead to a dead-end job can thoroughly sabotage the introduction of a CAD system into a design office.

Shift work is another trap. When CAD systems cost hundreds of thousands of dollars, firms had to use the equipment two or three shifts a day in order to pay for it. Not only does this isolate and demoralize those who work on the night shift, it also makes projects very difficult to coordinate. Since computers are expensive, even now, it is sometimes tempting to keep them operating as much as possible. While this may be helpful for training people after hours, it can be very disruptive if an office is split into two shifts. A common compromise is to overlap shifts, say 7AM to 3PM and 12PM to 8PM.

It is also possible to simply overemphasize computer-aided design. For example, when new employees begin work, their orientation should not be solely "meet the computer"; it is still important to introduce people and explain office customs. Likewise, if too much attention is paid to the progress of an individual or a project, an unnecessary amount of pressure can develop, and people start to worry that the system's failures will be attributed to them, personally. This is

FIGURE 8-1　A computer at every desk. Neeley/Lofrano Inc, Architects, San Francisco.

particularly true when instant productivity increases are expected. Often a manager will forget that real increases in efficiency not only require much practice, but that they only show up after much ground breaking has been done, such as the creation of base drawings or drawing libraries.

Managing the System

Each office has its own ways of organizing drafters, designers, and managers, and there is no reason why this system should change significantly as a CAD system is introduced. It may be, however, that the responsibilities at each level will change. For example, a project architect may be more concerned with graphic standards if his or her drawings will be converted directly to presentation drawings or working drawings; a drafter may become more responsible for making material choices when using drawing libraries with built-in attributes. These kinds of changes should be discussed among all concerned, because they can lead to mix-ups and bad feelings if they are not understood.

There is one new role that arises with CAD in all but the smallest practices. A **CAD manager** is someone who is responsible for planning and evaluating the CAD system, as well as for overseeing its day-to-day use. This person may be an experienced drafter, a management-level architect, or someone in between. There are two criteria for the role: First, this person should be interested in the nuts-and-bolts workings of the software and hardware, though not necessarily an

expert. Second, he or she should be intimately familiar with the procedures and requirements for taking an architectural design through whatever phases the system will be used for.

The CAD manager fills a number of roles, such as

- Recommending hardware and software choices,
- Organizing training schedules,
- Conducting training or introductions,
- Customizing the CAD system to the needs of the firm,
- Setting up working schedules and coordinating machine access,
- Suggesting and implementing drawing conventions,
- And, most importantly, seeing that projects move from phase to phase in a logical, efficient manner.

Essentially, the manager is responsible for seeing that the system is used effectively.

In a large firm, a CAD manager's job is full-time, since many workstations and projects require a great deal of attention. In a small firm, however, it is possible for an architect or drafter to fill the role adequately while participating in his or her usual projects. This need for a CAD manager may diminish over time, as practices are established and project managers become more capable of guiding a project through the nuances of computer-aided design, and as each user learns how to customize the system without violating office standards. Thus, in a midsized office, a job that may require a full-time manager initially may allow this person to return to project work after six months or a year.

SETUP AND BACKUP

In Chapter 4 we looked at a number of issues that must be addressed before drawing, such as layer schemes, drawing libraries, and software customization. Many of these are best handled through the implementation of office conventions. Setting up these standards must begin before the first project is started, though they may evolve indefinitely. They may be developed by an individual or by users' suggestions, but they should be coordinated by the CAD manager.

Staying Current

The most crucial single issue in operating a computer-aided design system is file management and backup. It is vitally important that everyone work with up-to-date copies of a drawing; since it's so easy to save one's copy on a hard disk at the end of the day, it's tempting to continue working on it the next day, even though someone else may have revised the original on another computer in the meantime. This is similar to the need to keep current sets of drawing prints in circulation, except that it is not as obvious when the original is being changed: there is no mylar original sitting on someone's desk. The techniques for communication will vary greatly depending on the number of people involved and the CAD system configuration, but in any circumstances, communication is crucial.

The most common solution to this dilemma requires a centralized location for the storage of a set of electronic master drawings. The container can be a box of master floppy disks that are updated at the end of each day, then copied onto each machine the following day, or a single, large capacity hard disk. In the latter case, drawings can be copied to the hard disk from floppy disks, or via a computer network, through which files may be passed back and forth as required. None of these procedures are simple to do, every day, without exception, but the hazard posed by mix-ups requires a central storage any time more than one person is working on a project.

When different people work on the same drawing simultaneously on different computers, they need to coordinate their work in order to be able to merge the new versions. If they are working on different areas or layers of a drawing, adding one to another is not particularly difficult with most software. However, if they are working on the same part of a drawing, combining them can be difficult. In this case, it's best for one or both to work on an alternative set of layers, to keep their work separate, just as if they were using tracing paper. Several different alternatives can be stored in a master drawing and reviewed later.

Alternatively, you may divide a project into several drawing files, by area or by groups of layers. Each piece should be kept on a single master floppy disk, and only the person who borrows a master disk may work on that area or layer set. This method is particularly useful with a very large project that must be subdivided into manageable-sized files anyway.

Staying Secure

One of the scariest aspects of learning to use a computer is the fear that a single mistake will cause a drawing to be "lost." Most programs include safeguards and warnings against taking the few actions that can really harm your work, but you are doubly secure if you know you have a copy of your work on disk. Some software

will always maintain an up-to-the-minute copy of your work on disk while others require that you *save* a copy at intervals. If a power outage can cause you to lose your drawing, then it is crucial that you make backup copies frequently, say, every hour or so. Since a hard disk malfunction can destroy data, it is also important to copy your work onto a backup disk (or tape, if you use a tape backup system) daily. If you are confident that your drawings are backed up, fears of losing your work should disappear.

Your backup disks or tapes can also help you to maintain a record of the evolution of a project. Sometimes you need to refer to an old version of a design: if you have a daily or weekly record of your project, you can reload an old version. If you want, you can extract parts of an old drawing and place them into the current version.

Institutions that deal with complex, irreplaceable records, such as banks, often maintain dozens of extra copies of their computer records, located at secure, scattered locations. Architectural drawings are no less valuable to the practice of architecture, but firms often keep entire projects on a single disk. Usually this is a matter of carelessness or laziness, rather than intent: a procedure for copying and storing backup disks may be planned, yet neglected, because it's "too much trouble." Obviously, losing a project in a computer malfunction or a fire is even more trouble. In addition to making sure that drawings are copied and stored securely every day, it is wise to maintain weekly backups outside the office, even if only at someone's house.

OFFICE AUTOMATION

Strictly speaking, computer-aided design includes graphics and integrated database capabilities, but design firms are also aided by a number of other computer applications, most of which relate directly to design.

PROCESSING WORDS, RECORDS, AND NUMBERS

One of the first areas of architectural practice to be computerized was writing and editing, since minicomputers and the first microcomputers were particularly good at these tasks. Although these same machines could also perform number-crunching miracles, it is only recently that architects have begun to use this capability. These are now fairly commonplace computer applications, so we will only look at them briefly in passing.

Word Processing and Specifications

Architects, despite the visual orientation of their profession, can produce large quantities of writing. It's not uncommon for an architect to spend part of every day writing memos, letters, proposals, reports, meeting notes, or project records, usually scribbled in haste and passed on to a secretary to type. Though time-honored, this technique is at best inefficient, since it requires everything to be written twice. A good typist can use a PC-based word-processing program to turn out a rough draft and leave it to be edited by a secre-

tary; however, a slow typist may find it a waste of time that might be better spent on other work. The decision is largely personal, but it makes sense to have computers and word-processing software available to anyone who writes.

When appearance is crucial, the software heavy artillery may be called for. Proposals and public relations brochures are often produced in-house and often require a combination of text and graphics. **Desktop publishing** software can be used to design page layouts, mix type fonts, and add illustrations to text. In combination with a laser printer, you can produce material of near-typeset quality. Ideally, you should be able to transfer drawings directly from your CAD system into a brochure or proposal, and using image-capture software (see Chapter 2) enables you to add and modify photographs. Ultimately, you can virtually eliminate cutting and pasting. Better still, you can eliminate the need for outside typesetting, with its attendant costs and deadlines. Since a page can be reprinted in seconds, the firm brochure can be revised any time a new project, drawing, or photo is added.

Construction specifications are perhaps the most demanding piece of writing that architects do. Even though standard specification forms have been used for years, specifications are nevertheless often written, or more often *adapted*, by specialist spec-writers. Specs tend to be complex descriptions of materials and construction methods, filled with terms that must be both comprehensible and legally valid, so this specialization is not without reason.

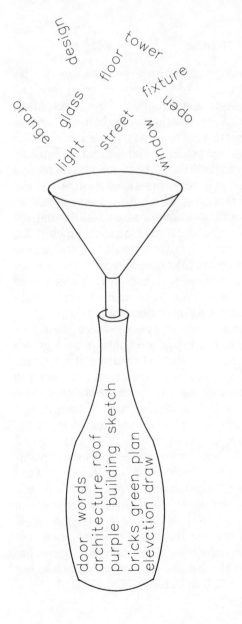

FIGURE 8-2   Although cost estimating, schedule-processing, or specification writing can generally be done on the same computer used for graphics, sometimes you may want to work on these as you draw. In lieu of a multitasking, windowing computer, it's not a bad idea to have a portable computer around the office. Neeley/Lofrano Inc, Architects, San Francisco.

Specification-writing is particularly well suited to computerized word processing, since specs often change very little from one job to another. Often whole sections can be reproduced with few or no changes. For this reason, "canned" spec packages like the AIA's **Masterspec** are invaluable. From a disk-based original, you can choose, then modify whatever sections are appropriate to the particular job you are doing. Very little writing or typing is required. These electronic originals can also be referenced to drawing libraries and attribute-linked databases, so that when a particular item is placed in a drawing, the appropriate specification is noted for later inclusion in the construction documents.

Getting Organized

In a design office, record keeping can be a particularly difficult chore, since many different kinds of records must be stored in an accessible manner. Usually every project has its own set of files, within which are kept correspondence, memos, meeting notes, transmittals, field notes, change orders, and so on. Each of these records covers one or more subjects, such as program requirements, site drainage, or doorknobs. Cross-filing, or placing copies or references in several places,

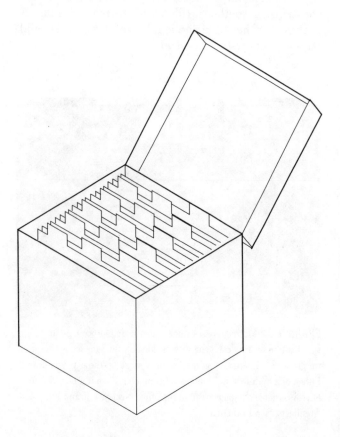

is often required. Keeping a complex filing system organized, current, and accessible can be a difficult task.

If, instead, these records are cross referenced by a database program, they can be kept on disk and located by subject, date, source, or other criteria. Each record is like a 3×5 card with many index tabs with which it can be pulled out. Some items, such as correspondence, may be separate letters in a file that are referred to by a "3×5 card" in the database, listing the topic, source, recipient and date. Change orders, on the other hand, may be typed as entries into a database form, then printed out as a final document. The full text remains in the database, subject to recall via its date, subject, destination, or number. This system may also be used to automatically tabulate the construction costs represented by change orders, perhaps divided up by subcontractors.

Number Crunching

Spreadsheet programs were largely responsible for the initial popularity of the personal computer and have since been adapted to many different uses. As we saw in Chapter 7, spreadsheets can be used for estimating construction costs throughout a project; they can also be used for tracking and estimating internal project costs. In addition, office management and accounting require very repetitive budgeting and record keeping, none of which makes sense to do by hand when there is a computer available. Specialized accounting software is available to handle much of this work, though a small firm can often do well with a good spreadsheet program. Like graphics software, spreadsheets can be customized with add-on packages. Called *templates*, these are designed to handle specific applications like accounting or project budgeting.

A project manager needs to know, accurately, how much money has been spent on a design project and how much is left. From this information, it is possible to plan which individuals will work on a project and how much time they can spend on it. Many of these calculations can be performed with a spreadsheet alone, but they can be kept up to date most effectively if the spreadsheet is linked to the office payroll and billing records. Templates and accounting programs are available that are oriented specifically toward architectural and engineering firms; like CAD software, they can be very helpful if they fit the way you work. It is important, however, to be sure that these programs can provide the specific information that you need to manage both a project and your office accounts. Software that attempts to do both tasks but does one badly will be a liability.

PROJECT MANAGEMENT

Since architectural project schedules are dependent on a variety of factors that are difficult to anticipate, they are notoriously difficult to plan and maintain. Design and drawing time are hard to estimate, consultants are sometimes unreliable, and unexpected delays are often imposed by clients, financial sources, and public agencies. Large and small firms alike face persistent scheduling problems that result from having to adjust to these uncertainties.

Computer-based project management (PM) was originally developed for very large construction, industrial, and aerospace projects. However, microcom-

puter PM systems have proved to be useful for much smaller applications, including the scheduling of architectural design work. Like CAD, it takes some time to learn and implement project management software, but once you begin using it, you can predict project schedules and personnel schedules more accurately and with much less effort.

Project management software is most effective with large projects that require the coordination of many *resources* (people and organizations) and many *tasks*. As you might expect, small projects are easier to set up, so there is reason to consider using it on either large or small jobs. It can also be limited to managing schedules and personnel *inside* a firm, or it can be

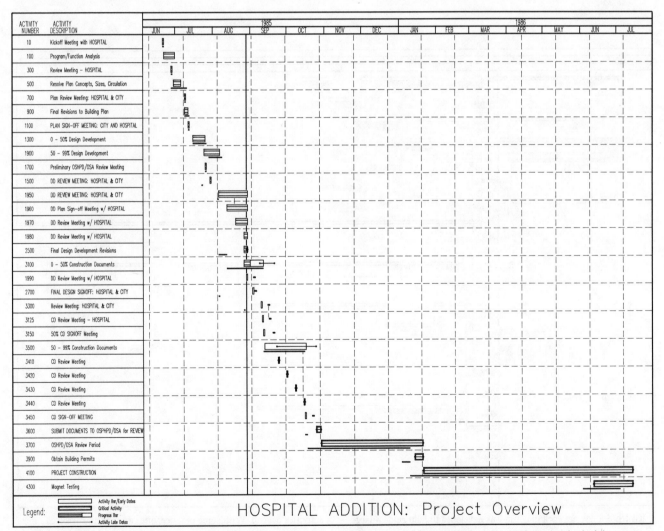

HOSPITAL ADDITION: Project Overview

FIGURE 8-3 This bar chart illustrates a project schedule that was developed in a few hours when planning the project, then kept up-to-date as the project progressed. Whenever a task was completed early or a meeting postponed, the schedule was updated and a new chart produced. This figure and 8-4 are externally oriented schedules; as opposed to internal job-management schedules, which are also useful. Both were produced using Primavera project management software. P. Bernstein, Kaplan/McLaughlin/Diaz, Architects.

applied just to scheduling *external* events such as meetings and submission deadlines.

In essence, project management software lets you list the tasks that make up a project, place them in order, estimate the minimum and maximum times for each, and assign resources according to available time and budget. You can also use the Critical Path Method (CPM) to specify which tasks are dependent upon the completion of others, and you can assign a *float* factor that determines the amount of leeway available in starting or completing a task. Once you have outlined these factors, you can view your project as a list of tasks or resources, as a *bar chart* (Figure 8-3) that illustrates when activities occur and which overlap, or as a *network* (Figure 8-4) that shows the critical path. The advantage to doing this on the computer is that any

time your schedule changes or a new task is added, the software will recalculate the entire schedule, enabling you to see the impact that changes will have on later tasks and completion dates. Another particularly useful function is called *resource leveling:* if you specify a maximum number of people that can work on a project or task at once, the software will calculate how much longer the task will take, then recalculate the schedule.

Project management occurs in two stages, *planning* and *monitoring*. Using traditional project management techniques, careful analysis of schedules, budgets, and staff use usually takes place in the planning stage of a project, when fees are being negotiated and personnel assigned. However, once a project begins, it is very difficult to manually update a

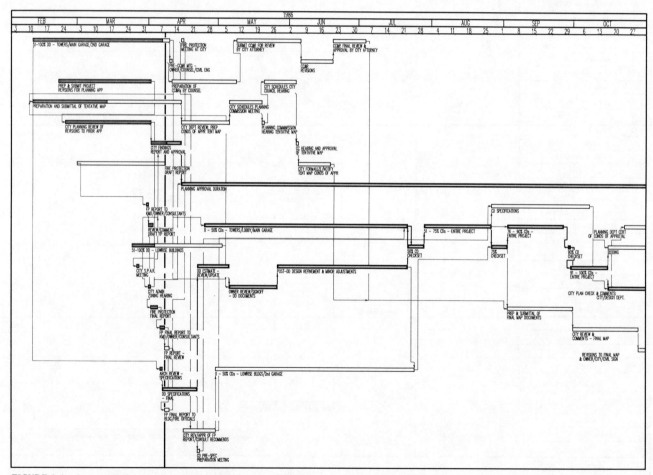

FIGURE 8-4 A network diagram was developed to help guide a large urban housing project through the design development and construction documents phases. The network illustrates both scheduling and sequencing, including the highlighted critical activities, upon which other activities depend. With some practice, one can read the arrowed sequences as if the network was a project road map. P. Bernstein, Kaplan/McLaughlin/Diaz, Architects.

schedule every time there is a delay or a change in the scope of the work. Management tends to become ad-hoc, and the monitoring of costs and schedules becomes less precise.

Using the computer, the planning stage can be used to set up goals for scheduling and resource allocation that are based on previous experience: each project management network can be based on a standardized model that is adapted to new projects by adding and subtracting tasks and resources. The creation of a fully detailed network is a laborious undertaking, prone to errors of omission; working from a standard model that reflects your office routines can help to begin a project easily and accurately. The model can help you avoid reinventing the wheel each time you begin a job.

Once a project begins, PM software can be used to monitor progress in relation to the targets you have established and measure the impact of changes in deadlines and resource availability. Monitoring with the computer is far easier than manual monitoring, since a project manager can periodically enter evaluations of project progress by simply noting the dates that certain milestones are passed and keeping track of the amount of time that is spent on each task. Some PM software permits time accounting to be integrated with office time card/payroll systems, so that reporting can be done automatically.

The graphic capabilities of computer-aided project management provide a potent dramatization of the implications of scheduling decisions. Changes to a schedule tend to have a rippling effect throughout the remainder of a project: when a client misses an approval deadline, there is a delay months hence that may cause another deadline to be missed, unless more people are assigned to the job. The resource leveling capability illustrates the tendency of tasks to act like balloons: if you shorten the time (compress the horizontal dimension), you must add people or work overtime (the vertical dimension expands), and vice versa.

Not all project management software is appropriate to architecture. The design professions commonly have activities that vary, day by day, in personnel availability, task sequences, and priorities, so software must be very flexible. Since it often must be used by people who are trained as architects and not as project management specialists, it is important that it be relatively easy to learn and convenient to use in the midst of a job. PM software is usually not appropriate to projects that can not be mapped out fairly clearly in advance or to unique jobs that cannot cover the costs of planning a whole new PM network. However, if you can develop standard models for project organization,

computer-aided project management can be a fruitful tool for getting and staying organized.

WORKING AMONG THE MACHINES

As efficiency rises in the computer-aided office, does job satisfaction follow? This question, spoken or unspoken, weighs heavily over the decision to automate a design firm.

The question is often raised in connection with the physical qualities of computers. After all, few people really want to spend forty hours a week staring at a TV screen: it's tiring. It's hard on your eyes and hard on your backside. (Of course, so is working at a drafting board. A mobile, high resolution monitor with no glare can be surprisingly comfortable for reasonable periods of time.) It's important to realize that breaks are necessary when you use a video screen for drawing (or writing or calculating, for that matter) and that many people can not work effectively at a video screen for more than about six hours a day. This is not, however, inconsistent with the way most firms operate: individuals often have more than one task pending at any given time, and people often take turns working on drawings. With CAD, it's a good idea to run plots and check the current work on paper frequently anyway.

Lurking behind the issue of job satisfaction is often a concern about increased pressure to produce and a dehumanization of the workplace. Since computers have been used to turn more than one kind of workplace into an electronic sweatshop, this is a legitimate concern. However, it is not something that is intrinsic to the tool: sweatshops are the product of management that values speed and profit over quality of work. Computers can be used toward this end very effectively, if

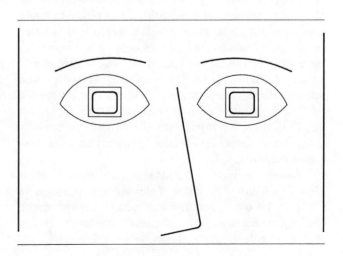

COMPUTERS AND THE DESIGN PROFESSION 176

managers choose to use them so. Computers do not cause this problem nor will they solve it. They can, however, make overwork even less palatable. In the interest of mental health and good eyesight, issues of working hours and the physical working environment need to be carefully addressed.

MORE WORK AND BETTER WORK

Architects design a small portion of all the buildings that are built, well under 10% by many estimates. Clearly there is room for professional designers to extend their services into new markets. We have seen that computers are automating some design tasks, perhaps bringing new kinds of work to some designers, taking work away from others. We have also seen that there is a risk of competitive fee cutting. Why should we expect a bigger cut of the pie?

MARKETING ARCHITECTURE

Marketing plays a key role in attracting architectural commissions. Architectural services can be marketed many ways, from personal contact to slick advertisements. Computers are having an impact on the way services are marketed, to be sure, but the widening range of services that designers can provide is also affecting *what* architects are offering.

Your design process itself can be a significant factor in obtaining commissions. It is important to show potential clients the efficiency and accuracy you can provide them. A client has reason to be concerned that a project will pass smoothly from phase to phase and be communicated clearly, at a carefully controlled cost, to the builder. As builders become familiar with computer-produced designs, they are beginning to expect better quality, trade-specific drawings and specifications; knowledgeable clients are concerned with this. Many clients are also stirred by increased opportunities for input into the process, especially interactive three-dimensional exploration of a proposed building.

Going beyond the traditional architectural practice, firms can offer some of the services outlined in Chapter 7—construction planning and management, facility management, and so on. Architecture is a wide-ranging profession, and it may be becoming more so. It

can be argued that a designer's involvement in the building and urban design processes has been limited more by the traditional and roles and legal structures of the industry than by logic: there may be valid reasons for architects to participate much more closely in planning, construction, and building management. If so, the graphic and information-handling capabilities of computers may prove to be the tool that makes this possible. In the long run, the most significant effect of computer-aided design may be expansion of the narrow base on which architects currently focus their services.

A BIGGER PIE

The specters of off-the-shelf, standardized buildings and fully automated expert systems are worrisome to many architects. Since it is possible to create a somewhat customized building with even a relatively simple parametric drawing program and a master design, these fears are not unfounded. Surely these kinds of programs will have an impact on the profession.

If architects are to turn increased efficiency to their advantage, they may have to make inroads into the 90% of construction that they aren't involved in. Much of this work is built on relatively low budgets, or is built according to standardized designs with little modification. This includes mass-produced housing, as well as large amounts of commercial and industrial construction. For the most part, it is lacking in the quality that architects are in business to provide— custom design.

As we have seen, drawing libraries and expert systems can reduce many of the time-consuming aspects of architectural work. By encouraging custom assembly of standard elements, they can lower production costs and, potentially, make lower-budget custom work more attractive to a firm. It will not be easy for architects to hold fees for more complex work at current levels while pursuing lower fee work, and it seems likely that individual firms will tend to specialize more and pursue work at one level or another. Nevertheless, if lower-budget work is more feasible, it is largely a matter of convincing developers, builders, and home-buyers that architects provide a service that is worth buying. If architecture is to continue to *be* a valuable service, architects must continue to offer the synthesis of site design, programmatic problem solving and building system design that humans can do better than a computer can do.

As the printing press replaced the scribal craft with typography, our *means* are changing. Computer-aided design opens new doors for designers, much as typography liberated writing and publishing. Our roles as architects are changing, and our design strategies will continue to evolve as our tools continue to change.

Any tool may be used well or badly, and computer-aided design is no exception. Architecture is and will continue to be based on the skill and intentions of architects. Computers can make both good and bad design easier to produce: perhaps this makes design skill more crucial than ever.

APPENDIX A
GLOSSARY

A

animation. A sequence of images displayed rapidly, producing the impression of movement. Real-time animation is produced as it is requested, rather than from a previously stored set of images.

application program. A computer program that is dedicated to a specific task, other than controlling the computer's operation.

array. To make multiple copies of a drawing element in a line, grid, circle or arc. The term also refers to a pattern of elements that results from the array process.

artificial intelligence. The concept that computers can be programmed to make decisions and "learn" from previous experience. Expert systems are generally considered a form of artificial intelligence.

assemblage. A design technique in which various predesigned components are combined.

associative dimensioning. A computer-aided drawing system in which dimensions are linked to specific drawing elements; when the elements are moved, the dimension lines are automatically moved and the dimensions are revised.

attribute. A descriptive tag attached to a drawing element. This text uses the term to refer to the numeric or textual tags that a CAD user may define. (CAD software also assigns attributes, internally, to describe characteristics like colors, layers, and linetypes.)

autoLISP. A version of the LISP programming language that has been adapted as a command language in AutoCAD.

automatic dimensioning. A computer-aided drawing system for adding dimensions to a drawing with minimal user input, according to previously defined rules for location and precision.

axis. A line on a coordinate system that is used as a reference for the location of objects on a plane or in space.

B

backup. To make copies of a file, to prevent loss of data in the event of hardware or software failure. Backups can often be made automatically with the aid of utility programs.

bar chart. A method of displaying project scheduling that portrays chronological sequences of activities.

BASIC. A high-level computer language widely used for instruction, business applications, and microcomputer programming.

batch. A set of instructions that tells a computer to perform a series of tasks, such as running several programs in a series.

Bernoulli Box. Trade name for a removable-cartridge disk drive, similar in speed and capacity to a hard disk.

bit. A binary number, either one or zero.

block. A group of drawing elements that can be manipulated as one. A block may be "redefined," whereupon all occurrences of the block are replaced with a new version.

block articulation. To add detail to a block, then redefine it so that each occurrence will be replaced and detailed accordingly.

blocking. In computer-aided space planning and schematic design, the allocation of space based on programmatic criteria such as adjacency and proximity desirability.

box. In computer-aided drawing, an area outlined on the display screen for the selection of drawing elements, or for zooming in or out. Synonymous with window and fence.

bug. An error in a program that will cause a malfunction in program operations.

built model. A three-dimensional model assembled from forms that represent actual construction elements.

byte. A group of bits, generally eight, that a computer can process as a single unit; sometimes referred to as a computer "word."

C

C. A high-level computer language that is particularly well suited to programs that are to be used with both the Unix and MS-DOS operating systems.

CAD. Computer-aided design.

CAD manager. A role in a design firm; a CAD manager has responsibility for coordinating and planning hardware and software systems, as well as advising project managers and architects on the use of the system.

CAD operator. A specialist in using a computer-aided design system. This term is often used to imply a lack of other design and drawing skills, and is a remnant of the days when CAD systems required full-time specialization to learn and use.

CAD/CAM. Computer-aided design and manufacturing.

CADD. Computer-aided design and drafting.

cathode ray tube. The "screen" or "picture tube" in a video monitor or television.

CD-ROM. Compact disk-read only memory; an information storage medium that can hold very large amounts of data. CD-ROM disks are read by lasers in disk drives that are similar to audio compact disks; they are similar also in that they are produced at a central location and cannot be written on by a user, and are thus ideal for widely used databases. CD-ROMs are also very durable.

CD-WORM. Compact disk-write once, read mostly; an information storage medium that is very similar to CD-ROM, but may be written on by a user, once. CD-WORM is an excellent archival storage medium.

cell. A synonym for "block".

clip. In the display of a drawing, the elimination of undisplayed drawing areas from the calculations performed by the computer. In the display of three-dimensional images, the elimination of all images behind or in front of a specified plane.

coprocessor. A processor that is designed to do specific tasks, such as mathematic calculations or graphic display control. CAD programs generally benefit greatly from the presence of coprocessors that can relieve the CPU of calculation-intensive activities.

command. An instruction given to a computer program using terms that the computer software is programmed to understand. Commands may be typed, picked from a menu with a pointing device, or spoken, depending on the specific hardware and software.

command language. A programming language that is accessible to users as they work within a program. Used for writing macros and new commands.

computer. An electronic machine that can process information according to programmed instructions.

construction document phase. The final design phase of an architectural project, in which a design is detailed, graphically and in specifications and material schedules, in a form that will be used for bidding and construction. Also referred to as the working drawing phase.

convention. An agreed-on standard, such as drafting standards, to which all work will conform.

coordinate system. A set of lines at right angles to each other that are used as a reference in locating objects on a plane or in space.

copy. To make an exact duplicate of a drawing element, a file, or anything else.

CPL. CAD programming language; a command language in VersaCAD.

CPM. critical path method. A technique for planning and tracking project progress according to a sequence of tasks that are interdependent, whose progress governs the scheduling of other activities.

CPU. Central processing unit. The processor that controls the execution of instructions. Original mainframe CPUs, assembled with vacuum tubes, occupied entire rooms; today's silicon chip CPUs are pocket-sized and often more powerful than their ancestors.

crosshair. A type of cursor.

CRT. Cathode ray tube.

cursor. A rectangle, blinking line, crosshair, or other icon that indicates the location on a computer display at which user input will occur.

curve fitting. Translating a multisegmented line into a curve around its vertices.

D

database. A collection of organized information. A list is a database; a drawing—a list of vectors, attributes, and other graphic information—is also a database.

database, alphanumeric. A collection of related records (text or numbers) that can be organized, sorted, and presented by a computer.

database, graphic. A collection of records that describe geometric elements and their attributed characteristics.

database management program. An application program used to manipulate information, generally in a format of fields (categories of data) and records (individual entries). Among other uses, these are applied in architecture to creating material schedules, based on information extracted from drawings.

debug. To correct errors (bugs) in a computer program.

dedicated computer. A computer that is designed to use only one type of software, such as graphics or word processing.

design development. The design phase that follows schematic design, in which decisions are generally made about specific materials, dimensions, and construction methods.

desktop publishing. Computer software systems that combine word processing and graphics with the ability to lay out and print pages in a manner similar to typesetting.

digitizing tablet. An electrically sensitive pad, from 6″ × 6″ to desk-sized, used in conjunction with a stylus or puck to move the screen cursor, pick items from a tablet menu, or trace drawing from paper to the computer. A tablet is an absolute pointing device, as it permits exact point location.

directory. A group of files that can be manipulated together as a group; directories have names and may include subdirectories.

display. An electronic device or system for presenting information visually; generally a video monitor, LCD, or plasma screen.

display adapter. See graphic adapter.

documentation. Written instructions supplied with a computer program.

drag. To move a drawing element on a display screen by attaching it to the cursor, then moving the cursor.

drawing library. A collection of drawings that are available to be inserted into other drawings. A drawing library can include symbols, architectural forms, text, building assemblies, rooms, buildings, or anything else that can be stored, on disk, as a drawing.

driver. A utility program that enables a program to work with a specific peripheral device.

DXF. A file format originated by AutoCAD for exchanging graphic information between programs. The DXF format is in ASCII (alphanumeric) format and can be read or written by any properly equipped graphics program.

E

element. Any distinct part of a drawing: a line, arc, circle, symbol, or block.

entity. A line, arc, circle, or other simple, single element.

expert system. A computer program that is modeled after the decision-making process used by a human "expert" in a particular field.

explode. To break up a defined block into its constituent elements. Synonymous with "unblock."

F

fence. In computer-aided drawing, an area outlined on the display screen for the selection of drawing elements or for zooming in or out. Synonymous with window and box.

file. An organized collection of data that can be treated as a single unit by computer programs. Programs themselves are composed of one or more files.

fillet. To cause two nonparallel lines to intersect, either at a right angle or in a curve of a specified radius.

flat database. A graphic database in which drawing elements are represented on a two-axis coordinate system. Elements may be given elevation and thickness dimensions in relation to a third, perpendicular axis, but they may only be drawn on the two-axis system.

floating point calculations. Calculations that are carried out using a number of decimal places for a high degree of precision. In a computer, floating point calculations can be speeded considerably through the use of a special coprocessor that is specifically designed to do these.

floppy disk. A readily portable information storage medium consisting of a thin, flexible, round sheet of plastic, housed in a paper or plastic sleeve. Floppy disks are available in various sizes, densities, and data capacities.

font. A typeface, characterized by size and style.

form. A drawing or portion of a drawing that represents a distinct architectural object.

form model. A three-dimensional model based on architectural shapes or objects.

framework. The invisible structure of a CAD drawing, which is based on the size and number of elements in a drawing and the relationships between them. Layer organization and the use of blocks play an important role in a drawing framework.

freeze. In the display of a drawing, the elimination of undisplayed drawing layers from the calculations performed by the computer.

front-end software. Computer programs that make other programs easier to use or more productive; some front-ends adapt programs to specific purposes or disciplines.

G

Gantt chart. See bar chart.

global. In computer terms, an action that affects all similar elements throughout a drawing or file.

graphic memory. Random access memory allocated specifically for image display and manipulation, usually in the form of RAM chips on a graphic adapter board.

graphic-based engineering. Engineering (such as structural, HVAC, lighting, acoustics, or site) that can be carried out by drawing objects to scale, which are analyzed by engineering software, based on the drawn dimensions and previously established criteria. Some (parametric) engineering software will redraw a drawing based on calculations.

graphic adapter. An electronic device for processing graphic information into a form that can be displayed by a monitor. It may be a circuit board or a single chip and it may be located in a computer or in a monitor. It often includes RAM chips allocated to graphic memory.

group. A collection of drawing elements. Some programs allow the selection of groups that may be referred to and manipulated together, without defining them as blocks.

H

handle. A reference point by which a block or group may be located. Synonymous with "insertion point."

hard disk. A large-capacity information storage device, generally fixed within a computer or in its own housing. Data capacities range from 5 megabytes to 900 megabytes.

hardware. The physical equipment that makes up a computer system.

hatch. To fill a specified area with a predefined pattern.

hatching. A pattern, consisting of lines, used to fill an area.

hidden-line removal. A technique in which a computer program automatically removes lines from a three-dimensional wireframe drawing, based on the location of planes and objects "in front" of lines.

high-level computer language. A set of commands and syntax with which sets of instructions can be written for computers. Unlike machine language, high-level languages use words and characters that are similar to spoken/written language.

HVAC. Heating, ventilating, and air conditioning.

I

IGES. See Initial Graphic Exchange Specification.

imaging system. A computer system (hardware and software) for capturing video images and manipulating (scaling, rendering, and combining) them.

Initial Graphic Exchange Specification. A system recognized by the National Bureau of Standards for transferring graphic information between computer programs.

input (noun). Instructions or data given to a computer by a user.

input (verb). To give instructions or add data to a computer program.

insertion point. A reference point by which a block or group may be located. Synonymous with "handle."

integer-based calculations. Calculations based on whole numbers. Integer-based calculations can be performed by a computer very rapidly, but without the accuracy of floating-point calculations.

integrated modeling. Three-dimensional modeling that includes the ability to draft, dimension, and plot two-dimensional drawings within a three-dimensional context. Two-dimensional elements and symbols may be drawn in specific working planes; modifications to the model database may be made while drafting.

interface. See user interface.

J

joystick. A pointing device that moves a cursor by pivoting a stick.

K

KB. See kilobyte.

keyboard. A manually operated device with which letters, numbers, symbols and instructions can be sent to a computer.

keyboard customizer. A utility program that enables a user to assign a series of keystrokes to a single key, to be invoked at any time while using another program.

kilobyte. 1,024 bytes, nominally 1,000 bytes.

L

LAN. Local area network; a type of microcomputer network.

layer. A means of grouping similar drawing elements so that they may be manipulated together. Analogous to sheets of tracing paper laid over each other, except that groups of layers may be managed together, as if they could be combined into a single sheet, then separated. Layers are referred to as "levels" by some software.

LCD. Liquid crystal diode; used in displays and some electrostatic printers.

LCD screen. A display using liquid crystal diodes; generally monochrome, although color LCD displays are also available.

LED. Light emitting diodes; a technology used in alphanumeric displays and some electrostatic printers.

level. In some CAD programs, this is synonymous with layer. We use the term here in the architectural sense, meaning a physical plane that differs in elevation from other levels.

light pen. A hand-held pointing device that registers position when pointed at individual pixels on a computer display. A button or sensitive tip allows points to be picked.

line-based drawing. A drawing method, typified by manual drawing, in which images are constructed one line at a time.

linetype. A categorization of lines by degree of continuity (continuous, dashed, dotted, or a combination) as displayed and/or plotted by a CAD program.

line weight. The width of a line, as displayed and/or plotted by a CAD program.

LISP. A high-level computer language, sometimes used in "artificial intelligence" programs. LISP stands for list processing, although some users claim it stands for "Lost In Stupid Parentheses," since it makes ample use of them.

local. In computer terms, an action that affects a single element.

local area network. LAN; a type of microcomputer network.

M

machine language. A highly specialized language used to instruct a computer; high-level languages are translated, or compiled, into machine language.

macro. A recorded or saved series of keystrokes or a short program that can be invoked within an application program.

mainframe computer. A large computer, generally designed for high speed and multiple simultaneous operations.

massing model. A three-dimensional model based on space defining forms, such as rooms or buildings. Similar to a volumetric model.

MB. See megabyte.

megabyte. 1,048,576 bytes, nominally 1,000,000 bytes or a 1,000 Kilobytes.

menu. A list of commands, macros, or frequently used terms that is displayed on screen or on a digitizing tablet. Menu items may be selected by pointing to them, or, sometimes, by typing the first letter of a displayed item at the keyboard.

microcomputer. A small, desktop-sized computer, generally designed for a single user.

microdisk. A small floppy disk housed in a rigid plastic sleeve.

microprocessor. A processor that is entirely contained on a chip of silicon.

minicomputer. A medium-sized computer, generally capable of supporting multiple users and multiple simultaneous operations.

modem. A device for passing digital data from one computer to another over analog communication links, such as phone lines. Modems are available in several speeds, measured in bits per second. An acronym for modulator/demodulator.

modification. Changing or editing a drawing in any manner.

mouse. A hand-held relative pointing device with one to three buttons, used to move the on-screen cursor, enter commands, and pick points. A mechanical mouse registers position with a rolling ball on its underside; an optical mouse uses a light that reflects on a small pad.

move. To relocate an element or group of drawing elements from one location or layer to another.

MS-DOS. A microcomputer operating system; virtually identical to PC-DOS.

multitasking. The ability to perform several different operations, using separate programs, simultaneously on the same computer. Often these tasks are displayed within windows on the screen.

multiuser. A computer system that can be used by several people, at different terminals, at the same time.

N

nested block. A block that is part of a larger block. One block may have many nested blocks, and a nested block may, in turn, have blocks nested within it.

network. (Applied to project management) A graphic representation of the interrelationships between activities in a project.

network. (Applied to computers) Two or more self-contained computers that are linked in order to share information and programs.

O

object. A group of drawing elements; an object may be treated as one element or its individual components may be addressed separately.

object snap. A computer-aided drawing mode in which picked points will occur at specified points of previously drawn objects, such as the "end," "middle," or "tangent."

object-based drawing. A drawing method that uses a computer to construct images by adding predrawn shapes and symbols together.

operating system. A set of programs that enable a computer CPU, memory, and peripheral devices to function with applications programs.

origin. The intersection of x, y, and z axes on a system of Cartesian coordinates.

orthogonal mode. A computer-aided drawing mode in which all lines will be either horizontal or vertical.

OS/2. A microcomputer operating system.

overlay drafting. A drawing production technique that uses transparent film and an alignment mechanism to produce drawings on a number of sheets that may be printed together, as one. Similar to CAD layering.

P

paint. To render an image using a bit-mapped graphics program.

parameter. A numeric variable that can be used to determine a drawing dimension; more generally, any rule for proceeding with a task, such as creating a specific kind of drawing.

parameter file. A table of dimensional specifications that instruct a parametric design program to use specific values when rectifying drawings. This table, often in spreadsheet format, may contain formulas for automatic calculation of dimensions, based on variables specified by the user.

parametric drawing. A computer-aided drawing method in which variable numeric values may be used to specify dimensions, which cause drawings to be drawn accordingly by a computer program.

Pascal. A high-level computer language used for a wide range of applications.

pattern. A predefined, repeating arrangement of drawing elements that can be used to fill in a specified area, a process called hatching. "Pattern" is also used by some programs as a synonym for "block."

payback period. The length of time in which the savings made possible by a piece of hardware or software equal the cost of the item.

PC. See personal computer.

PC-DOS. A microcomputer operating system; virtually identical to MS-DOS.

perceptual model. A three-dimensional model based on the architectural shapes that one experiences in moving through a space.

peripheral. Hardware that is distinct and separate from the enclosure housing a computer's CPU, such as monitors, printers, plotters and digitizing tablets.

personal computer. A computer that is intended to be used by a single person. The term generally refers to a stand-alone microcomputer, although PCs can be linked in networks to each other, to peripheral equipment, and to larger computers.

pixel. A single dot on a monochrome display screen, three dots on a digital color display screen (red, blue, and green); the smallest screen increment that can be manipulated by a computer. In a video monitor, a pixel will glow when struck by a beam from a cathode-ray gun.

plotter (electrostatic). A large dot-matrix printer that uses, typically, laser, LCD or LED technology to draw CAD graphics on paper. Vector graphics must be converted to raster graphics in order to be plotted by a dot-matrix plotter.

plotter (pen). A mechanical device that uses one or more pens to draw vector graphics on paper, velum, or plastic film.

poché. Any pattern, hatch, or solid tone used to fill in a wall in a two-dimensional drawing.

polyline. A line that may contain multiple connected segments at angles to each other. Some software allows a polyline to be varied in width or fitted to a curve.

primitive. A line, arc, circle, or other simple, single element.

printer, dot matrix. A device that places text or graphics on paper by printing closely spaced dot patterns. Dot matrix mechanisms include printhead-and-ribbon, ink jet, and electrostatic.

printer, electrostatic. A type of dot-matrix printer that uses a laser beam, LCDs, or LEDs to place an image on paper. Capable of relatively high resolution.

processor. A component of a computer that manipulates data according to specific instructions that are encoded within it, in conjunction with instructions received from external programs (software).

program (architectural). A set of instructions for the design of an architectural project.

program (computer). A set of instructions that tells a computer to perform specific tasks. Programs are written in special computer languages and are stored on electronic media, such as floppy disks.

programming language. See "high-level language."

projected drawing. See three-dimensional projection.

prompt. A symbol, statement, or question displayed on a computer screen as a cue for a user to enter data or a command.

puck. A hand-held pointing device with one or more buttons and wire crosshairs for picking points and menu items on a digitizing tablet.

R

RAM. Random access memory.

random access memory. RAM, rapidly addressable, volatile memory, usually in the form of silicon chips. RAM must be constantly supplied with power or the information stored within it will be lost.

raster graphics. A system in which graphics are stored and drawn as individual dots located on a grid. Also called bit-mapped graphics.

real-time animation. See animation.

real-world scale. In computer-based drawing and modeling, the concept that a designer can work with actual, rather than scale, units using a display that allows an image to be expanded and contracted.

rectification. The process by which parametric drawing programs transform a drawing based on dimensional parameters.

redefine. To change a block in such a way that all occurrences of the block within a drawing are automatically changed.

redraw. (Applied to computer display) To either regenerate or refresh a display, depending on the terminology of a particular program. Used here for "refresh."

refresh. To redisplay a graphic image as stored in a computer's memory, without recalculating vectors. Generally, this process is very fast. Usually synonymous with redraw.

regenerate. To fully recalculate and redisplay the vector graphics on a computer display. With a complex drawing and slow hardware or software, this process can take minutes.

replacement. The exchange of one drawing element with another. When the element has been defined as a symbol or block, redefinition will cause all occurrences of a block to be replaced.

resolution. The fineness or courseness, in rows of dots, that a computer graphic adapter and monitor are capable of displaying, measured in rows of dots. Common CAD resolutions range from 600×350 dots to 1700×1200.

resource leveling. In computer-aided project management, a program capability for setting targets for resource use and calculating schedules accordingly.

resources. In computer-aided project management, resources represent skilled people and the value placed on their services.

RISC. Reduced instruction set computer; a computer designed to operate with a relatively small number of preprogrammed operations. RISC computers can operate at high rates of speed and are well suited to graphics.

rule-based system. A computer program that carries out operations based on a set of rules, or "if-then" criteria. A rule system can be used to produce complex drawings (or other products) based on minimal direct input by the user.

S

scale. (verb) To expand or compress a drawing element.

schedule. In architectural terminology, a list of materials and/or construction methods.

schematic design. The initial design phase of an architectural project.

section/elevation. A multilayered architectural drawing that includes both sections and elevations, on different layers.

semiautomatic dimensioning. A computer-aided drawing system for adding dimensions to a drawing that requires only that the user specify the location of witness lines and arrows.

service bureau. A company that provides computer-aided drawing services. Some service bureaus also provide training.

snap. A computer-aided drawing mode in which all picked points will fall on a grid, at a user-specified spacing (snap resolution).

software. A set of instructions that tells a computer to perform specific tasks. Software is written in special computer languages and is stored on electronic media, such as floppy disks.

solid model. A three-dimensional model based on shapes that are treated as solid forms by a computer.

A solid model may generally be viewed as either a wireframe image or with shaded surfaces.

spatial database. A graphic database in which forms may be represented on a three-axis coordinate system; lines, planes, and shapes may be drawn in any orientation. The resulting representation is a three-dimensional model.

spatial modeling. See three-dimensional modeling.

spreadsheet. An electronic table (or computer program for creating one) that displays data in columns and rows, and links cells (each column and row intersection) with formulas for performing mathematic operations.

stacking. In computer-aided space planning and schematic design, the assignment of areas to specific floors, based on programmatic criteria.

stretch. To move one part of a drawing element while leaving another part in place, increasing or decreasing the length of connecting lines or curves.

stylus. A pencil-like pointing device with one button or a sensitive point, used for picking points and menu items on a digitizing tablet.

subdirectory. A directory that is included within another directory; a subdirectory may include other lower level subdirectories. This arrangement is comparable to a tree structure, with the first directory called the root directory, and subdirectories branching out.

substitution. The exchange of one drawing element with another. See replacement.

surface model. A three-dimensional model based on planes.

surface shading. A technique by which shapes representing planes and curved surfaces in three-dimensional drawings and models are filled with tones and patterns. Surface shading may tone surfaces according to user-specified light sources, simulate shadows, and produce semitransparent tones to represent translucent planes.

symbol. A drawing that is used as a graphic notation or as a representation of an individual architectural form. Some CAD programs use the term "symbol" to refer to all complex objects that may be manipulated as single objects. We use the term "block" for all such elements to avoid confusing single objects with the broader range of large and small blocks.

T

template. A set of related symbols, stored together in a drawing library.

text. Alphanumeric characters. In a drawing, these may be entered directly at a keyboard, or transferred from a word processing program.

three-dimensional modeling. Representation of lines, planes, shapes or solids in space, in any plane, including nonorthogonal planes. Two-dimensional drawings may be extracted by "cutting through" a model. Models may be displayed as wireframes, shaded surfaces, or solid models, depending on the capabilities of the software. Models may be viewed from any viewpoint, inside or out, often in either perspective or parallel-line views.

three-dimensional projection. A means of displaying two-dimensional drawings as three-dimensional images by stretching or extruding them along a third, perpendicular axis. 3-D projections can not be used to create new drawings in planes that are not parallel to the original (i.e., sections from projected plans).

two-and-a-half-D drawing. See three-dimensional projection.

two-dimensional drawing. Drawing with points, lines, arcs, circles, and complex objects in a single plane.

U

unblock. To break up a defined block into its constituent elements. Synonymous with "explode."

Unix. A computer operating system that supports multiple users and multitasking; Unix exists in many versions, which have been modified to be used with a variety of computers.

user interface. The means by which a person interacts with a computer program. Many programs use either menus or command lines, or both, in conjunction with keyboards and pointing devices.

V

VDT. Video display terminal, a computer display that includes a CRT monitor, and may include other peripherals; by definition, a VDT is remote from the computer itself.

vector. A mathematic value representing a direction and distance. Vectors are used in storage and display of CAD graphics.

vector graphics. A system in which graphic images are stored and drawn as vectors.

viewpoint. A user-selected point in space from which a three-dimensional image will appear to be seen.

virtual machine. When a computer is to run different programs simultaneously without any interaction, it may function as if it contains two or more separate computers inside itself, which are referred to as virtual machines. This capability must be supported by the operating system.

virtual memory. Mass data storage—such as a hard disk—that is used by a computer as if it was electronic random access memory. Computers and operating systems that allow the use of virtual memory can support much larger programs than those that do not.

volumetric model. A three-dimensional model based on space defining forms, such as rooms or buildings. Similar to a massing model.

W

what-if. A study conducted with a computer by changing the parameters (numbers, rules, formulas, or graphics) of a situation (a spreadsheet, project management chart or floor plan, for example) and observing the results.

window. In computer-aided drawing, an area outlined on the display screen for the selection of drawing elements or for zooming in or out. Synonymous with box and fence.

wireframe. A three-dimensional projection or model in which the edges or outlines of objects are displayed as lines. Usually all lines are displayed, unless hidden lines are removed.

word processor. A computer program that manipulates text. Generally used as a typewriter with editing capabilities; some can also be used for combining text and graphics.

working drawings. Graphic documents that illustrate the precise details and dimensions of an architectural project.

workstation. A computer or computer terminal that is fully equipped for architectural or engineering graphics. Formerly used to refer specifically to minicomputer terminals.

Z

zoom. To expand or contract an image on a computer display: the effect is much like changing scale in drafting, but the user views a drawing in real units, regardless of the zoom magnification.

APPENDIX B
RESOURCES

COMPUTER SOFTWARE

Each of the following programs was evaluated, used, or both, in the preparation of this text. A brief description of each is included; for more detailed, current information, contact the manufacturer. All programs use the MS-DOS operating system, unless noted.

AutoCAD is a multipurpose drafting program, available in numerous configurations. It includes a variety of interface configurations, sophisticated editing and dimensioning capabilities and a user programming language. It offers options for three-dimensional projection and modeling, with hidden line removal. Surface shading and perspective views are available through the *AutoShade* module. Many architectural applications programs are available for customizing AutoCAD, such as Autodesk's *AutoCAD AEC*, which includes symbol libraries, parametric capabilities, and a digitizing tablet menu system. AutoCAD is available for Unix-based computers, as well as MS-DOS computers.

Autodesk, Inc.
2320 Marinship Way
Sausalito, CA 94965

ARRIS is a Unix-based microcomputer version of Sigma Design's minicomputer CAD software, and includes architectural drafting and three-dimensional surface-modeling capabilities. Modules are also available for space planning and database management. The software may be used in conjunction with the Sigma high-end system.

Sigma Design
7306 South Alton Way
Englewood, CO 80112

DataCAD is an architectural drafting program with add-on modules for accounting, costing, and material scheduling capabilities. It includes architectural symbol libraries, as well as drawing, editing, and dimensioning tools that are oriented specifically toward architecture, and a three-dimensional capability that offers perspective views.

Microtecture
218 West Main Street
Charlottesville, VA 22901

In-A-Vision is a drawing program with limited CAD capabilities, useful for design studies and presentation graphics. It includes symbol libraries and works through Microsoft's **Windows** software, offering compatibility with other Windows programs.

Micrografx, Inc.
1820 N. Greenville
Richardson, TX 75081

Lumen-Micro is an interior-lighting analysis program that performs engineering calculations for direct and indirect lighting. It can display results graphically, using three-dimensional graphics with perspective views and automatic surface shading.

Lighting Technologies
3060 Walnut Street, Suite 209
Boulder, CO 80301

MegaCADD Design Board Professional is a three-dimensional modeling program that is based on drawing shapes, and includes architecture-specific modeling tools. It includes multiple simultaneous views, hidden-line removal, perspective, axonometric and two-dimensional drawing extraction, automatic walk-around and walk-through capabilities, and links to numerous two-dimensional drafting programs. Mega-CADD's *Design Board Illustrator* is a bit-mapped "paint" program that can be used to render images extracted from MegaCADD's Design Board Professional.

MegaCADD, Inc.
The Court in the Square
401 Second Avenue South
Seattle, WA 98104

Personal Architect includes two separate, partially-integrated programs: a three-dimensional modeling "design" module, and a "drafting" module. The volume-oriented design module includes automatic surface shading and hidden line removal, as well as parametric capabilities in its "Technology File" system. The drafting module includes sophisticated editing capabilities and a user programming language, and is compatible with Computervision's high-end CAD systems.

Computervision, Inc.
Personal Systems Business Unit
201 Burlington Road
Bedford, MA 01730

Primavera Project Planner is a project management program with capabilities for resource leveling, bar charts and network diagrams. Primavera can handle very large projects; graphics may be plotted with pen plotters or dot-matrix printers.

Primavera Systems, Inc.
Suite 925
Two Bala Plaza
Bala Cynwyd, PA 19004

Solid Vision is a three-dimensional modeling program that is oriented toward architectural applications. It includes capabilities such as 3-D object substitution, surface shading, hidden line removal, and 2-D drawing extraction. It also includes drafting tools such as dimensioning and lettering, which function in both horizontal and nonhorizontal planes.

ISICAD
2411 W. La Palma Avenue
Anaheim, CA 92803

Synthesis is a parametric drawing program that is used with AutoCAD. It offers the capability of rectifying existing drawings, as well as creating and modifying master drawings according to a parameter spreadsheet.

TransformerCAD, Inc.
2300 James Street, Suite 201
Bellingham, WA 98225

Versacad is a general-purpose drafting program that includes architecturally-oriented tools and symbol libraries. It has elaborate capabilities for grouping elements and includes a user programming language. Versacad offers an optional three-dimensional surface modeling and shading module, as well as a database management module.

Versacad Corporation
7372 Prince Drive, Suite 106
Huntington Beach, CA 92647

DRAWING SOURCES

Several CAD software companies contributed drawings and other artwork to this book. In addition, the following architectural and graphics firms contributed their work and provided numerous insights and suggestions.

Arch.1
San Mateo, California

Buday Wells, Architects
Houston, Texas

David Baker & Associates
Berkeley, California

Creative Technologies, Inc.
Santa Cruz, California

Heard and Associates
Chicago, Illinois

Kaplan McLaughlin Diaz
San Francisco, California

NBBJ Group
Seattle, Washington

Neeley/Lofrano Inc.
San Francisco, California

James Stewart Polshek and Partners
New York, New York

Wallace, Floyd Associates
Boston, Massachussetts

PHOTO CREDITS

Chapter One Opener: Mark Lauden Crosley.
Chapter Two Opener: Photo courtesy of Sony Corporation of America. Photographer: Nicholas Basilion.
Chapter Three Opener: Courtesy of Russo & Sonder, Architects. Photo by Douglas Wramage.
Chapter Four Opener: Mark Lauden Crosley.
Chapter Five Opener: Stella Kupferberg.

Chapter Six Opener: Reprinted from *Architecture & Engineering Systems*, Jan/Feb 1986. Design: Faith Keating. Rendering: Judeanne Winter. Computer image: Sigma Design.
Chapter Seven Opener: Richard Blair.
Chapter Eight Opener: Courtesy of Russo & Sonder, Architects.
Page 169: Courtesy of Digital Equipment Corp.

INDEX

Window (boundary), 70
Window (display), 25, 116, 117
Wireframe, 12, 127–129
Word processing programs, 5, 23, 171, 172
Working drawings, 45, 55–58, 93, 101, 104, 124, 126, 141, 150, 167, 169

Workstations, 25, 166, 167, 169
Writing, 170–172, 175, 177

Z
Zoom, 38–40, 57